GOD AS DYNAMIC ACTUALITY: A PRELIMINARY STUDY OF THE PROCESS THEOLOGIES OF JOHN B. COBB, JR. AND SCHUBERT M. OGDEN

James E. Caraway

University Press of America™

Copyright © 1978 by

University Press of America, Inc.™

4710 Auth Place, S.E., Washington, D.C. 20023

All rights reserved

Printed in the United States of America

ISBN: 0-8191-0485-X

Library of Congress Catalog Card Number: 78-61388

CONTENTS

John B. Cobb, Jr. and Schubert M. Ogden are among those contemporary theologians who recognize the problem of the reality of God as the central theological problem. Both men reject the attempts to do theology without God and assert that if there is to be theology it must be a theology which affirms the reality of God in a conceptuality understandable to contemporary man. The factors which serve as unifying forces in the theologies of these two men, however, are not confined to their agreement in regarding the same theological problem as of central concern. Having asserted that the problem of the reality of God is the central contemporary theological problem, both Ogden and Cobb agree that the resources for conceptually delineating a solution to the problem are available in the philosophical explication of Alfred North Whitehead and Charles Hartshorne, both of whom see "God" as the fundamental religious dogma to which all others are subsidiary. Moreover, both Cobb and Ogden agree with the central demand which Whitehead requires of any adequate doctrine of God. This demand is that "God is not to be treated as an exception to all metaphysical principles, invoked to save their collapse. He is their chief exemplification." (PR 521). The acceptance by both Cobb and Ogden of the attempt to develop a doctrine of God which meets Whitehead's demand provides assurance that they will remain theological allies regardless of what other divergence of emphasis they may entertain. While the acceptance of the basic Whiteheadian demand by both Cobb and Ogden legitimizes a combined study of their work, their difference in emphasis and approach to the problem of God insure a variety which saves a combined study from mere repetition.

Cobb finds the possibility for a conceptualization of a doctrine of God understandable to contemporary man in the philosophy of Whitehead. He, therefore, delineates Whitehead's doctrine of God, stressing that the Whiteheadian system--which views God as the one who envisages all possibilities for becoming, provides the subjective aim for the initial phase of each entity's becoming, lures each entity toward fulfillment, and preserves each entity in a unity of multiplicity which does not negate the entity's individuality--contains the resources for developing a coherent doctrine of God which modern man will find acceptable. However, Cobb sees points of incoherence in Whitehead's system. He, therefore, attempts to alter the system so that it will be more coherent than that of Whitehead himself. The alterations he proposes intend to depict God as functioning in a way more like that of other actual entities than did Whitehead's concept of God. Cobb proposes that God be viewed as a person rather than an actual entity, that he be understood as omnispatial and non-temporal. He proposes that the function of envisaging eternal objects directly and providing subjective aims not be assigned to God alone, but that actual occasions be understood as participating in some sense in these roles, although God would always function as such in a decisive way.

By developing in detail a Whiteheadian doctrine of God, Cobb performs the task which Ogden considers requisite for an adequate doctrine of God today. Ogden analyzes the problem of contemporary "atheism," and concludes that all men in some sense believe in God. He reasons: Characteristic of all men today is a basic confidence in the abiding worth of life. This confidence must be grounded in something. "God" is the name properly given to the ground in reality itself of our basic confidence in life's final meaning.

Ogden and Cobb serve to complement each other in important respects, for Ogden analyzes the problem, the solutions to which are explicated in Cobb's developed Whiteheadian doctrine of God. This work is an attempt to explicate and critically analyze their contribution toward formulating a doctrine of God.

Preparation of a study such as this can never be accomplished without the guidance and help of others. I am deeply indebted to Professor Gene Bianchi of Emory University with whom I not only discussed my original ideas for this study, but, what is more, he patiently read and criticized the study as it progressed. I also want to express my appreciation to Profesor Ivor Leclerc, Professor Ted Runyon, and Professor Jack Boozer, all of Emory University, and Bishop Mack B. Stokes, formerly of Emory University, for their helpful suggestions and insightful and critical analysis. Professor Cobb and Professor Ogden were most helpful in making available to me whatever I requested of them. I am especially indebted to Professor Cobb for voluntarily exceeding my requests for material by making available several of his essays which were not available through publication.

I am particularly grateful to Ms. Patty Smith who painstakingly typed the final manuscript for publication, often insightfully interpreting my somewhat less than legible handwritten notes. Thanks is likewise due to Ms. Nancy Parkey who assisted with proofreading and suggestions relative to the final text, and Ms. Jane Caraway who kindly accepted the difficult task of corresponding with publishers as well as proofreading the final text. I acknowledge with gratitude the help of all of these without whom my study could not have been completed.

INTRODUCTION: THE REALITY OF GOD AS THE
CENTRAL THEOLOGICAL PROBLEM

That the problem of God is now one of the central
problems of contemporary theology--if not the central
problem--is hardly to be questioned.   Kenneth Cauthen,
in a discussion of "The Challenge of Science and
Secularization" in Science, Secularization, and God
addresses the heart of the matter when he says:

> ...while there are many countervailing
> factors in the complex history of modern
> Western culture, the last few centuries
> have, by a steadily growing logic, brought
> us to an unprecedented point which compels
> us to face with radical seriousness the
> question as to whether man is alone in a
> neutral cosmos.   What we confront is 'a
> new self-containing comprehensive concep-
> tion of reality' (Heim) in which a growing
> number of people find appeals to a tran-
> scendent, purposive God neither credible
> nor relevant.   This is the situation that
> lies behind the widespread recognition
> that the reality of God and meaningful
> language about him has become the central
> issue in contemporary theology.[1]

Langdon Gilkey observes that the "primary problem" of
theology is "to discover how the God who has almost
disappeared may appear to us again in power and
truth."[2]   He further notes that "only if we can legitimately discourse about that dimension and category of
deity, about God and his works can we speak of other

---

[1]Kenneth Cauthen, Science, Secularization and God,
p. 14.

[2]Langdon Gilkey, "Dissolution and Reconstruction
in Theology," Frontline Theology, (Dean Peerman, ed.),
p. 33 Cf. also Gilkey, "Theology," Great Ideas Today,
1967 (Mortimer J. Adler, ed.) Chicago: The Encyclope-
dia Britannica, Inc., 1967, pp. 239-270.

1

theological issues and problems of which these divine works are the presupposition."[1]

John B. Cobb and Schubert M. Ogden represent two theologians whose approach to theology today is summed up in these assertions of Cauthen and Gilkey. They recognize with Cauthen that "the reality of God and of meaningful language about him has become the central issue in contemporary theology."[2] They, too, would say with Gilkey that "however God may be known, the knowledge of his reality is logically prior to all else; no revelation, no Christ of faith, no ecclesiology is ultimately possible or intelligible if the category of deity remains totally empty."[3]

In their attempt to speak to the "primary problem" of theology today, in their attempt to speak meaningfully of the reality of God, both Cobb and Ogden turn to the resources available through the philosophies of Whitehead and Hartshorne. Whitehead is one philosopher who has found it necessary to speak of God as a primary and pervasive constituent of an adequate description of reality. Although his influence among theologians was eclipsed by the recent Barthian dominance of theology, the importance of his philosophy as conducive to explicating the Christian faith is once again being recognized. In him and Hartshorne both Cobb and Ogden find a conceptuality which enables them to explicate the reality of God in a manner understandable to contemporary man.

That John B. Cobb would concur with the assertion that the central theological problem is that of the reality of God can be observed immediately upon examination of his book A Christian Natural Theology.[4] Noting that "we live in a time when the categories in which the Christian message has traditionally been presented have lost all meaning for major segments of the population,"[5] Cobb observes:

---

[1]Gilkey, op. cit., p. 33.

[2]Cauthen, op. cit.

[3]Gilkey, op. cit.

[4]John B. Cobb, A Christian Natural Theology, Philadelphia: The Westminister Press, 1965.

[5]Ibid., p. 13.

The crux of the matter has to do with the
concepts of man and God....For much of the
culture that is growing up about us and
within us, 'God' has become an empty sound.
This is no longer a problem only for those
Christians trying to communicate with a
special segment of the intelligentsia estranged from the church. It has become
the problem of the suburban pastor in his
dealings with his most sensitive church
leaders and youth. Perhaps most of all it
has become the problem of the perceptive
minister in dealing with himself and his
own understanding of his ministry."[1]

Cobb notes that theologians, in response to this
situation, have taken one of three approaches. First,
those theologians who have been opposed to natural
theology have taken the position that such an approach
is to be treated as of no fundamental importance for
the gospel message. While some have been indifferent
to the stance of natural theology, others have taken
the position that an abandonment of natural theology
is a positive gain, for thereby false ideas of God
are destroyed and the way is cleared for the encounter
with the truly transcendent God revealed only in Jesus
Christ.[2] Other theologians have offered a second alternative, namely, that the emptiness of the term "God"
requires that we either abandon the use of this word
altogether or else redefine it in categories that are
meaningful to modern man, categories such as love,
depth dimension, Mitmenschlichkeit.[3] The third
alternative, which Cobb himself views as both useful
and possible, is the attempt "to restore the term
'God' to meaningful discourse while at the same time
maintaining some real continuity with the historic use
of the term."[4] That Cobb, just as Ogden sees such an
attempt as "the sole theme of all valid Christian

---

[1]Ibid., p. 14.
[2]Cobb, A Christian Natural Theology, pp. 13-14.
[3]Ibid., p. 14.
[4]Ibid.

theology,"[1] is evidenced when he says:

> To me it appears that the struggle to restore
> the meaningfulness of the word 'God', which
> means to justify the horizon in which this
> word can have its appropriate reference, is
> a matter of ultimate importance for the
> health, even the survival, of Christian
> faith.[2]

Both Odgen and Cobb, then, would concur that the
theme of the reality of God is "the one essential point
to all authentic Christian faith and witness,"[3] for in
today's world the crucial theological question for many
men is simply whether the word "God" has any meaning.
To speak of God's activity in the world as revealed
by Christ is meaningless in a situation in which the
word "God" has no significance, and the reality to
which it refers is called in question. According to
Ogden the theme of the reality of God has "become the
central problem of Protestant theology, if not of
Christian theology generally."[4] In fact Ogden stresses
that "this theme is, in the last analysis, the sole
theme of all valid Christian theology, even as it is
the one essential point to all authentic Christian
faith and witness."[5] As attestation of this point,
Ogden cites a statement of Charles Hartshorne:

> In its earliest stages religion means
> certainty about many things. But we now
> see that he is most religious who is
> certain of but one thing, the world-embrac-
> ing love of God. Everything else we can
> take our chance on; everything else, includ-
> ing man's relative significance in the world
> is mere probability.[6]

John Cobb's mentor, Alfred North Whitehead, makes
virtually the same observation when he says:

---

[1] Schubert Ogden, The Reality of God, p. 14.
[2] Cobb, op. cit., pp. 14-15.
[3] Ibid., pp. 14-15.
[4] Ogden, op. cit., p.x.
[5] Ibid., p. ix.
[6] Ibid., p. x., from Charles Hartshorne, Beyond
Humanism, p. 44.

4

"Today there is but one religious dogma in debate:
What do you mean by 'God'? And in this respect,
today is like all its yesterdays. This is the fundamental religious dogma, and all other dogmas are
subsidiary to it."[1]

The present study is an attempt to explicate the
developing thought of Schubert Ogden and John B. Cobb
insofar as they attempt to speak of the certainty of
"this one thing" or "the fundamental religious dogma"
of which their mentors Hartshorne and Whitehead,
respectively, have spoken. But, the tie which binds
Ogden and Cobb in their attempts is far stronger than
their mere agreement that the reality of God is the
central theological problem today. Nor is the consideration of the two together based merely on the fact
that they are philosophical-theologians of the type
known as process-theology. Rather, Ogden and Cobb are
considered together in this study for they both attempt
to develop a doctrine of God on the basis of the
primary demand which Whitehead makes for any adequate
doctrine of God. They together accept Whitehead's
dictum that "God is not to be treated as an exception
to all metaphysical principles, invoked to save their
collapse. He is their chief exemplification."[2] The
acceptance of this demand by Cobb as well as Ogden,
and their continued efforts to maintain the Whiteheadian demand throughout their attempted formulation
of a doctrine of God both legitimizes a combined
study of their attempts and indicates that, regardless
of their divergence from one another, they will be
theological allies at this central point. This study
therefore will attempt to present not only an explication of the two theologies, but also will include
critical comments and a consideration of the interrelation of the doctrine of God as developed by Cobb and
Ogden.

---

[1]Whitehead, Religion in the Making, p. 66.
[2]Process and Reality, p. 521.

I. JOHN B. COBB'S WHITEHEADIAN DOCTRINE OF GOD

In <u>A</u> <u>Christian</u> <u>Natural</u> <u>Theology</u>, John Cobb depicts his stance in relation to Whitehead's philosophy in the following words:

> In most of this book, I have identified myself fully with the position I have ex-pounded on Whitehead's authority. Even in the preceding chapter, where I focused upon the development of his views, I largely identified myself with my presentation of his thought in <u>Process</u> <u>and</u> <u>Reality</u>. White-head's philosophical reasons for affirming God and his attempt to show that God is not an exception to all categories appear[1] to me philosophically responsible and even necessary.[2]

Cobb's close identification with Whitehead's thought makes it necessary that we first--even as he has done--delineate summarily the main aspects of the Whiteheadian system.[3] The problem is not merely that of explicating Whitehead's doctrine of God, for the interpenetrating complexity of the system requires

---

[1]Cf. Whitehead's contention: "For nothing, with-in any limited type of experience, can give intelli-gence to shape out ideas of any entity at the base of all actual things, unless the general character of things requires that there by such an entity. (Alfred North Whitehead, <u>Science</u> <u>and</u> <u>the</u> <u>Modern</u> <u>World</u>, "God", p. 156.). "...God is not to be treated as an exception to all metaphysical principles, invoked to save their collapse, He is their chief exemplification." (White-head, <u>Process</u> <u>and</u> <u>Reality</u>, p. 521.).

[2]Cobb, <u>A</u> <u>Christian</u> <u>Natural</u> <u>Theology</u>, p. 176.

[3]As Cobb notes in reference to Whitehead in <u>A</u> <u>Christian</u> <u>Natural</u> <u>Theology</u>: I am so profoundly and overwhelmingly indebted to him for the fundamental structure of my thought, and I begin my own reflection on each topic so deeply influenced by my understanding of his philosophy, that the book is also a book about

that Whitehead's concept of God can only be discussed in the context of a survey of the system as a whole. Therefore, Cobb's discussion of Whitehead's philosophy is to be considered first.

A. An Introduction to Whitehead's Philosophy

The central philosophical problem is an attempt to determine "the kinds of things that are and how they are related to each other,"[1] or in other words, the basic philosophical problem is the question of the relationship of material things and mental things. Is one to ascertain his view of reality by an observation of sticks, stones, mountains, human bodies and animals, or is one to get at the really real by a reflection on the nature of conscious experience, and hence intuit some notion of mentality? Are these approaches fundamentally different? Or is there some more inclusive method by which we can understand both?

Most philosophers have tried to overcome dualism in one of three main ways. First, one can understand matter as an appearance to mind.[2] The basis of our notion of matter is sense experience. Sense experience is fundamentally mental for only mentality can have conscious experience. Hence, the notion of matter should be explained in terms of sensuous qualities. A second approach is that of emphasizing the material, asserting that minds are functions of matter.[3] This is the attempt to understand subjective experience or the mental as merely a product of material force. In the twentieth century, however, the physical sciences have been confronted with the possibility that the notion of matter is not fully illuminative of their field of investigation. To empha-

---

Whitehead. (Ibid., p. 17.). "The book as a whole can make no sense apart from a basic understanding of some main features of Whitehead's philosophical position." (Ibid., p. 18.).

[1] Cobb, A Christian Natural Theology, p. 23.

[2] Ibid., p. 24

[3] Ibid.

size the material was appropriate so long as atoms could be regarded in a substantial way as the ultimate stuff of the universe. The inadequacy of this assumption was revealed when it was discovered that the atom itself was not static substance, mere matter, but rather, a dynamic entity, composed of protons, electrons and neutrons. Hence, mental experience seems to warrant more consideration than the mere subsumption of it under materialistic categories. While some merely admitted the ultimate unintelligibility of the universe, others attempted to subsume duality under some more comprehensive unity. As Cobb asserts: "This might mean that some kind of reality underlies our subjective mental states as well as that which seems objective to them; it might mean that all reality participates in both mentality and materiality without in fact being either."[1]

Whitehead's philosophy is representative of this attempt to find a single type of reality explanatory of both the mental and material. In his endeavor, Whitehead seeks to replace the traditional philosophy of substance or stress on static structure with a philosophy of organism. Emphasizing that philosophical method involves generalization from the concrete particulars to the universals, Whitehead asserts that such a generalization must be based on description rather than deduction, and this description, to be adequate, necessitates a description of dynamic process rather than a morphological description, i.e. a description of static structure. Moreover, any description must begin with immediate experience. Whitehead makes this clear when he asserts that, "the elucidation of immediate experience is the sole justification for any thought; and the starting point for thought is the analytic observation of components of this experience."[2] Of this procedure, Cobb observes:

> We might call his procedure phenomenological except that at no time did Whitehead dismiss from his thought the relevant knowledge about physics, physiology, and

---

[1]Ibid., pp. 24-25

[2]Whitehead, Process and Reality, p. 6.

psychology. It would be best to say that
he began with human experience as we all
know it, and as he further understood it
in the light of science, and then presented
the question as to what must be the case[1]
in order that this experience can occur.

In his elucidation of immediate experience,
Whitehead, having criticized traditional philosophy
for dealing too much in abstract terms, endeavored to
begin his investigation with the most concrete facts
of human experience. The most concrete fact of
existence is not that of any given experience as a
whole, but rather a particular indivisible unit of
the given experience. As Cobb points out:

> ...what must be assumed, in order that
> human experience (and the ultimate par-
> ticles of nature) can be understood,
> are successive 'actual occasions of ex-
> perience.' Rather than being a continuous
> flow, experience comes to be in discrete
> and indivisible units. These momentary
> occasions succeed each other with a rapid-
> ity beyond any clear grasp of conscious at-
> tention. The direct analysis of any single
> occasion of experience is impossible.[2]

These "discrete and indivisble" units Whitehead calls
actual entities or actual occasions. Actual entities
are defined by Whitehead as:

> the final real things of which the world
> is made up. There is no going behind
> actual entities to find anything more
> real. They differ among themselves:
> God is an actual entity, and so is the most
> trivial puff of existence....these actual
> entities are drops of experience complex
> and interdependent.[3]

---

[1]Cobb, A Christian Natural Theology, p. 28.
[2]Ibid., pp. 28-29
[3]Whitehead, Process and Reality, pp. 27-28.

Actual entities,[1] then, are the actualities of Whitehead's organismic universe. They are the most con-

---

[1]Professor Leclerc in his exposition of Whiteheadian thought discusses Whitehead's reasoning in
choosing the phrase "actual entity" as signifying the
basic reality. Leclerc notes that Whitehead consciously avoids the use of the ambiguous words "being"
or "substance", and utilizes instead the phrase "actual entity". The phrase "actual entity" is used to
denote "the things that are actual...which exist in
the fullest sense." (Ivor Leclerc, Whitehead's Metaphysics: An Introductory Exposition, p. 21.). As
Leclerc further notes: "In English the word 'entity'
has come to be used for 'thing' in this very general
sense. It is derived from the Latin esse, and denotes
anything which 'is' or 'exist', in any sense of 'being'
or 'existing'; anything of which we can say: 'it
is....Since we do think about and thus distinguish a
large number of 'entities' which do indubitably 'exist'
in some sense or other, Whitehead explicitly and tech-
nically accepts this usage of 'entity' in this completely general sense; philosophically he regards it
as entirely justified." (Leclerc, Ibid., p. 22.). In
order to concretize the general 'entity', Whitehead
combines with it the word 'actual'. As Leclerc notes:
"...to distinguish those entities with which metaphysics is primarily concerned from all others, Whitehead employs the term 'actual'. The word 'actual', in
Whitehead's usage, connotes 'existence' in the 'full'
as opposed to the 'dependent' sense. Accordingly, a
'thing which is actual', an 'actual thing', or more
precisely, 'an actual entity,' is an entity which is
a 'fully existent' entity. That is to say, the word
'actual' in the phrase 'actual entity' is intended to
distinguish, as fully existent, the entity in question
from all other entities." (Leclerc, Ibid., p. 22.).
Whitehead observed in The Concept of Nature that the
word "entity" is simply the Latin equivalent for
"thing," and likewise, in Science and the Modern World
(pp. 178-179.), he noted that the generality of the
notion of "entity" was such that it may be taken to
mean anything which can be thought about, for any
something which is merely the object of thought may
be called an "entity." The phrase "actual entity" in
contradistinction, points to that which is concrete
and fully existent.

crete facts of experience.

In order to understand reality, then, Whitehead asserts that one must begin with immediate experience, and one finds upon beginning with immediate experience "actual occasions of experience" in "discrete and indivisible" units. Whitehead stresses that any model by which one understands reality or any part of it must be derived from human experience, for there is simply nowhere else to turn. This is not to suggest that all actual entities are like human ones in an all inclusive way. For example, it would be absurd to suppose that electrons enjoyed vision or touch. But sense data are not the sole constituents of experience, for the entity's "feeling"[1] of being among things is the primary factor in experience.[2]

----

[1]A "feeling" is a positive prehension. In Whitehead's words: "This word 'feeling' is a mere technical term; but it has been chosen to suggest that functioning through which the concrescent actuality appropriates the datum so as to make it its own." (Whitehead, Process and Reality, p. 249.). "This notion of a direct 'idea' (or 'feeling') of an actual entity is a presupposition of all commom sense." (Ibid., p. 83.). "Each actual entity is conceived as an act of experience arising out of data. It is a process of 'feeling' the many data, so as to absorb them into the unity of one individual "satisfaction". Here 'feeling' is the term used for the basic generic operation of passing from the objectivity of the data to the subjectivity of the actual entity in question." (Ibid., p. 65.).

[2]Cobb presents Whitehead's contention when he observes: "Sense experience plays a considerable role, but at the outset we must be clear that for Whitehead it does not play the foundational role. He shows that the assumption that sense data alone are given in experience is disastrous for philosophy. Certainly it would put an end to any possibility of finding aspects of human experience attributable also to electrons, for it would be absurd to suppose that subatomic particles enjoyed vision or touch. There is, of course, the experience of the patch of green. But there is also the experience of some thing that is green and that occupies a region of space in a particular geometric relation to my body. This experience of thingness, Whitehead insists, is not dependent

It is with reference to this aspect of the actual entity that Whitehead uses the term "physical pole." An actual entity has both a physical pole and a mental pole. The physical pole of the entity represents "the physical impact of the world upon the occasion of experience."[1] The physical pole is "that by which we experience ourselves as related to, and our experience as derivative from, events in our recent past."[2] In Donald Sherburne's words: "The physical pole is that aspect of an actual entity wherein it makes no contribution of its own, but merely receives what is given for it from the past."[3] In describing the physical pole, reference has been made to "the physical impact of the world," and to the entity's receiving "what is given for it from the past." These considerations point to the presupposition of some actuality which serves as the ground or basis for the becoming actuality under consideration. This basis is itself actual entities.[4] Actual entities are the ultimate facts, but they are in the process of "perpetual perishing." As they perish, they are somehow taken up in the creative advance, through the process of prehension pass into other actual entities, and achieve "objective immortality." Explaining the "past" which becomes the given world of the "physical pole," Cobb notes:

---

on a process of learning. We do not first experience only sense data and then later learn by experience that these represent entities. The simplest animal acts as if it were aware of being among things and not simply sensa. The sense of there being a reality other than an experience given to us in the experience is absolutely primitive. Indeed, our knowledge of physiology shows us, if immediate introspection does not, that sense experience is the secondary and not the primary factor in experiencing." (Cobb, A Christian Natural Theology, pp. 29-30.).

[1] Ibid., p. 30.

[2] Ibid.

[3] Donald W. Sherburne, A Key to Whitehead's Process and Reality, p. 228.

[4] This statement presupposes the "ontological principle," which will be discussed subsequently.

Each actual occasion comes into being
against the background of the whole past
of the world, That past is composed of
innumerable actual occasions that have
had their moment of subjective immediacy
and have 'perished.' As perished, they
have not become simply nothing. Rather,
they have their own mode of being, which
Whitehead calls 'objective immortality.'
That means that they are effective as objects
to be prehended by new occasions. They are
the efficient causes explaining why the new
occasions embody the characteristics they
do in fact have. If, for example, someone
wants to explain my experience, he must
point to my past experiences and to the
immediately past events that have been tran-
spiring in my environment and in my body.[1]

The physical pole can be analyzed into "physical prehensions," or "physical feelings," which are "the
feeling of one momentary occasion of another momentary
occasion."[2] The occasion that is felt is always in
the past of the occasion that is feeling. That is
to say, the cause always precedes the effect. Whitehead's contention is that the:

relation of prehension is always asym-
metrical. The earlier occasion has
'causal efficacy'[3] for the later. The
later occasion 'prehends'[4] the earlier.
These terms cannot be reversed. In
other words there is no causal relation
between contemporary occasions.[5]

---

[1]Cobb, A Christian Natural Theology, p. 38.

[2]Ibid., p. 31.

[3]Whitehead, Process and Reality, p. 125.

[4]Ibid., pp. 28-29.

[5]Cobb, op. cit., p. 31; Whitehead, Process and
Reality, pp. 95, 188, 192.

Cause and effect are not simultaneous as the common sense view often supposes. On the macrocosmic level this seems to be the case, but the microcosmic entities force a rejection of such an assertion of simultaneity. In retrospect we can see that the assertion of simultaneity of cause and effect renders the sense of the influence of the past upon the present unintelligible.[1] If, in our conscious experience we view a green field, it is presented to us as if it were simultaneous with our experience of seeing it.[2] But if we reflect on this experience we realize that thousands of events have occurred each one having causal efficacy for its successor and each one contributing to the human experience.[3] Some quality is present in the presented data which when abstracted we call greenness. The many received data must be transformed into one patch of green. The process of transforming[4] or transmuting the multiplicity of received data into one patch of green is a mental operation. Such a mental operation, however, involves the introduction of some quality not present in the data, for the data merely present the quality of greenness, while the acts of abstraction and transmutation are performed by the experient.[5] This conceptualization, i.e. the abstraction and transmutation, of the data given in the physical pole, Whitehead calls "the mental pole." In Whitehead's words: "The mental pole originates as the conceptual counterpart of the operation of the physical pole. The two poles are inseparable in their origination. The mental pole starts with the conceptual registration of the physical pole."[6] As Sherburne **explains: "The mental pole is that aspect of an**

---

[1]Cobb, A Christian Natural Theology, p. 31.

[2]This dimension of our total experience Whitehead calls "presentational immediacy." Cf. Cobb, p. 32; Whitehead, Process and Reality, p. 189ff.

[3]Cobb, op. cit., pp. 30 and 32.

[4]Whitehead, Process and Reality, p. 40.

[5]Cobb, op. cit., p. 33. Of the received data Cobb says: "there must be some quality, somehow analogous to greenness, that they do possess and contribute to the experience, but the human occasion is here introducing an element of novelty." (p. 33.).

[6]Whitehead, Process and Reality, p. 379.

actual entity which responds to what is given."[1] The
mental pole, then, is the subject acting as "a determinate of its own concrescence." The mental pole is
"the subject determining its own ideal of itself."[2]
In Process and Reality Whitehead explains the twofold
nature of actual entities when he says:

>   In each concrescence there is a two-
> fold aspect of the creative urge. In one
> aspect there is the origination of single
> causal feelings; and in the other aspect
> there is the origination of conceptual
> feelings. These contrasted aspects will
> be called the physical and mental poles
> of an actual entity. No actual entity
> is devoid of either pole; though their
> relative importance differs in different
> actual entities. Also conceptual feelings
> do not necessarily involve consciousness;
> though there can be no conscious feelings
> which do not involve conceptual feelings
> as elements in the synthesis.
>
>   Thus an actual entity is essentially
> dipolar, with its physical and mental poles;[3]

---

[1]Sherburne, op. cit., p. 228.

[2]Whitehead, op. cit., p. 380.

[3]Regarding a proper interpretation of this
dipolarity, Sherburne offers a statement of caution:
"the terms 'physical pole' and 'mental pole' may not
be the happiest of terms to introduce into a philosophy that repudiates the Cartesian dualism and insists
that actual entities are the only finally real actualities. Certainly Whitehead has no intention of re-
introducing the old concepts of mind and matter, and
it is emphatically not the case that actual entities
in the physical world have only physical poles and
that mental poles are present only in the higher
organisms. 'No actual entity is devoid of either pole,
though their relative importance differs in different
actual entities....Thus an actual entity is essentially
dipolar, with its physical and mental poles; and even
the physical world cannot be properly understood without reference to its other side, which is the complex
of mental operations. (PR 366.). On the other hand,
this does not mean 'that these mental operations in-

16

and even the physical world cannot be
properly understood without reference
to its other side, which is the complex of mental operations. The primary mental operations are conceptual
feelings.[1]

The individual actual entities interact with one
another through what Whitehead calls "prehension." A
prehension is a "feeling"[2] of one actual entity as
involved with another. It is the feeling by one
momentary occasion (i.e. actual entity) of another
momentary occasion. Prehensions are described by
Whitehead as "Concrete Facts of Relatedness,"[3] for
they "are the vehicles by which one actual entity becomes objectified in another, or eternal objects
obtain ingression into actual entities."[4] Prehensions,
then, are what the actual entity is composed of.
Each prehension consists of three factors: the
subject which is in the process of prehending, that
is, the actual entity in which the prehension is con-
cretized, the datum which is being prehended, and the
subjective form which is how the subject prehends the
the datum.[5] These prehensions are of two species:
Positive prehensions which are called simply "feelings"
and negative prehensions which are said to "eliminate
from feeling."[6] Prehensions as the concrete facts of

---

volve consciousness, which is the product of intricate
integration' (PR 379.)." Sherburne, pp. 228-229.

[1]Whitehead, _Process and Reality_, p. 366.

[2]With regard to the difference between 'feeling'
and 'prehension,' Cobb notes: "The only difference
between 'feeling' and prehension' in Whitehead's
technical vocabulary is that only positive prehensions
are called feelings." (Cobb, _A Christian Natural
Theology_, p. 31.).

[3]Whitehead, _Process and Reality_, p. 32.

[4]Sherburne, _op. cit._, p. 235.

[5]_Ibid._; Whitehead, _Process and Reality_, p. 35.

[6]Whitehead, _Process and Reality_, p. 35.

relatedness and that of which the acutal entity are composed are integral in the actual entity's becoming. As the actual entity in its process of becoming pre- hends other actual entities, it moves toward fulfill- ment or concrescence."[1] The coming together of diverse becoming actual entities into a unity results in a concrete actual entity. This "concresced" actual entity becomes datum for prehension by another actual entity.

The stress that actual entities are the finally real things apart from which there would be nothing at all serves to indicate that "each actual occasion comes into being against the background of the whole past of the world."[2] This is to say that the "per- ished" actual occasions serve as efficient causes ex- planatory of why the new entity embodies the charac- teristics it in fact has. For example, one explains experience on the basis of past experience. But Whitehead stresses that the influence of the past in determining what the entity becomes in the present is not complete or absolute, although many psychologists view the influence of the past upon the determination of the present complete. In this view if all the details of an entity's past experience along with the aspects impinging upon the entity's present were known, then an accurate prediction of its future actions could be made. Whitehead, nevertheless, holds to "the univer- sal practical assumption" that we are free.[3] Entities are, according to Whitehead, both determined and free. As Cobb explains Whitehead's position:

---

[1]"The word 'Concrescence' is derivative from the familiar Latin verb meaning 'growing together.' It also has the advantage that the participle 'concrete' is familiarly used for the notion of complete physical reality. Thus concrescence is useful to convey the notion of many things acquiring complete complex unity." (F.S.C. Northrop and Mason W. Gross, Alfred North Whitehead, p. 927.).

[2]Cobb, A Christian Natural Theology, p. 38.

[3]Ibid., p. 39.

that is, the determination of the past is
real but not absolute. What I have been
in the past, and what the world
as a whole has been may narrowly limit
what I can become in the next moment.
But within those limits it is still my
decision in that moment how I shall react
to all these forces impinging upon me.[1]

Cobb stresses that this freedom or self-determination
is not necessarily a matter of consciousness, for the
freedom or self-determination occurs prior to the
consciousness of it.[2] Although in the human occasion
there may or may not be some consciousness of the
self-determination, "clearly conscious decision
would be a very special case of decision generally."[3]
Whitehead attributes some element of freedom or
self-determination to every entity.[4] The assertion
that the freedom of an actual entity is not necessarily
a matter of consciousness is clarified when one notes
that in conscious experience one is for the most part
concerned with groupings of actual entities rather
than an individual actual entity. As Whitehead notes:

----

[1]Ibid., p. 39.

[2]Ibid.

[3]Ibid.

[4]As Cobb explains Whitehead's position: "In vast
numbers of occasions this freedom is used only to reenact the past. But there are signs in modern physics
of an ultimate spontaneity at the base of things.
Not only is it clear that in principle man can never
predict the behavior of individual electrons, it is
also clear that the reason for the success of his
predictions when he deals with larger entities is
that so many of the ultimate actual entities are involved, even pure chance or spontaneity on the part
of each individual can allow for great precision in
predicting the behavior of the group. There is no
basis for exact prediction about individuals. For
this reason, Whitehead's assignment of freedom as
well as the vast causal influence of the past even to
such minute entities as electrons seems to be in accord with the world revealed to us by science."
(Ibid., p. 39.).

"It is only when we are consciously aware of alien
mentalities that we ever approximate to the conscious
prehension of a single actual entity."[1]

For his description of groupings of actual
entities Whitehead employs the terms nexus, society,
and enduring object. A society is "any group of occasions characterized by any real interconnectedness
at all..., however, loose the connectedness may be."[2]
A nexus which "illustrates" or "shares in" some type
of social order[3] is a society. "When a nexus is
characterized by some common trait exemplified by each
of its members in dependence of some of the others,
the nexus is called a 'society.'"[4] A society is
self-sustaining. It is its own reason.[5] When the
actual entities of a society are temporally contiguous
and successive, that is when they display what Whitehead calls serial or personal order,[6] the society is

---

[1]Ibid., p. 40, note 42; Whitehead, Process and
Reality, p. 387.

[2]Cobb, A Christian Natural Theology, p. 40.

[3]Whitehead, Adventures of Ideas, p. 203. In
Adventures of Ideas (p. 203.)and Process and Reality
(pp. 50-51.), Whitehead defines Social Order as
follows: "A nexus enjoys 'social order' where (i)
there is a common element of form illustrated in the
definiteness of each of its included actual entities,
and (ii) this common element of form arises in each
member of the nexus by reason of the conditions
imposed upon it by its prehensions of some other
members of the nexus, and (iii) these prehensions
impose that condition of reproduction by reason of
their inclusion of positive feelings of that common
form is the 'defining characteristic' of the society...
The common element of form is simply a complex
eternal object exemplified in each member of the
nexus.... Thus the defining characteristic is in-
·herited throughout the nexus each member deriving it
from those other members of the nexus which are
antecedent to its own concrescence." (Whitehead,
Process and Reality, pp. 50-51.).

[4]Cobb, op. cit., p. 40.

[5]Whitehead, Adventures of Ideas, p. 203.

[6]Whitehead explains 'personal order' in the
following: "A nexus enjoys 'personal order' when (a)

20

called an enduring object. An enduring object, then,
is a nexus which "forms a single line of inheritance
of its defining characteristic."[1] "In such a society,"
Cobb points out, "no two occasions exist at the same
time, but at each moment one such occasion occurs,
prehending all the preceding occasions in the society,
reenacting the defining characteristic of the society,
and mediating this pattern to its successor."[2]

Whitehead's distinction between the individual
actual entities and their groupings, i.e. the distinction between the individual actual entity and nexus,
societies, and enduring objects, points to his understanding of the subject-object schema, a schema which
Whitehead believes to be fundamental to experience.[3]
Yet, Whitehead disagrees with and offers correctives
for the traditional interpretation of the subject-
object schema.[4] In the first place, the actual
entity experienced as an object is in its own nature
also a subject. If one is focusing upon individual
actual entities, the only difference one finds between
them is that subjects are in the present while the
object is always past.[5] In the second place, Whitehead rejects the traditional view that objects are
contemporary with subjects and given in sense experience, and rather stresses that the true objects of experience are neither the presented sensa nor the contemporary entities in the region on which the sensa
is projected. In the third place, Whitehead notes
that our confusion with regard to the subject-object
schema has resulted frc our failure to distinguish

---

it is a 'society,' and (b) when the genetic relatedness
of its members orders these members serially." (Process and Reality, p. 51.).

[1]Ibid.

[2]Cobb, op. cit., p. 41.

[3]Ibid., p. 44; Cf. Adventures of Ideas, pp. 175
and 190. On pp. 175f. Whitehead notes his agreement
with the subject-object schema, but points to necessary correctives of the traditional view.

[4]Cobb, op. cit., pp. 44-45.

[5]Cf. Adventures of Ideas, paragraph 9, p. 178.

between individual actual entities and societies.[1]

We have begun our study at the point at which Whitehead himself begins, and we have posited actual entities as the most concrete fact of experience, explaining their relation to one another on the basis of prehension. In doing this, we have not yet made reference to the "ground" or the basis of the actual entities themselves. To this we now turn, and in so doing we must sketch briefly Whitehead's category of the ultimate, the category which expresses the general principle presupposed by all other aspects of Whitehead's philosophy of organism. This category includes three notions: "creativity," "many," and "one." The ultimate metaphysical principle for Whitehead is creativity.[2] Creativity underlies all things with no exception. Even God is subordinate to this ultimate category. Creativity is crucial to an understanding of process, for it points to the

------

[1]Cobb clarifies Whitehead's position when he says: "...we correctly resist the idea that sticks and stones as such have subjectivity.... The society as a whole has no subjectivity, but this is because it has only the individuality of a particular form or pattern, not that of a truly individual entity. The inertness and passivity of the stick or stone as a corpuscular society gives us no grounds for positing a similar inertness or passivity on the part of the protonic and electronic occasions of which the society is composed. It is to these and not to the sticks and stones that Whitehead refers as subjects in their moment of immediacy and as objects for new subjects when that moment is past. (A Christian Natural Theology, p. 45.).

[2]Sherburne's observation with regard to the principle of creativity may be informative at this point: "Whitehead's understanding of creativity does not do violence to the ontological principle; creativity is not, nor does it point to, some kind of entity or being more real than actual entities. It is, rather, descriptive of the most fundamental relationship participated in by all actual entities. '"Creativity" is the universal of universals characterizing ultimate matter of fact.' (PR 31.).'" (Sherburne, A Key to Whitehead's Process and Reality, p. 218.).

presupposition of the whole system, that of "on-goingness," "generation after generation of actual entities succeeding one another without end."[1] That this is the case is indicated when Whitehead says: "The ultimate metaphysical principle is the advance from disjunction to conjunction, creating a novel entity other than the entities given in disjunction."[2] This statement also indicates that creativity as the ultimate metaphysical principle is the principle of novelty. The notion of creativity must be viewed in relation to the other two notions constituent of Whitehead's category of the ultimate, those of "many" and "one." Creativity is the advance from disjunction to conjunction in which a novel entity is created. The relation of "many" and "one" with regard to this novel entity is explained in Whitehead's words:

> The novel entity is at once the together-
> ness of the 'many' which it finds, and
> also it is one among the disjunctive 'many'
> which it leaves; it is a novel entity dis-
> junctively among the many entities which
> it synthesizes. The many become one and
> are increased by one.[3]

One other aspect of Whitehead's philosophy must be mentioned before his doctrine of God can be pre-sented. Whitehead diverges from traditional philoso-phy in the application of what he calls the ontological principle. This divergence and the principle by which it is indicated is best presented in his own words:

> The notion of 'substance' is trans-
> formed into that of 'actual entity;' and
> the notion of 'power' is transformed in-
> to the principle that the reasons for
> things are always to be found in the com-
> posite nature of definite actual entities--
> in the nature of God for reasons of the
> highest absoluteness, and in the nature
> of definite temporal actual entities for
> reasons which refer to a particular

---

[1] Ibid.

[2] Whitehead, _Process_ _and_ _Reality_, p. 32.

[3] Ibid.

23

environment. The ontological principle
can be summarized as: no actual entity,
then no reason.[1]

This principle makes it unequivocally clear that every
particular condition has its reason either in some
actual entity in the actual world of that particular
condition or else in the elements of the subject in
the process of concrescence.[2]

We have thus far attempted to present a synopsis--
as viewed by Cobb--of the particular aspects of Whitehead's philosophy, the understanding of which is
necessary before we can delineate his doctrine of
God. Moreover, such a presentation has seemed necessary in the light of Cobb's indebtedness to and close
identification with Whitehead's philosophy.[3] We have
seen that the basic realities of Whitehead's organismic
philosophy are actual entities which, through the
process of prehension reach concrescence or fulfillment. The basic principle applicable to this process
is that of creativity, the movement from disjunction
to conjunction. With these considerations, and with
the summary "no actual entity, then no reason," in
mind, we proceed to Whitehead's doctrine of God.

---

[1]Ibid., p. 28.

[2]Cf. Process and Reality pp. 36 and 373.

[3]Cf. Cobb, A Christian Natural Theology, pp. 176,
17, and 18.

B. Whitehead's Doctrine of God[1]

At the beginning of his development of a doctrine of God Whitehead totally rejects the appeal to God on the part of thinkers who required him for the solution of the problem of the order of nature. Of such an approach Whitehead says:

> My point is that any summary conclusion jumping from our conviction of the existence of such an order of nature to the easy assumption that there is an ultimate reality which, in some unexplained way, is to be appealed to for the removal of the perplexity, constitutes the great refusal of rationality to assert its rights.[2]

Later, in another significant passage, he asserts:

> In a sense all explanation must end in an ultimate arbitrariness. My demand is, that the ultimate arbitrariness of matter of fact from which our formulation starts should disclose the same general principles of reality, which we dimly discern as stretching away into regions beyond our powers of discernment.[3]

These two passages are significant for consideration

---

[1]It must be noted that the following presentation is an attempt to explicate Whitehead's doctrine of God as viewed by John Cobb. The attempt here is to present Cobb's interpretation without--for the present --questioning the validity of such vis-a-vis Whitehead's philosophy per se.

In Chapter 4 of A Christian Natural Theology, Cobb summarizes Whitehead's doctrine of God as presented in Science and the Modern World, Religion in the Making, and Process and Reality.

[2]Cobb, op. cit., p. 137, from Whitehead's, Science and the Modern World, pp. 134-135.

[3]Ibid.

at the outset of our delineation of Whitehead's
doctrine of God for two reasons. First, they point
out that God is to be an integral--and not peripheral--
aspect of Whitehead's overall philosophy, no deus ex
machina. Second, they present Whitehead's contention
that God rationally fits into his philosophical
system, for God conforms to the same general characteristics of reality which may be discerned in the
most concrete facts of existence. This highly negative attitude toward introducing God as an explanatory
principle in philosophy is reaffirmed when Whitehead
says: "God is not to be treated as an exception to
all metaphysical principles, invoked to save their
collapse. He is their chief exemplification."[1] God,
then, for Whitehead, is the ultimate metaphysical
reality that underlies and expresses itself in every
concrete occurrence of actuality or value. He does
so through three types of envisagement, namely, the
envisagement of eternal objects, the envisagement of
possibilities of value relative to the synthesis of
eternal objects, and by the envisagement of the actual
matter of fact in the context of its total situation.[2]
Explaining this activity, Cobb notes:

> ...the ultimate metaphysical reality that
> underlies and expresses itself in every
> concrete occurrence of actuality or value
> 'envisages'[3] possibilities both in pure
> abstraction and in their relevance for

---

[1]Whitehead, Process and Reality, p. 521.

[2]Whitehead describes this activity of God when
he says: "The underlying activity, as conceived
apart from the fact of realization, has three types
of envisagement. These are: first, the envisagement
of eternal objects; secondly, the envisagement of
possibilities of value in respect to the synthesis of
eternal objects; and lastly the envisagement of the
actual matter of fact which must enter into the total
situation which is achievable by the addition of the
future. But in abstraction from actuality, the
eternal activity is divorced from value." (Science
and the Modern World, pp. 154-155.).

[3]Cobb observes later: "Perhaps 'envisaging'
means no more than taking account of." (Cobb, op.
cit., p. 138.).

actual entities, as well as 'evisaging'
the actual entities themselves.[1]

Of utmost significance in his description of
divine activity is Whitehead's caution: "But in
abstraction from actuality, the eternal activity is
divorced from value."[2] Whitehead has asserted that
there is "one ultimate reality actualizing itself in
all the entities we can know or think."[3] This reality
is not static substance undergoing change, but rather,
it is itself the active ongoingness of things.[4] "What
this means," says Cobb, "is that the occurrence of
events, the sheer fact that something happens, is not
itself accidental and is not subject to explanation by
anything beyond itself."[5] This eternal activity is
totally formless. If it is to occur it must do so in
some definite way, that is, it must occur in some
actual entity. Yet, how is one to explain how that
which is essentially indeterminate becomes determinate?
How is the eternal activity, which in abstraction from
actuality is divorced from value,[6] to become determinate within actuality? In itself it is completely
indeterminate; it is "divorced from value." According
to Whitehead, then, the situation requires that we
"posit an additional metaphysical principle which
functions to provide the requisite determination.[7] He
refers to this principle as the principle of determination,[8] the principle of limitation,[9] or the principle
of concretion.[10]

These considerations lead us to recall the
ontological principle "no actual entity, no reason."

---

[1]Ibid., p. 137.

[2]Whitehead, Science and the Modern World, pp.
154-155.

[3]Cobb, op. cit., p. 139.

[4]Ibid.

[5]Ibid.

[6]Whitehead, Science and the Modern World, pp.
154-155.

[7]Cobb, op. cit., p. 140.

[8]Whitehead, Science and the Modern World, p.
257.

[9]Ibid., p. 256.

[10]Ibid., p. 250.

In abstraction from reality the divine activity is
divorced from value.[1] The reason for this divine
activity must itself be found in actuality, for apart
from the actual entity there is no reason.[2] Recalling
the ontological principle leads one to understand why
the starting point for Whitehead's assertions about
God is a consideration of God as actual entity. Every
actual entity has an aim toward fulfillment. This
Whitehead calls the subjective aim. But this aim for
fulfillment must itself derive from somewhere. It cannot come into being from nowhere, out of nothing, and
somewhere must be some actual entity.[3] The becoming
actual entities do not carry in themselves any regula-
tive principle for concretion or synthesis. Something
must provide the aim. Something must provide the principle of limitation by which the eternal objects, the
eternal possibilities for becoming, are translated from
a mere welter of disjunctive data to a concrete, limited, defined actuality. Hence, there must be a unique
actual entity which provides the subjective aim[4] for

---

[1]Cobb, op. cit., p. 137; Whitehead, Science and
the Modern World, pp. 154-155.

[2]"...the reasons for things are always to be found
in the composite nature of actual entities..." Whitehead, Process and Reality, p. 28.

[3]Leclerc, Whitehead's Metaphysics, p. 190.

[4]Sherburne explains "subjective aim" in the following: "The subjective aim of an actual entity is
the ideal of what that subject could become, which
shapes the very nature of the becomimg subject. The
doctrine that each actual entity is causa sui means
that there is not first a subject, which then sorts out
feelings; it means, rather, that there are first feelings, which, through integrations, acquire the unity
of a subject. Process doesn't presuppose a subject;
rather, the subject emerges from the process. 'This
doctrine of the inherence of the subject in the process
of its production requires that in the primary phase of
the subjective process there be a conceptual feeling of
subjective aim: the physical and other feelings originate as steps towards realizing this conceptual aim
through their treatment of initial data.' (PR 342.).

This subjective aim arises in the primary phase
of each actual entity as a result of its hybrid physical
feeling of God. As primordial, God prehends conceptually the realm of eternal objects; as consequent, he
prehends physically the actualities of the world as

28

each becoming actual entity, for without some aim
toward fulfillment the possible actual entities would
represent merely a welter of disjunctive data. The
explanation must be found in an actual entity, for
as Whitehead has stressed: "God is not to be treated
as an exception to all metaphysical principles, invoked to save their collapse. He is their chief
exemplification."[1] Whitehead's contention is, then,
that there must be a unique actual entity which provides the possibility for the concrescence of the
various actual entities. Professor Leclerc explains
Whitehead's conclusion in these terms:

> What is necessary is a criterion
> in terms of which a decision can be
> made between a wealth of alternatives,
> so that a definite concrescence of
> this data can begin.[2] There must
> accordingly be a unique actual entity
> Whitehead maintains, capable of pro-
> viding that criterion. That is to
> say, this unique actual entity 'is
> the principle of concretion--the
> principle whereby there is initiated
> a definite outcome from a situation
> otherwise riddled with ambiguity.'[3]

This unique actual entity which serves as the principle
of limitation or concretion, Whitehead calls "God."
He stresses that this has been the object of man's

---

they arise....As superject, God offers for each
actual entity, as its subjective aim, a vision of
what that entity might become....Subjective aims,
then, constitute the means by which God works in the
world." (Sherburne, op. cit., 244.).

[1]Whitehead, Process and Reality, p. 521.

[2]Or as Cobb explains: "An actual entity cannot
come into being apart from antecedent limitations.
The actual entity cannot settle for itself the logical
or cosmological relations to which it will conform.
If this is not predetermined for it, it can have no
basis for entering into those relations with the past
apart from which it cannot occur at all." (Cobb, op.
cit., p. 141.).

[3]Leclerc, op. cit., 192-193.

worship in all religions,[1] and he identifies it with
the God of the higher religions and especially with
the God of the Christian faith.[2] Hence, God is "that
actual entity from which each temporal concrescence
receives that initial aim from which its self-causation
starts."[3] To sum up, then, God is that actual entity

---

[1]Cf. Cobb, op. cit., p. 142.

[2]Of special significance are passages from pp.
520-521 of Process and Reality which reveal Whitehead's
close affinity with Christianity: "...many variations
in detail respectively fashion God in the image of an
imperial ruler, God in the image of a personification
of moral energy, God in the image of an ultimate philosophical principle. Hume's Dialogues criticize un-
answerably these modes of explaining the system of
the world....The history of theistic philosophy exhibits various stages of combination of these three diverse ways of entertaining the problem. There is,
however, in the Galilean origin of Christianity yet
another suggestion which does not fit very well with
any of the three main strands of thought. It does
not emphasize the ruling Caesar, or the ruthless
moralist, or the unmoved mover. It dwells upon the
tender elements in the world, which slowly and in
quietness operate by love and it finds purpose in the
immediacy of a kingdom not of this world. Love neither
rules, nor is it unmoved; also it is a little oblivious
as to morals. It does not look to the future; for it
finds its own reward in the immediate present."
     Commenting on this aspect of Whitehead's thought,
Sherburne notes: "When Whitehead states that he does
not conceive of God under the image of the ruling
Caesar, or the ruthless moralist, or the unmoved
mover, but rather in the spirit of the 'brief Galilean
vision of humility' that 'dwells upon the tender
elements in the world, which slowly and in quietness
operate by love,' (PR 520.), he is implicitly referring to his doctrine of God as source of subjective
aims. God works slowly because there is no compulsion
upon an actual entity to accept the proffered lure--
it is possible for a subjective aim to suffer simpli-
fication and modification in the successive phases of
concrescence." (Sherburne, A Key to Whitehead's
Process and Reality, pp. 244-245.).

[3]Whitehead, Process and Reality, p. 521.

which provides the initial aim of each becoming actual
entity, and hence the principle of limitation, the
basis for conjunction rather that disjunction, and
the principle of concrescence.

In discussing Whitehead's concept of God as
developed in Science and the Modern World, Cobb has
shown that there are three attributes of the divine or
substantial activity. First, the substantial activity
is the sheer ongoingness of things and as such is
"totally formless and neutral with respect to form."[1]
Secondly, this substantial activity which envisages
all pure possibilities for becoming--i.e. all eternal
objects--can only occur in a definite way. This points
to the fact that: "In concreto, substantial activity
is given only in actual entities which are called its
modes."[2] Thirdly, in order to explain how that which
is entirely indeterminate becomes, in the world we
know, quite determinate, Whitehead feels compelled to
posit a third metaphysical principle, the principle
of limitation, concretion or determination.[3] Whitehead calls this principle of limitation or concretion
"God," and declares that it is in fact the object of
man's worship in all religions. This means, in the
first place, that his argument for the third attribute
of the substantial activity is an agrument for the
existence of God. In the second place, the identification of the principle of limitation with the God
which is the object of religious worship means that
Whitehead has rejected an identification of the
religious God with the metaphysical ultimate or absolute.[4] Cobb notes that for the former consequence
Whitehead has never been forgiven by those who believe
that sophisticated thought has learned to do without
God, while for his rejection of the identification of
the religious God with the metaphysical absolute he in
turn has been rejected by most theologians. But
Whitehead's reasoning for such a stance is revealed in
his feeling that "religious concern is characterized
more decisively by goodness than by ultimacy."[5]

---

[1]Cobb, A Christian Natural Theology, p. 139.

[2]Ibid., p. 140; Whitehead, Science and the Modern
World, p. 255.

[3]Ibid.

[4]Ibid., p. 142. [5]Cobb, op. cit., p. 143.

He further explains his position when he points out
that if God is regarded as:

> the foundation of the metaphysical
> situation with its ultimate activity,
> ...there can be no alternative except
> to discern in Him the origin of all
> evil as well as of all good....If He
> be conceived as the supreme ground
> for limitation, it stands in his very
> nature to divide the Good from the
> Evil.[1]

In his chapter on God in Science and the Modern
World, Whitehead notes the limitations of metaphysics
when he says of Aristotle's attempt: "It did not
lead him very far towards the production of a God
available for religious purposes. It may be doubted
whether any properly general metaphysics can ever,
without the illicit introduction of other considerations get much further than Aristotle."[2] Whitehead,
does, nevertheless, view Aristotle's metaphysical
attempts as representative of "a first step without
which no evidence on a narrower experiential basis
can be of much avail in shaping the conception."[3]
Given the limitation of metaphysics, he notes that
"what further can be known about God must be sought
in the region of particular experiences, and therefore
rests on an empirical basis."[4] Cobb notes that such
a conviction on Whitehead's part led him to an investigation of religion, which, in turn, led to his
writing of the second series of the Lowell Institute
Lectures published in Religion in the Making.[5]

In Science and the Modern World metaphysics
was seen as merely a first step, but a necessary first
step in the knowledge of God, a step to which additional knowledge could be added from religious experience.

---

[1]Whitehead, Science and the Modern World, p. 161.
(258.).

[2]Ibid., p. 156. (249.).

[3]Ibid., p. 156. (250.).

[4]Whitehead, Science and the Modern World, p. 161;
Cf. Cobb, op. cit., p. 144.

[5]Cobb, op. cit., p. 144.

In Religion in the Making, however, Whitehead asserts
that "religion 'contributes its own independent evidence which metaphysics must take account of in
framing its description.'"[1] Cobb notes that this
shift in the understanding of the relation of religion
and metaphysics may be largely verbal, yet Whitehead's
new emphasis is "more on reciprocity and less on the
dependence of religious knowledge on prior philosophical doctrine."[2] Yet, Religion in the Making is primarily based on the further development of Whitehead's
philosophical thought.[3] Whitehead does not import
into his philosophy religious doctrines that have
achieved dominance in particular religious traditions.
On the contrary, he rejects the view that religious
experience provides evidence for affirming that God is
personal.[4] But he does affirm that religion offers
evidence to support the concept of a rightness
in things which is partially conformed to and partially disregarded.[5] Moreover, through religion also

---

[1]Ibid., from Whitehead, Religion in the Making,
p. 76.

[2]But note the complete quotation from Whitehead:
"Thus rational religion must have recourse to metaphysics for a scrutiny of its terms. At the same
time it contributes its own independent evidence,
which metaphysics must take account of in framing its
description." Note also Whitehead's initial remarks
in his discussion of "Religion and Metaphysics" in
Religion in the Making "Religion requires a metaphysical backing; for its authority is endangered by
the intensity of the emotions which it generates.
Such emotions are evidence of some vivid experience;
but they are a very poor guarantee for its correct
interpretation." (p. 81.). Cobb notes that this
change may be accounted for by the broad definition
of metaphysics which Whitehead employs in Religion in
the Making: Cf. note p. 82: "By 'metaphysics' I
mean the science which seeks to discover the general
ideas which are indispensably relevant to the analysis
of everything that happens."

[3]Cobb, op. cit., p. 144.

[4]Ibid.; Cf. Religion in the Making, pp. 60-64.

[5]Cobb, op. cit., p. 145; Cf. Religion in the
Making, p. 60: "There is a large concurrence in the
negative doctrine that this religious experience does
not include any direct intuition of a definite

33

we learn that "our existence is more than a succession of bare facts."[1]

According to Cobb, then, Religion in the Making represents a repetition, supplementation and alteration of the doctrine of God developed in Science and the Modern World. Cobb illustrates this interpretation in Whitehead's own words: "The universe exhibits a creativity with infinite freedom, and a realm of forms with infinite possibilities; but...this creativity and these forms are together impotent to achieve actuality apart from the completed ideal harmony, which is God."[2] Cobb points out that this is fundamentally a simple restatement of the position presented in Science and the Modern World, but it also supplements the position presented there by referring to God as a "completed ideal harmony."[3] God considered as the "conceptual ideal harmony" functions as the principle of limitation "by ordering the infinite possibilities of the eternal objects according to principles of value."[4] Hence, is evidenced the fact that the envisagement of the eternal objects which was designated as a dimension of substantial activity in Science and the Modern World is attributed to God. This envis-

---

person or individual. It is a character of permanent rightness, whose inherence in the nature of things modifies both efficient and final cause, so that the one conforms to harmonious conditions, and the other contrasts itself with an harmonious ideal. The harmony in the actual world is conformity with the character."

[1]Cobb, op. cit., p. 145.

[2]Ibid,; Whitehead, Religion in the Making, pp. 119-120.

[3]Cobb, op. cit., p. 145. As Cobb further elaborates this position: "In other passages this is stated in a variety of ways. God is said to hold 'the ideal forms apart in equal, conceptual realization of knowledge, '--so that as concepts, they are grasped together in the synthesis of omniscience.' (RM 153.). God is a conceptual fusion of values, 'embracing the concept of all such possibilities graded in harmonious, relative subordination.'" (Ibid.).

[4]Ibid., pp. 145-146.

agement is not a function additional to the principle of limitation, but rather explains how that principle operates.[1]

Cobb notes a further change in Whitehead's concept of God as presented in Religion in the Making. In Science and the Modern World, Whitehead's stress had been that "God is not concrete," which assertion, says Cobb, certainly meant that God was not actual.[2] Cobb had already cautioned that Whitehead's concept of an underlying activity which envisaged possibilities for becoming could not be interpreted anthropomorphically, for the underlying activity was regarded as not being actual.[3] Yet, in Religion in the Making, God is consistently referred to as an actual entity. This assertion does not reject the view that God functions as the principle of limitation. It rather supplements the view by asserting that it is an actual entity which functions as the principle of limitation.[4]

The assertion that God is an actual entity rather than a nonconcrete principle makes it possible to attribute to him[5] characteristics other than those

---

[1]Ibid., p. 146.

[2]Ibid.

[3]Cobb, op. cit., p. 146; Cf. also pp. 137-138. Cobb quotes from Whitehead to support his case: "The underlying activity, as conceived apart from the fact of realization, has three types of envisagement. These are: first, the envisagement of eternal objects; secondly, the envisagement of possibilities of value in respect to the synthesis of eternal objects; and lastly, the envisagement of the actual matter of fact which must enter into the total situation which is achievable by the addition of the future. But in abstraction from actuality, the eternal activity is divorced from value." (Cobb, p. 137; from Science and the Modern World, pp. 154-155.). Yet, Cobb seems to ignore the segments of the quote: "...as conceived apart from the fact of realization" and "...in abstraction from actuality, the eternal activity is divorced from value."

[4]Cobb, op. cit., p. 146.

[5]Perhaps Fritz Guy's cautionary statement is noteworthy at this point: "Whitehead regularly used the pronoun 'he' in referring to God, but this was

which the latter designation would allow. Hence,
Whitehead speaks of God as having purpose,[1] knowledge,[2]
vision,[3] wisdom,[4] consciousness,[5] and love.[6] It has
been noted earlier that Whitehead emphasizes the impossibility on the part of religious experience to
justify our speaking of God as personal. Moreover, he
criticizes the Semitic conception of God as a personal
creator,[7] and denies that there is adequate warrant for
religious experience to declare the actuality of God.[8]
Yet, the declaration that God is actual entity, and

------

merely following convention and not an indication of
'personality' in God (cf. RM 60-64) as in traditional
Christian thought. Had Whitehead used a different
proper noun to refer to God (such as 'Eros,' which
occurs occasionally in AI), he would certainly have
used 'it' rather than 'he' where such a pronoun was
required. His reason for using 'God' was that 'the
contemplation of our natures, as enjoining real feelings derived from the timeless source of all order,
acquires that 'subjective form' of refreshment and
companionship at which religions aim' (PR 47.)."
(Fritz Guy, "Comments on a Recent Whiteheadian Doctrine
of God," Andrews University Seminary Studies, Volume
4, July, 1966, p. 109, note 11.

    [1]Whitehead, Religion in the Making, pp. 100, 101,
152.

    [2]Ibid., p. 148.
    [3]Ibid., p. 151.
    [4]Ibid., p. 154.
    [5]Ibid., p. 152.
    [6]Ibid.

    [7]Cobb, op. cit., p. 147; Religion in the Making,
pp. 66-69.

    [8]Cobb, op. cit., p. 147; Cf. Religion in the
Making, pp. 66-70. Cobb's description of this aspect
of Whitehead's stance is: "He even denies that
religious experience provides adequate warrant for
affirming the actuality of God, since 'the Eastern
Asiatic concept of an impersonal order to which the
world conforms' is given equal status with other
doctrines." The segment of this quote which consists
of a quote from Religion in the Making, p. 66 seems
to be taken somewhat out of context. Whitehead does
not seem to be saying that "impersonal order" renders

the utilization of personalistic language to describe
God is presented in the more philosophical part of
Religion in the Making.[1] Cobb explains this change
in Whitehead's thought when he says:

> Apparently the basic reason for the change
> in tone and language is that the function
> of providing limitation to ensure order
> and value could be assigned only to an
> actual entity. Once God is regarded as an
> actual entity, the use of personalistic
> language follows naturally, for our basic
> clue to the nature of an acutal entity is
> given in our own immediate human experience.[2]

The former part of Cobb's reasoning is substantiated
when Whitehead asserts: "The definite determination
which imposes ordered balance on the world requires an
actual entity imposing its own unchanged consistency
of character on every phase.[3]

While these words of Whitehead serve to assert
the necessity of an actual entity to impose "ordered
balance on the world," they also indicate that this
required entity is indeed a unique or special type
of actual entity. This actual entity differs from

---

proof of actuality of God an impossibility. He does
say, however, that such proof is problematic in that:
"Any proof which commences with the consideration of
the character of the actual world cannot rise above
the actuality of this world. It can only discover
all the factors disclosed in the world as experienced.
In other words, it may discover an immanent God, but
not a God wholly transcendent. The difficulty can
be put in this way: by considering the world we can
find all the factors required by the total metaphysical
situation; but we cannot discover anything not included in this totality of actual fact, and yet explanatory of it." (p. 69.).

[1]Whitehead, Religion in the Making, p. 147.

[2]Cobb, op. cit., p. 147.

[3]Whitehead, Religion in the Making, p. 92.

all others in that it is non-temporal.[1] The fact that
God is non-temporal, however, does not entail that he
"confront every new temporal entity with his ideal
envisagement of value in just the same way."[2] This
is indicated by the following passage from Religion
in the Making:

> He is the binding element in the
> world. The consciousness which is in-
> dividual in us, is universal in him:
> the love which is partial in us all-em-
> bracing in him. Apart from him there
> could be no world, because there could
> be no adjustment of individuality. His
> purpose in the world is quality of at-
> tainment. His purpose is always embodied
> in the particular ideals relevant to the
> actual state of the world. Thus all
> attainment is immortal in that it fash-
> ions the actual ideals which are God in
> the world as it is now. Every act
> leaves the world with a deeper or a
> fainter impress of God. He then passes
> into his next relation to the world with
> enlarged or diminished, presentation of
> ideal values.[3]

This passage also serves to indicate another new
element presented in Religion in the Making. That
God "then passes into his next relation to the world
with enlarged or diminished presentation of ideal

---

[1]Cobb, op. cit., p. 147; Cf. Whitehead, Religion
in the Making: "These formative elements (of the
temporal world) are: ...The actual but non-temporal
entity whereby the indetermination of mere creativity
is transmuted into a determinate freedom. This non-
temporal actual entity is what men call God--the
supreme God of rationalized religion." (p. 88.).
And later: "His completion, so that he is exempt from
transition into something else, must mean that his
nature remains self-consistent in relation to all
change." (pp. 95-96.).

[2]Cobb, op. cit., p. 148.

[3]Whitehead, Religion in the Making, p. 152.

values,"[1] asserts that he is to be understood as
affected by the world. God not only envisages eternal
objects but also actual entities. God makes possible
order and value in the world, and the world acts
upon God, which, in turn, affects God's new relation
to the world.[2] There is interaction between God
and the world. Hence, "the general principle of the
interaction of actual entities is applied to God
who now appears as the supreme actual entity."[3]

It has been noted that changes have occurred
in Whitehead's doctrine of God. In Science and the
Modern World four metaphysical principles were presented, namely, the underlying substantial activity
and its three attributes: eternal objects, actual
entities and the principle of limitation.[4] In Religion
in the Making certain changes are made. In the first
place, the substantial activity is now called creativity and the complete interdependence of the four
principles is stressed rather than the predominance
of one.[5] Second, God is now conceived as an actual
entity and the four metaphysical principles can
be said to have been reduced to three. These are
creativity, eternal objects and actual entities, which
include God as a special actual entity, the "special"
serving as a reminder that there is a major difference
between God as non-temporal and the temporal actual
entities.[6] Hence, Cobb terminates his delineation of
Whitehead's doctrine of God in Religion in the Making
by summarily concluding:

> He is an actual entity who envisages and
> orders the realm of eternal possibilities.
> He adds himself to the world as the vision
> of ideal possibility, from which every new
> occasion takes its rise, thereby ensuring
> a measure of order and value in a situation
> that could otherwise be only chaotic and
> indeed could achieve no actuality at all.
> The world, in its turn, reacts upon him so
> as to affect the way in which he, in his
> turn acts upon it.[7]

---

[1] Ibid.
[2] Cobb, op. cit., p. 148.
[3] Ibid.
[4] Ibid., pp. 148-149.

[5] Ibid., p. 149.
[6] Cobb, op. cit., p. 149.
[7] Ibid.

Having offered this summary, Cobb notes that Whitehead adds "nothing really new" to his doctrine after Religion in the Making. "All the ingredients are here,"[1] but other important questions are dealt with in Process and Reality, "the greatest of Whitehead's philosophical writings."[2] These include a delineation of the relation of God to creativity, the status of eternal objects in relation to God's envisagement, a consideration of the way the world acts upon God, and an attempt to harmonize such action with the doctrine of God as non-temporal.[3] We now turn to these considerations.

Whitehead has thus far described reality in terms of actual entities, eternal objects, or pure possibilities for realization, and the underlying metaphysical principle of creativity, which depicts the sheer ongoingness of nature. The actual entities exist momentarily, perish, and as perished become data constitutive of their successors.[4] Of Whitehead's understanding of this situation Cobb observes: "No one of these factors singly and no combination of them can explain the concrete particularity of what in fact becomes. Unless we affirm that this concrete particularity is an illusion, we must acknowledge that another factor is working."[5]

Each actual occasion has a subjective aim at a determinate satisfaction. It prehends eternal objects and temporal entities in its past in terms of this aim. But, how does the subjective aim occur? If it is said that each occasion produces its own aim out of nothing an account regarding the randomness of its choice would still be requisite. The initial phase of the subjective aim of an occasion--i.e. its initial aim--is given to the occasion "to determine its limits by the principle of limitation which transcends every temporal occasion and which Whitehead calls God."[6] The question of how this aim is derived

---

[1] Ibid.
[2] Ibid., p. 150.
[3] Ibid., pp. 149-150.
[4] Cobb, op. cit., pp. 150-151.
[5] Ibid., p. 151.
[6] Ibid.

from God is crucial.[1]

In our ordinary language aim is understood
indiscriminately in three ways: as a pure possibility
one strives to actualize, as the actualization of
a possibility, and as the act of aiming. This same
ambiguity can be seen in Whitehead's usage, but it
need cause no confusion,

> for the eternal object can constitute
> the aim only when an occasion is act-
> ively aiming at its realization; the
> satisfaction aimed at is always the
> actualization of some determinate pos-
> sibility (eternal object); and
> the act of aiming is always directed to-
> ward such an actualization.[2]

Focusing upon the act of aiming itself, Cobb
points out that, in the first place, the initial aim
determines what locus or standpoint each occasion
will occupy. Hence, the occasion comes to be within
a perspective which is already settled for it.[3]
Second, the subjective aim determines the kind of
satisfaction at which the occasion will initially aim,
and thus influences the satisfaction actually attained.[4] The initial aim, then, is always at the best
possible actualization, given the situation, but it
also includes indetermination waiting to be deter-

---

[1]Note Cobb's explanation of Whitehead's stance:
"In Science and the Modern World, we noted how Whitehead first criticized the introduction of God into
philosophical systems and then himself introduced him.
There was no strict contradiction. What Whitehead
objected to there and again in later writings was not
the introduction of God as an explanatory factor as
such, but the failure to explain how God performs the
requisite function. (Process and Reality 78, 219, 289;
The Function of Reason 24; Adventures of Ideas 171.).
Yet, Whitehead's own treatment there is highly vulner-
able to that criticism, and in Religion in the Making
does not entirely escape the same objection. In
Process and Reality, the way God functions as the
principle of limitation is extensively articulated for
the first time." (Cobb, op. cit., p. 150.).

[2]Ibid., p. 152. [3]Ibid., pp. 152-153.
[4]Ibid., pp. 153-154.

mined by the occasion itself in its subsequent development.[1]

Hence, the actual entity's concrescence is not totally arbitrary. Each has an initial aim which determines the range of possibilities and places it within a settled perspective. This initial aim is derived from God, and it is through provision of the aim that God functions in his role as the principle of limitation. God functions as the principle of limitation by ordering the eternal objects. Two things must be noted with reference to this ordering. In the first place, God's ordering of eternal objects is primordial or eternally unchanging.[2] Second, the ordering specifies the initial aim for each occasion.[3] Cobb recognizes the tension involved in attempting to entertain both these assertions. He explains how one unchanging order can provide the aim for each occasion, when he says:

> The solution seems to be that the eternal
> ordering of the eternal objects is not
> one simple order but an indefinite variety
> or orders. God's ordering of possibilities

---

[1]Explaining this aspect of Whitehead's thought Cobb asserts: "Some particular possibility must be ideal, given the situation. But closely related to this possibility are others, appropriate to the situation although deviating from the ideal. The initial aim thus involves the envisagement of a set of related and relevant possibilities from among which the final satisfaction of the occasion will in fact be chosen. These are all bounded by the definite limits required for the maintenance of minimal order. Yet they allow for so large a measure of self-determination that higher levels of order are subject to destruction by occasions that reject the ideal possibilities they confront in favor of others of lesser value. Whitehead shows here the sensitive balance between the freedom and the determinism of the cosmos, and how order is sustained and enhanced while constantly threatened by the possibility of decay." (p. 154.).

[2]Cobb, op. cit., p. 155; Process and Reality, p. 46; 523-534.

[3]Ibid.

42

is such that every possible state of the
actual world is already envisioned as possible and every possible development from
that actual state of the world is already
envisioned and appraised. Thus, the one
primordial ordering of eternal objects
is relevant to every actuality with perfect specificity.[1]

Cobb here refers to what Whitehead calls the "primordial nature of God,"[2] that is God as "the unlimited
conceptual realization of the absolute wealth of
potentiality."[3] This means that in his primordial
nature God conceptually realizes all of the varied
possibilities for fulfillment of all possible actual
entities. But merely as primordial, he is "deficiently
actual" in two ways. First, his feelings are only
conceptual, and as such lack the fullness of actuality.
Second, mere conceptual feelings apart from their integration with physical feelings are devoid of consciousness. His conceptual feeling for all possibilities come from his own creative act apart from any
particular course of things. "He is the unconditioned
actuality of conceptual feeling at the base of
things."[4] As such, he entertains conceptually or
envisages all unchanging possibilities for realization.
This is the immutable character of God.

It has been noted that the initial aim of each
occasion is derived from God. But how does a particular eternal object or set of eternal objects become
effective in a novel occasion? Cobb notes that Whitehead "tells us little more than that the initial
aim is derived from God,"[5] but he does suggest further

---

[1]Ibid., pp. 156-157; Process and Reality, p. 134.

[2]The primordial nature of God and the consequent
nature of God do not admit to division in actuality,
but for purposes of discussion the concepts must be
abstracted from actuality and discussed separately.

[3]Whitehead, Process and Reality, p. 521.

[4]Ibid., p. 522.

[5]Cobb, op. cit., p. 156.

explanation. God, like all other actual entities, has an aim at intensity of feeling. This aim is primordial, determining the ordering of eternal objects. Yet, this general aim, to be efficacious, must be actualized in specific occasions. Hence, God entertains for each occasion the aim for its ideal satisfaction. He desires its realization. "If God entertains such a propositional feeling," notes Cobb, "we may conjecture that the new occasion prehends God in terms of this propositional feeling about itself and does so with a subjective form of appetition conformal to that of God."[1]

In identifying God with the principle of limitation, and in asserting that God is an actual entity, Whitehead indicates his contention that only something actual could perform the role of limitation.[2] In fact, apart from actual entities, nothing can have influence or be effective. But what of eternal objects? They must be effective; they must be the reason for something, or else they would be superfluous to the system. Moreover, the principle of limitation itself operates only by their graded effectiveness for new occasions. But they are not actual entities.[3] Hence, how are they operative and effective? Since they are not actual entities their effectiveness must be by virtue of some agency beyond themselves.[4] They can affect

---

[1]Ibid., pp. 156-157.

[2]This is merely a continued affirmation of the ontological principle which states "that every condition to which the process of becoming conforms in any particular instance, has its reason either in the character of some actual entity in the actual world of that concrescence, or in the character of the subject which is in process of concrescence....This ontological principle means that actual entities are the only reasons." (Process and Reality, pp. 36-37.).

[3]Cobb, op. cit., p. 158.

[4]In support of this contention, Cobb notes Whitehead's assertion: "Apart from God, eternal objects unrealized in the actual world would be relatively non-existent for the concrescence in question." (Cobb, p. 158, note 87, from Process and Reality, p. 46.).

events only in being envisaged by God. God is therefore not merely the principle of limitation but--as
the one upon whom the effectiveness of the pure possibilities for becoming, the eternal objects, depends--
also the principle of potentiality.[1] In Process and
Reality Whitehead affirms that the eternal objects
are presupposed by virtue of God's envisagement. God's
relation to eternal objects is presupposed by all other
actual entities.[2] God's ordering of eternal objects
is also requisite for all realization of novelty.

Thus far we have focused primarily upon the
primordial nature of God. We have seen that God in
his primordial nature envisions all the possibilities
for actualization. He is the principle of limitation,
potentiality, and novelty.[3] This is the permanent,
unchanging aspect of God. He establishes the subjective aim of each actual entity, but within a perspective which gives it freedom so that it virtually
chooses its own path of fulfillment, guided by God's
lure, or by the appetition or desire for fulfillment
which God has given it. In his primordial nature,
then, God functions in such a way that out of a welter
of disjunctive data there issues conjunction. It was
noted earlier, however, that the primordial nature of
God cannot be considered apart from the consequent nature. Whitehead makes this clear when he says of
God that:

> he is the principle of concretion--the
> principle whereby there is initiated a
> definite outcome from a situation other-
> wise riddled with ambiguity....But God,
> as well as being primordial, is also
> consequent. He is the beginning and the
> end. He is not the beginning in the
> sense of being in the past of all members.
> He is the presupposed actuality of con-
> ceptual operation in unison of becoming
> with every other creative act.[4]

---

[1]Cobb, op. cit., p. 158.
[2]Ibid., p. 160.
[3]Cf. Ibid., pp. 158, 160, 161.
[4]Whitehead, Process and Reality, p. 523.

This passage indicates the distinction which Whitehead intends to make by focusing on the one hand on the dimension of God which involves permanency and immutability, the primordial nature of God, and on the other hand on the dimension of God in which the actual occasions affect God. The primordial nature of God emphasizes his all-inclusive, unchanging aspects. But in the consequent nature of God we see the "becoming" of God himself. As Whitehead summarizes: "God's conceptual nature is unchanged, by reason of its final completeness. But his derivative nature is consequent upon the creative advance of the world."[1]

The consequent nature of God is God's physical pole, that is, his consequent nature is his prehension of the temporal actual entities. Since there is a succession of these actual entities, there is a succession in God's prehension of them as actual which suggests temporality on the part of God. God's prehension of the temporal actual entities, however exemplifies a completeness lacking in the prehension of data by other actual entities. God prehends the actual completely and without the perishing exemplified in all other actual entities. Hence, as consequent, God is everlasting. Every achievement of value is preserved in God's consequent nature everlastingly. Some aspect of every occasion is preserved everlastingly in God.[2]

In his consequent nature God is conscious.[3] His primordial nature consists merely of conceptual feelings which are never conscious. But his consequent

---

[1]Ibid., pp. 523-524.

[2]Cobb, op. cit., pp. 162-163.

[3]Perhaps Whitehead's use of "conscious" and "unconscious" requires some elaboration at this point. In Process and Reality, Whitehead consistently refers to God in his primordial nature as unconscious while in his consequent nature, he is conscious. Cf. Process and Reality p. 521 in which Whitehead says of God that as primordial: "His feelings are only conceptual and so lack the fullness of actuality. Secondly, conceptual feelings, apart from complex integration with physical feelings, are devoid of consciousness in their subjective forms." Note also

46

nature consists of the interweaving of conceptual and physical feelings requisite of consciousness.[1] In his consequent nature, God realizes the world as it becomes, and transforms it by his wisdom. He judges the world, and through his infinite patience adjusts the possibilities of fulfillment so that even when an actual entity negatively prehends his lure for feeling (i.e. deviates from the possibility of ideal fulfillment offered by God) God's judgment is nevertheless "the judgment of a tenderness which loses nothing that can be saved."[2] Since all of this is presented with great clarity and precision in Whitehead's own words, I take the liberty to quote a rather lengthly passage from Process and Reality which summarizes God's action in his consequent nature:

> The wisdom of subjective aim prehends
> every actuality for what it can be in such
> a perfected system--its sufferings, its
> sorrows, its failures, its triumphs, its
> immediacies of joy--woven by rightness of
> feeling into the harmony of the universal
> feeling, which is always immediate, always

Whitehead's contention that "...when we make a distinction of reason and consider God in the abstraction of a primordial actuality, we must ascribe to him neither fulness of feeling, nor consciousness." (Process and Reality, pp. 521-522.). This is in agreement with Whitehead's reminder that "consciousness presupposes experience and not experience consciousness." (p. 85.). As Whitehead explains: "Consciousness is how we feel the affirmation-negation contrast." (p. 372.). Commenting on Whitehead's understanding of this aspect of consciousness, Sherburne notes: "An affirmation-negation contrast involves holding together in a unity as one datum a feeling of a nexus of actual entities and a feeling of a proposition with its logical subjects members of the nexus." (Sherburne, p. 214.). The primordial nature of God rules out consciousness as thus understood.

[1]Ibid., p. 164; Whitehead, Process and Reality, p. 521.

[2]Whitehead, Process and Reality, p. 525.

many, always one, always with novel advance, moving onward and never perishing.
The revolts of destructive evil, purely
self-regarding, are dismissed into their
triviality of merely individual facts;
and yet the good they did achieve in individual joy, in individual sorrow, in
the introduction of needed contrast, is
yet saved by its relation to the completed
whole. The image--and it is but an image--
the image under which this operative
growth of God's nature is best conceived
is that of a tender care that nothing be
lost.

The consequent nature of God is his
judgment on the world as it passes into
the immediacy of his own life. It is the
judgment of a tenderness which loses nothing that can be saved. It is also the
judgment of a wisdom which uses what in
the temporal world is mere wreckage.[1]

This passage also serves to indicate that the principle
of universal relativity is applicable to God himself.
Just as God in his consequent nature prehends the
actual entities, so also the actual entities prehend
God's consequent nature.[2]

We have seen that the universe includes a three-
fold creative act. First, there is God in his
primordial nature, "the one infinite conceptual
realization."[3] Second, there is the free physical
realization in the temporal world, that is the actual
entities in their becoming. Third, there is the
ultimate unity of the multiplicity of actual entities
with the primordial conceptual fact. This entire
creative process may be stated in terms of the interrelation of God and the world. The consequent nature
of God is his fulfillment as he receives the multiplicity of actuality into his own actualization. It
is God as really actual, not merely conceptually actual as in his primordial nature.

---

[1]Whitehead, Process and Reality, p. 525.
[2]Cobb, op. cit., p. 164.
[3]Whitehead, Process and Reality, p. 525.

Thus we see that the consequent nature of God
is composed of the unity of a multiplicity of elements
which have individual self-realization. It is just
as much a multiplicity as it is a unity.[1] Each
entity in its full satisfaction or in its realization
of its full potential retains its self-identity. "Thus
the actuality of God must also be understood as a
multiplicity of actual components in process of
creation. This is God in his function of the kingdom
of heaven."[2] At this stage of realization, however,
there is no mere static unity. The principle of
creativity is still operative. As Whitehead points
out: "Neither God, nor the World, reaches static
completion. Both are in the grip of the ultimate
metaphysical ground, the creative advance into
novelty."[3]

Whitehead sums up his whole philosophy by pointing out that there are four phases in which the
universe accomplishes its actuality.[4] It will be
noted that God is central in this accomplishment.
First, there is the phase of conceptual origination,
which is deficient in actuality, "but infinite in its
adjustment of valuation."[5] This is God's primordial
nature. Second, there is the temporal phase of
physical origination giving rise to the multiplicity
of actualities. This is directed by God's establishing
subjective aims. Third, is the phase of perfected
actuality, "in which the many are one everlastingly,
without the qualification of any loss either of

---

[1]Cf. Whitehead's antitheses, Process and Reality,
p. 528.

[2]Whitehead, Process and Reality, p. 531; Cf.
the chapter entitled "Peace" in Adventures of Ideas.
The concept "kingdom of heaven" is a designation applied to the fully realized consequent nature of God
as he receives the multiplicity of actuality into His
own actualization. The concept is only used once in
Whitehead's delineation of his doctrine of God in
Process and Reality, and therefore does not permit of
further elaboration here.

[3]Ibid., p. 529.

[4]The parallel with Nicolus Cusanus' four creative
phases is interesting to note.

[5]Whitehead, Process and Reality, p. 532.

individual identity or of completeness of unity."[1]
God functions as the ground of this phase, or the
principle of limitation and concretion which directs
by his lure for feeling. In the fourth phase of
creativity the creative action completes itself. This
is accomplished throughout all dimensions of creativity
by God's "infinite patience" and tender care that
nothing be lost.[2]

We have noted at the outset that Whitehead has
stressed that metaphysics could not go far toward
delineating an idea of God which would be both available and acceptable for religion. In his later formulations, however, the doctrine of God as an actual
entity was seen to be required as an explanatory
principle without which there would be no entity at
all. Yet, Whitehead stresses the difference between
his doctrine of God and traditional theological formulations. In the first place, he repudiates the
doctrine of God as an unmoved mover and as eminently
real.[3] Second, he rejects the attribution to God of
any characteristics which make him an exception to the
metaphysical categories descriptive of all other
aspects of actuality.[4] Third, he emphasizes that both
God and the world presuppose each other so that ontological or temporal priority can be assigned to

---

[1]Ibid.

[2]Ibid., p. 525.

[3]"So long as the temporal world is conceived as
a self-sufficient completion of the creative act, ex-
plicable by its derivation from an ultimate principle
which is at once eminently real and the unmoved mover,
from this conclusion there is no escape: the best
that we can say of the turmoil is, 'For he giveth his
beloved--sleep.'" (Process and Reality, p. 519.).

[4]"...God is not to be treated as an exception to
all metaphysical principles, invoked to save their
collapse. He is their chief exemplification."
(Process and Reality, p. 521.).

neither.[1]

> God and the World stand over against each
> other expressing the final metaphysical
> truth that appetitive vision and physical
> enjoyment have equal claim to priority in
> creation. But no two actualities can be
> torn apart: each is all in all. Thus
> each temporal occasion embodies God and
> is embodied in God.[2]

These three emphases underscore the difference between
Whitehead's doctrine of God and that of traditional
theism. He opposes the one-sided emphasis on the

---

[1]This is made clear in his famous **antitheses**,
immediately prior to which he cautions that in presenting these he has not abandoned his rationalism, for
"in each antithesis there is a shift of meaning which
converts the opposition into a contrast." (Process
and Reality, p. 528.). These antitheses are:
   "It is as true to say that God is permanent
and the World fluent, as that the World is permanent
and God fluent.
   "It is as true to say that God is one and the
World many, as that the World is one and God many.
   "It is as true to say that, in comparison with
the World, God is actual eminently, as that, in
comparison with God, the world is actual eminently.
   "It is as true to say that the World is immanent
in God, as that God is immanent in the World.
   "It is as true to say that God transcends the
World, as that the World transcends God.
   "It is as true to say that God creates the World,
as that the World creates God.
   "God and the World are the contrasted opposites
in terms of which Creativity achieves its supreme task
of transforming disjoined unity, with its diversities
in contrast. In each actuality these are two concrescent poles of realization--'enjoyment' and 'appetition,'
that is, the 'physical' and the 'conceptual.' For
God the conceptual is prior to the physical, for the
World the physical poles are prior to the conceptual
poles." (Process and Reality, p. 528.).
   [2]Ibid., p. 529.

permanence, eminent actuality, unity, transcendence,
and creative power of God. He affirms these only in
polar tension with other factors which traditional
theism usually negates of God.[1]

---

[1]Cobb, op. cit., p. 166.

C. John Cobb's Whiteheadian Doctrine of God

    In the preceding we have examined some basic
notions of Whitehead's philosophy along with a brief
summary of Whitehead's doctrine of God. We have felt
this presentation to be necessary because of Cobb's
close adherence to and indebtedness to Whitehead's
philosophy. Of his own position Cobb notes: "I have
identified myself fully with the position I have expounded on Whitehead's authority."[1] Moreover, Cobb
finds "Whitehead's philosophical reasons for affirming
God and his attempt to show that God is not an exception to all the categories...philosophically responsible and even necessary."[2] Nevertheless, Cobb
asserts that at several points Whitehead's answers
create more problems "than would some alternative
answers."[3] While Cobb sees that Whitehead's interpretation of God entails that God as actual entity exemplify the categories necessary to all actual occasions, he, nevertheless, stresses that there are
other features of actual occasions besides the
strictly necessary ones. He argues that if Whitehead
is to make his system more coherent, he must interpret
God as conforming to these aspects of actual occasions
as well as the strictly necessary features. With
these considerations of Cobb in mind, we turn to his
attempt "to develop a doctrine of God more coherent
with Whitehead's general cosmology and metaphysics
than are some aspects of his own doctrine."[4] Cobb's
attempt includes five areas of Whitehead's thought.
These include: God as Actual Entity, God and Time,
God and Space, God and the Eternal Objects, and God
and Creativity. The first task, then, is an attempt
to explicate Cobb's doctrine. Only then can we examine the contention that it is more coherent than
some aspects of Whitehead's own doctrine.

----

[1]Cobb, A Christian Natural Theology, p. 176.

[2]Ibid., p. 177.

[3]Ibid.

[4]Ibid., p. 176.

1. God as Actual Entity

We first examine Cobb's evaluation of Whitehead's conception of God as an actual entity.

Cobb believes that there are inconsistencies, that is, contradictions in Whitehead's philosophy, but such contradictions are minor and easily remedied.[1] But there is more to incoherence than mere logical inconsistency. A system is also incoherent if it contains "arbitrary disconnection of first principles."[2] It is Cobb's contention that Whitehead's system is subject to such a critique in that the four ultimate elements of his system--i.e. actual entities, God, eternal objects, and creativity--are arbitrarily disconnected. Although Cobb views Whitehead as moving far toward overcoming such disconnectedness and incoherence, he, nevertheless, asserts "that one can go, and therefore should go, further yet."[3]

According to Cobb, Whitehead is inconsistent in his development of God as an actual entity in that he deals too often with the consequent and primordial nature of God as if they were genuinely separable entities.[4] Also, his writings frequently imply that God is merely an addition of these two natures.[5] Cobb feels that this criticism is justified by several considerations. In the first place, where Whitehead introduced God as a systematic element in his philosophy, he did so by treating God merely as one attribute of the substantial activity without attempting to assimilate God to any other of the categories. Secondly, in the doctrine of God developed in Process and Reality, which exemplifies a direct continuity with the earlier delineation, most of the references to God are references to the primordial nature of God. Finally, when Whitehead does discuss the consequent nature of God, he stresses that, unlike the primordial nature, the consequent nature is fully actual. But it is not stated with precision that God is actual by virtue of his con-

---

[1]Ibid., p. 177.
[2]Ibid., p. 177; Cf. Process and Reality, p. 9.
[3]Ibid.
[4]Cobb, A Christian Natural Theology, p. 178.
[5]Ibid.

sequent nature. Yet, even this is not enough, for
what must be said is not merely that God is actual by
virtue of his consequent nature, but rather it must
be said that God is actual by virtue of his being an
actual entity, and his being an actual entity entails
both primordial and consequent natures.[1]

We have noted that Cobb further criticizes Whitehead for frequently writing as though God were merely
an addition of these two natures, with the primordial
nature performing some functions while the consequent
nature performs others. Cobb rejects this interpretation as misleading, for although actual entities are
unities composed of both a mental and a physical pole,
they, nevertheless, are not exhaustively analyzable
merely in terms of these two poles. Such an attempt
to analyze an actual entity merely in terms of the
addition of the analyzation of the two poles taken
individually, would omit the subjective unity, concrete
satisfaction, the power of decision and self-creation
requisite of an actual entity.[2] In stressing that any
analysis of an actual entity must consist primarily of
a consideration of the entity as a unity, Cobb notes:
"It is always the actual entity that acts, not one of
its poles as such, although in many of its functions
one pole or another may be primarily relevant."[3]
Although Cobb feels that Whitehead "must certainly
have meant to say this also about God," he, nevertheless, asserts that Whitehead is misleading in his
"separate and contrasting" treatment of the two
natures.[4]

Realizing these problems in Whitehead's philosophical endeavor, Cobb proposes to attempt "to explain
the way in which God is related to actual occasions,
eternal objects, and creativity in such a way that at
no point do we attribute to him a mode of being or relation inexplicable in terms of the principles operative elsewhere in the system."[5]

---

[1]Ibid.
[2]Ibid., p. 178.
[3]Ibid.
[4]Ibid.
[5]Ibid., p. 179.

The first problem which Cobb faces is that of how God's ordering of eternal objects is primordial and eternally unchanging, while at the same time having the ability to specify the initial aim for each new occasion.[1] How can God's aim for satisfaction for every occasion be wholly timeless and yet become effective and relevant at particular moments?

Cobb approaches the problem by analyzing a possible way in which the subjective aim of an entity arises. The initial aim is a feeling of a proposition accompanied by the subjective desire for its actualization. A proposition is a togetherness or nexus of actual entities with some eternal object. In temporal occasions the initial aim is always an aim at some intensity of feeling both in the entity itself and in its relevant future. It is the aim at some intensity for the future, i.e. the unrealized intensity, which gives rise to tensions between that which is and that at which the entity is aiming. But in God no such tension exists because the ideal aim for himself and for the world coincide.[2] Cobb explains this by noting that "we may simplify and say that God's aim is at ideal strength of beauty and that this aim is eternally unchanging."[3]

Yet, Cobb notes that there must be some tension even in God between immediate and more remote realizations of intensity. This contention is clarified in Cobb's discussion of knowledge on the part of God. He says:

---

[1]Ibid., p. 179-180; Cf. p. 155 where the tension between these two areas of God's activity is first noted.

[2]This same point is presented clearly in an unpublished essay in which Cobb asserts: "In terms of concern, human subjects care for some few others in some partial way and in some painful tension with their preoccupation with themselves. The divine experience has perfect sympathy with all other experiences and seeks their richest fulfillment in no tension with its self-concern." (John B. Cobb, "Affirming God in a Non-Theistic Age." p. 4.)

[3]Cobb, A Christian Natural Theology, pp. 180-181.

In terms of knowledge, human experience at
best in a faltering and distorted way cor-
responds with some tiny segment of the
reality that exists over against it. The
divine experience is ideally related to all
reality without distortion and limitation.
God knows what is actual as actual and what
is possible as possible.[1]

Although Cobb can say that the divine knowledge is
"ideally related to all realtiy without distortion and
limitation," the tension is presented in that God
knows the possible ideal actualization for the world
but only as possibly actual, not actually actual. The
tension in knowing what is possible while not yet
knowing the possible will be actualized designates a
tension even within God. This is true because God
sees the possible merely as possible and not as actual
until it is actually actualized.

How individual aims can be timeless and yet become relevantly effective in particular moments of
time is exemplified by a consideration of the situation of man. Man's aim at realization is an aim involving both his immediate moment of becoming and his
future satisfaction. He aims at actualizing himself
in the present in such a way that his future aim will
continue to have possibility for fulfillment, or perhaps better stated, his present aim is such that its
realization provides that the possibilty for his
future realization will be greater. Within the context
of his aim there will be occasions of experience other
than his own about which he must entertain some propositional feeling.[2] Hence, there will be a large interweaving of secondary aims within the context of his
primary aim for ideal satisfaction. His aim for his
own ideal satisfaction will remain constant, but it

---

[1]Cobb, "Affirming God in a Non-Theistic Age," p.4.

[2]Cf. "A Whiteheadian Christology," an unpublished
essay in which Cobb discusses the way in which one
actual entity is present "in" another actual entity.
The problem is also dealt with in "The Finality of
Christ in a Whiteheadian Perspective," The Finality of
Christ (Dow Kirkpatrick, ed.) pp. 122-154.

will take different forms as it prehends the data of
changing situations.[1]

While in man there is some degree of selfishness,[2] there is nothing selfish in God's aim at his
own satisfaction. God's aim at satisfaction can be
described as an aim at universal satisfaction. As
Cobb explains Whitehead's position which is at the
same time his own: "The divine experience has perfect
sympathy with all other experiences and seeks their
richest fulfillment in no tension with its self-concern."[3] Given this exception, there is no reason why
in other respects an analogy between man's aim and
God's may not be affirmed. Hence, it is to be affirmed
that God's aim with respect to intensity of ideal satisfaction or ideal strength of beauty is unchanging
and indifferent as to how this satisfaction is attained.[4] Yet, as has been noted previously, it is
God's aim which accounts for the limitation by which
individual occasions achieve definiteness. Therefore,
his aim must involve feelings with regard to each becoming occasion's aim at satisfaction. Cobb explains
God's relation to and action upon other becoming occasions when he says:

> God's subjective aim will then be so to
> actualize himself in each moment that the
> propositional feeling he entertains with
> respect to each new occasion will have
> maximum chance of realization. Every
> occasion then prehends God's prehension
> of the ideal for it, and to some degree
> the subjective form of its prehension
> conforms to that of God. That means
> that the temporal occasion shares God's
> appetition for the realization of that
> possibility in that occasion. Thus,

---

[1]Cobb, A Christian Natural Theology, p. 181.
[2]In the anthropological section of A Christian
Natural Theology Cobb discusses "Man as Responsible
Being," denying a rigid selfishness on the part of
man. Cf. pp. 92-134, 181.
[3]Cobb, "Affirming God in a Non-Theistic Age,"
p. 4.
[4]Cobb, A Christian Natural Theology, p. 181;
Whitehead, Process and Reality, pp. 160-161.

God's ideal for the occasion becomes the
occasion's ideal for itself, the initial
phase of its subjective aim.[1]

Cobb affirms that the interrelation between God and
man can be understood in this way, and can serve to
provide an analogy between "at least some" temporal occasions and occasions in their future. As examples
Cobb notes that the human occasion may often actualize
itself in such a way that other occasions in the body
will be influenced. Also, the human occasion attempts
to actualize itself in such a way that it will influence future occasions in its own experience. Finally,
the human occasion attempts to influence future occasions in the experience of others. Such influence
indicates that a new occasion in becoming will be influenced by the aim which prior occasions have had for
it. This entails a modification of Whitehead's sharp
distinction between the initial aim and the initial
data within the initial phase of a new occasion.[2]
This new occasion prehends all the entities in its
past and is influenced by them, an influence which
entails that at least some of the subjective form the
new entity takes will be directly referable to the influence of past occasions. Among these influential
entities is God whose influence "will always be by far
the most important one and, in some respects, prior to
all the others."[3] The subjective aim for the new
occasion will consist of a synthesis and adaptation of
the various aims for it.

Cobb's analysis at this point deviates from Whitehead's in at least two ways:[4] In the first place,

---

[1]Cobb, A Christian Natural Theology, p. 182.

[2]Ibid.

[3]Ibid., p. 183.

[4]Cobb recognizes this deviation while at the
same time noting: "It would be possible to support
this analysis in some detail by citation of passages
from Whitehead that point in this direction." (Cobb,
A Christian Natural Theology, p. 183.).

Cobb rejects the positing of God's aim as an exclusive function of the primordial nature of God. Cobb sees such a rejection as necessarily entailed by the denial that God's unchanging aim alone adequately explains how God functions in relation to the world. In the second place, Cobb's position denies that the initial phase of the becoming occasion's subjective aim need be derived exclusively from God. Cobb's position views the new occasion's initial aim as deriving from a complex of its predecessors only one of which is God.[1]

Finally, in discussing Whitehead's concept of God as actual entity, Cobb notes that Whitehead is mistaken in treating God's causal efficacy for the world, his action in his consequent nature, quite separately from his action in his primordial nature. Cobb notes that if God is an actual entity he will be prehended by each new occasion, but that such prehension will not be confined merely to the prehension of God's initial aim for the new occasion. The objectification of God's initial aim for each new occasion by that occasion need not exhaust God's objectification in that occasion.[2] Whitehead rightly insisted, Cobb feels, that God could be prehended by an occasion in some way other than through objectification of the initial aim. Cobb, feels, however, that Whitehead on the one hand wrongly identifies the initial aim with the primordial nature of God, while, on the other hand, he wrongly identifies all other prehensions of God with the consequent nature. Cobb admits that Whitehead's writings regarding the consequent nature of God do attribute the synthesis of physical and conceptual prehensions in the consequent nature of God.[3] Yet, believing that Whitehead has separated the primordial nature of God from the consequent nature, Cobb sees need to caution that there be no sharp distinction between the reception of the initial aim and the reception of other prehensions of God.[4]

Having offered these objections and cautions

---

[1]Ibid.
[2]Ibid., p. 184.
[3]Whitehead, Process and Reality, p. 524.
[4]Cobb, A Christian Natural Theology, p. 184.

regarding the Whiteheadian development of God as an
actual entity, Cobb summarily offers his view:

> According to my view, the actual oc-
> casion is initiated by a prehension of all
> the entities in its past, always including
> God. Some of these entities, always in-
> cluding God, have specific aims for this
> new occasion to realize. The subjective
> aim of the new occasion must be formed by
> some synthesis or adaptation of these aims
> for which it is itself finally responsible.
> In addition, the past entities, including
> God, will be objectified by other eternal
> objects. What these other eternal objects
> will be, complex or simple, is determined
> partly by the past entities and partly by
> the new subjective aim.[1]

Having presented this modified view of God as actual
entity, Cobb then proceeds to delineate his adaptation
of Whitehead's concept of God's relation to time.

2. God And Time

In an unpublished essay Cobb sums up his interpretation regarding the problem of God and time when
he asserts:

> In terms of time, human subjects are consti-
> tuted by a limited set of closely interwoven
> experiences with a definite beginning point.
> God has had no such beginning point. And
> whereas human life is lived toward death,
> the divine life will continue forever with
> no such violent interruption.[2]

Having noted Cobb's affirmation that God is everlasting, we turn to a consideration of his attempt to present a coherent position of the relation of God and
time by means of a modification of Whitehead's doctrine
of God. When Whitehead discusses the relation of God

---

[1]Ibid., pp. 184-185.
[2]Cobb, "Affirming God in a Non-Theistic Age," p.4.

and time, he does so by focusing primarily on the primordial nature of God. Hence, God's primordiality, nontemporality, and eternity is emphasized.[1] Yet, when Whitehead discusses the consequent nature of God, that aspect of God which is affected by the world, he necessarily introduces process into God. He does not deny the temporality of the world of events which affect God. Rather, he maintains, on the one hand, that there is real becoming in God, while on the other hand, he denies that God is temporal.[2]

Such an approach is possible because Whitehead distinguishes between two types of process.[3] Cobb points out that when Whitehead speaks of "Time," he is referring to physical time. That is to say, he is referring to the transition from one actual occasion to another.[4] Time, in this sense, is neither prior to actual occurrences as in Newtonian thought, nor is it viewed merely as the way that the mind orders flux as in Kantian thought. Actual occasions, whose internal relations with past occasions include time as an important aspect of such relations, are, from the standpoint of physical time atomic. Though temporally extended, such extension "happens all at once as an indivisible unit."[5]

Although in terms of physical time the actual entity can be said to become all at once, the process of the becoming of an actual occasion can be analyzed. The process has a beginning, namely, the initial phase, and an end, the point at which it reaches satisfaction thereby becoming datum for prehension by other becoming occasions. Cobb clarifies this position when he explains:

---

[1]Cobb, A Christian Natural Theology, p. 185.

[2]Ibid.

[3]"Time" refers to the physical time derived from the transition from one actual occasion to another. The other type of process has to do with the process internal to the beoming occasion.

[4]Cobb, A Christian Natural Theology, p. 185; Cf. Process and Reality, pp. 107, 196, 442-444.

[5]Ibid., p. 186.

> For every perspective other than its own,
> the occasion either is not at all or is
> completed. One cannot observe, from with-
> out, an occasion in the process of becoming.
> From the perspective of the becoming occasion,
> of course, the situation is different. It
> does experience itself as a process of be-
> coming and indeed only as such.[1]

From the standpoint of physical time, then, the occasion's own perspective is the experience of itself in
a process of becoming.

The question, then, is how does Whitehead relate
God, the nontemporal actual entity, to time and
process. Cobb notes that Whitehead makes a threefold
distinction between God and other actual entities. In
the first place, God is nontemporal while all other
actual entities are temporal. All actual entities
other than God perish as soon as they have become.
God, however, in his primordial nature is eternal.
That is, God's primordial nature is wholly unaffected
by process in any sense. It affects the world while
remaining unaffected by it.

Secondly, while other actual entities perish,
God is everlasting. By everlasting Whitehead means
"the property of combining creative advance with the
retention of mutual immediacy."[2] In God, the earlier
elements are not lost as new ones are added. Whatever
God receives in his consequent nature is retained in
its full immediacy everlastingly. The loss which
other entities experience with the passage of "time"
is not attributable to God.

Finally, the description of God as nontemporal
does not entail that there is no process in God. Both
"before" and "after" can be used meaningfully in describing God-in-process, for God who knows the actual
as actual and the possible as possible,[3] can be described before he has prehended a certain actual occasion and after he has prehended the same occasion.
Time and history are real, both for temporal occasions
and for God. God both affects temporal events and is
affected by subsequent temporal events.

---

[1]Ibid., p. 187.   [3]Cf. pp. 67-68.
[2]Whitehead, Process and Reality, pp. 524-525.

Having described these distinctions which Whitehead makes regarding God and other actual occasions, Cobb maintains that the simplest way to understand this description of God would be "to regard God, like human persons, as a living person."[1] Although Cobb realizes that Whitehead clearly depicted God as an actual entity rather than as a living person, he presents the following thesis for subsequent development:

> It is clear that Whitehead himself thought
> of God as an actual entity rather than as a
> living person. The thesis I wish to develop
> is that despite this fact, the doctrines he
> formulated about God compel us to assimilate
> God more closely to the conception of a living
> person than to that of an actual entity.[2]

This thesis having been proposed, Cobb immediately presents his defense of the contention that Whitehead's system would be more coherent were God considered more closely analogous to a living person rather than an actual entity. The first point of the argument has to do with Whitehead's recognition of process in the consequent nature of God. As we have seen this process is either one of two types. It is either the process which occurs between occasions or the process which occurs within an occasion.[3] Whitehead's insistence that God is an actual entity requires that the process assigned to God be that which occurs within an occasion.[4] If this is the case, then a problem with regard to God's relation to the world immediately

---

[1]Cobb, A Christian Natural Theology, p. 188.

[2]Ibid., p. 188. Explaining this way of understanding God Cobb asserts: "A living person is a succession of moments of experience with special continuity. At any given moment I am just one of those occasions, but when I remember my past and anticipate my future, I see myself as the total society or sequence of such occasions. God, then, at any moment would be an actual entity, but viewed retrospectively and prospectively he would be an infinite succession of divine occasions of experience."

[3]Cf. note 3, p. 74.

[4]Cobb, A Christian Natural Theology, p. 188.

arises. The process which is internal to an occasion has no efficacy for other occasions except indirectly as it reaches satisfaction hence becoming datum for objectification by other becoming occasions. Hence, if the process attributed to God is merely internal process, then it cannot directly affect the world, as Whitehead maintains.

A further problem with regard to the attribution to God of mere internal process is to be noted when we recall the indissoluble unity of the primordial and consequent natures of God. In considering God's function as principle of limitation, the activity is not attributable merely to the causal efficacy of God's consequent nature. Consideration must also be given God's efficacy as provider of the initial aim for each occasion. Such a relationship is like that of the consanguinity of completed occasions and subsequent occasions. It is not like that of the phases of internal process within a single occasion.[1] Hence, Cobb's conclusion is that "we must recognize that the phases in the concrescence of God are in important respects more analogous to temporal occasions that to phases in the becoming of a single occasion."[2]

---

[1] Ibid., p. 188-189.

[2] Ibid., p. 189. Cobb defends himself against the possible objection that it may be his formulation of Whitehead's thought rather than Whitehead's thought itself which is incoherent, by observing: "If only the primordial nature of God were causally efficacious for the world, and if it were indifferent to time, then, the problem would not arise. But if, as I hold, God can function as principle of limitation only by entertaining a specific aim for each becoming occasion, that aim must take account of the actual situation in the world. In that case, the problem does arise. Furthermore, since Whitehead unquestionably affirms the causal efficacy of the consequent nature of God the problem also occurs for his explicit formulation. We must either reject this doctrine of the causal efficacy of the consequent nature and also affirm that an entirely static God can have particular efficacy for each occasion, or else we must recognize that the phases in the concrescence of God are in important respects more analogous to temporal occasions than to phases in the becoming of a single occasion." (Cobb, A Christian Natural Theology, p. 189.).

The attribution to God of merely internal process offers the same problem when God's satisfaction is considered. In all other entities satisfaction is attained coincident with the completion of the entity. If God is a single entity never to be completed, neither can he know satisfaction. Yet, Whitehead explicitly refers to the reality of God's satisfaction.[1] Cobb's conclusion is, therefore, that "satisfactions are related to the successive phases in God's becoming as they are related to temporal actual occasions, and not as they are related to successive phases of becoming of such occasions,"[2] There are, then, according to Cobb, two respects in which Whitehead's account of God is more closely analogous to that of a living person than to an actual entity. These are, in the first place, his description of God's causal efficacy in relation to the world, and in the second place, his consideration of God's satisfaction.

Cobb next considers whether there are any systematic reasons for Whitehead's affirming that God is an actual entity rather than a living person. He notes that there are two characteristics attributable to living persons which Whitehead wants to deny of God. These are lack of self-identity through time, and loss of what is past. According to Whitehead, then, "God must, without qualification, be self identically himself, and in him there must be no loss."[3] Cobb's contention is that these two characteristics can be maintained of God even if God is considered to be analogous to a living person. God's self-identity through time would be maintained because his prehension of all other entities would not be something other than prehension of his own past since all these entities would be retained in his consequent nature.[4] Loss occurs in the temporal world because of the fragmentary way in which past occasions are reenacted in the pres-

---

[1]Cobb, A Christian Natural Theology, p. 189; Cf. Process and Reality, pp. 48, 135.

[2]Ibid., pp. 189-190.

[3]Ibid., p. 190.

[4]Earlier, in his discussion of personal identity, Cobb maintained that "such identity is attained to the degree that there are immediate prehensions by each new occasion in the person of the occasions constituting the past of that person." A Christian Natural

ent. Moreover, the memory of an experience loses a
very important part of the experience. God, however,
"vividly and consciously remembers in every new occasion all the occasions of the past. His experience
grows by addition to the past, but loses nothing."[1]
This is an important aspect of Cobb's argument, for it
helps him to face a possible objection. He admits the
validity of the possible objection that the concrete
individuality of the past in its own subjective immediacy is lost. He argues, however, that this loss is
no loss of value, for "the living person now enjoys a
new experience that includes everything in the old
and more."[2] While in humans the passage of time entails loss of beauty of past occasions and the movement toward the time when as living persons they will
be no more--thus negating the compensation of novel
experiences--no such loss occurs in God with the passage of time. Finally, one may object to identifying
God as a living person on the grounds that his envisagement of the eternal objects is one primordial and
unchanging act rather than an endless succession of
acts. Cobb notes, however, that this argument is
essentially arbitrary, for while we describe our
gazing at an object for one minute as a single act, as
many as six hundred acts may have taken place.[3] Insofar as each successive act is the same, it may well
be described in our normal language as a single act.
Similarly, God's one envisagement of all possibilities
maintained identically from moment to moment, may, in
our normal language, be described as a single unchanging and eternal act.

Having offered these considerations, Cobb reaches
the conslusion that "the chief reasons for insisting
that God is an actual entity can be satisfied by the
view that he is a living person, that this view makes
the doctrine of God more coherent, and that no serious
new difficulties are raised."[4]

Theology, p. 190; Cf. also pp. 77-78.

[1]Ibid., p. 191.
[2]Ibid.
[3]Ibid.
[4]Ibid., p. 192.

3. God And Space

While Whitehead seems to assert the metaphysical
necessity of time in the sense of successiveness, he
does not affirm the same necessity with regard to
space. There may be numerous dimensions in some other
cosmic epoch, but God would remain unalterably God in
any cosmic epoch. Since space is, however, an important factor in the only world we know, then the question of God's relation to space may be legitimately
considered.[1]

In any consideration of space it must be emphasized that the primary reality is actual entities.
Although every actual occasion actualizes a spatiotemporal region which constitutes its standpoint, it is
the actual occasion that is primary. Space is affirmed
merely as a dimension in which actual entities prehend
each other producing in us the experience of spatial
extension.[2] Every occasion occupies as its standpoint
some region in the extensive continuum, a continuum
constituted by space and time. Does the fact that
other occasions occupy such a region lead us to assert
that God likewise occupies a spatio-temporal region?
Cobb points out that logically there are only three
possible answers to this question. It may be that God
occupies some particular region. Or his being may be
such that it is irrelevant to regions. Finally, he
may occupy the entire continuum.

---

[1]Reference to several of Cobb's subsequent articles will indicate both his reliance on Whitehead and
his continued maintenance of the position delineated in
the following. Cf. e.g.: "The Finality of Christ in
a Whiteheadian Perspective," The Finality of Christ,
Dow Kirkpatrick, ed.; "The Objectivity of God,"
Christian Advocate, Mar. 9, 1967; "Affirming God in a
Non-Theistic Age," unpublished; "A Whiteheadian Christ-
ology," unpublished, Cf. esp. Part I. of this article,
"How God is Present," which presents an analysis of
God's objectification in another actual entity;
"Speaking About God," Religion in Life, Volume 36,
Spring, 1967.

[2]Cobb, A Christian Natural Theology, p. 193.

Cobb easily dismisses the first possibility on
philosophical grounds. Any spatial location of God is
impossible since God is related with equal immediacy to
all actual occasions.[1] The choice between the other
two alternatives, however, is quite difficult. There
is an important sense in which God can be said to
transcend space, for his being is independent of spatiality.[2] Yet, the question whether God is to be
characterized by spatiality when considered in relation to a spatial epoch is still to be entertained.
Whitehead himself gives no explicit answer to this
question. According to Cobb, both nonspatiality and
omnispatiality of God are equally allowed by Whitehead's metaphysics.[3] The choice between the two,
therefore, can be made only on the basis of coherence.
To ascertain coherence, Cobb presupposes that "that

---

[1]Ibid., p. 194.

[2]Ibid., p. 194.

[3]The contention that nonspatiality and omnispatiality of God are equally allowed by Whitehead's
metaphysics is delineated by Cobb in the following:
"Normally we think of unmediated prehensions as prehensions of occasions immediately contiguous in the
spatiotemporal continuum. This suggests the doctrine
of omnispatiality. Indeed, if contiguity were essential to unmediated prehensions, it would be necessary
to posit God's omnipresence throughout space. However, even apart from consideration of God, we have
seen that Whitehead qualifies this principle. He holds
that in our cosmic epoch, prehension of the physical
poles of other occasions seems to be dependent on
contiguity, but that prehensions of the mental poles
of other occasions may not be dependent on contiguity.
By this principle we could explain our prehension of
God's primordial nature and God's prehension of our
mental poles quite apart from any spatial relations.
Further, since no metaphysical problem is involved in
affirming that physical experience may also be prehended apart from contiguity, the doctrine of the radical nonspatiality of God is compatible with all of
the functions attributed to God by Whitehead. Indeed,
since his thinking about God was largely formed with
the primordial nature in view, it is probable that
nonspatiality was assumed by him." (Ibid., p. 194-
195.).

doctrine of God is always to be preferred which, other
things being equal, interprets his relations with the
world more, rather than less, like the way we interpret
the relations of other entities."[1] Applying this principle, we must readily assert that God, like all other
occasions, has a definite standpoint. But we must go
further and say, that since God is related to every
occasion with equal immediacy, such a standpoint could
not favor one part of the universe over against others.
Therefore, the standpoint must be all-inclusive.[2]

Such a position that God's standpoint is all-
inclusive would have to be rejected if actual standpoints could not include the regions that comprise
other actual standpoints. Cobb argues that such regional inclusion of standpoints is to be affirmed. In
the first place, although Whitehead neither affirmed
nor developed the implications of the doctrine of regional inclusion,[3] it is, nevertheless implicit in his
cosmological assertions, compatible with his metaphysical doctrines and with his understanding of the relation of space and time to actual occasions.[4] In the
second place, the doctrine of regional inclusion is
compatible with the doctrine that contemporaries do not
prehend each other. This compatibility can be asserted, for each of the entities participating within the
regional relationship would still prehend the other
only when it had achieved satisfaction.[5] Finally,
Cobb notes that just as spatiotemporal regions of the
occasion of the human person include the spatiotemporal
regions of numerous occasions in the brain, analogously
the region of God includes the regions comprising the
standpoints of all the contemporary occasions in the
world. Such regions would be included not in a single
occasion of the divine experience, but in a succession
of divine experiences.[6] Hence, Cobb contends that the
affirmation that God, like all other occasions, has an

---

[1] Ibid., p. 195.

[2] Ibid.

[3] That is, that actual standpoints can include the
regions that comprise other actual standpoints.

[4] Cobb, A Christian Natural Theology, p. 195.

[5] Ibid.

[6] Ibid., pp. 195-196; Cf. also pp. 89-91.

actual standpoint, is coherent while at the same time
it avoids treating God as an exception to other actual
entities. His contention, then, is that:

> In terms of space, men and all actual sub-
> jects other than God have a particular
> perspective and external environment. God
> is omni-spatial. The region he occupies
> contains all the regions occupied by other
> entities. This means that whereas the
> vast majority of our relations are medi-
> ated through entities spatially between us
> and other subjects, God is immediately rel-
> evant to every subject.[1]

---

[1]Cobb, "Affirming God in a Non-Theistic Age,"
p. 4.

4. God and the Eternal Objects

In discussing Whitehead's treatment of the relation of God to eternal objects Cobb's contention is that Whitehead maintained coherence in his delineation of this relationship in Religion in the Making, for he presented God's envisagement of the eternal objects as fundamentally the same as the envisagement possible to other actual entities.[1] But in Process and Reality, Whitehead radically differentiates between the way in which God prehends the eternal objects and the way in which they are prehended by other actual entities. Insofar as this differentiation remains, there is incoherence in the system. Hence, Cobb's effort is centered around the attempt to restore the relation of God and the eternal objects to the situation described in Religion in the Making, a situation in which the relation between God and the eternal objects "belongs to no totally different mode from that of other actual entities to the eternal objects."[2]

In Whitehead's consideration of the relation between God and the eternal objects in Process and Reality, Cobb sees incoherence arising at two points. The incoherence is evidenced by the fact that God seems to function in his presentation of eternal objects to actual occasions in a way radically different from that in which actual occasions present eternal objects to each other. The two points of incoherence, according to Cobb, are God's provision of the initial

---

[1]As Cobb notes: "In Religion in the Making, we read that 'the forms (i.e. eternal objects) belong no more to God than to any one occasion.' God is seen as envisaging all the eternal objects as well as all actual occasions, but Whitehead does not see this envisagement as fundamentally different in kind from that possible to other occasions." (Cobb, A Christian Natural Theology, p. 196.).

[2]Cobb, A Christian Natural Theology, p. 198.

aim and his provision of relevant novel possibilities.[1]
For Whitehead, God seems to function as the ground for
both the initial aim and the relevant novel eternal
objects. In the preceding section, "God As Actual
Entity,"[2] Cobb has already defended the thesis that
we can view past actual occasions as also being contributory to the initial aim of an occasion without
detracting from God's role as the decisive and supreme
agent.[3]

The question remains, however, can God's role in
the origination of novelty be explained so that he
functions in a way not radically different from that
in which other occasions relate to each other? Cobb
explains that Whitehead goes far toward establishing
coherence in that he stresses that God so orders the
otherwise disjunctive eternal objects that the prehension of one eternal object suggest that of
another. Such a prehension of the novel eternal object is a hybrid prehension[4] of God. Considered in
detail, Cobb presents the following summary of Whitehead's position:

A past actual occasion is objectified
by eternal object X. This eternal object
is then reenacted in the new occasion by a

---

[1]Ibid., p. 199.

[2]Cf. my discussion of Cobb's position in "God
As Actual Entity," pp. 63-73, esp. pp. 70-71.

[3]Cf. Cobb, A Christian Natural Theology, pp. 182-
183, 200.

[4]Perhaps some clarification should be made regarding the various types of prehensions, included in
which are the following: physical prehensions, positive prehensions, pure and impure prehensions, conceptual prehensions, negative prehensions. Their differentiation is summed up by Sherburne in the following: "Physical prehensions are prehensions whose data
involve actual entities; conceptual prehensions are
prehensions whose data involve eternal objects. Both
physical and conceptual prehensions are spoken of as
pure; an impure prehension is a prehension in a later
phase of concrescence that integrates prehensions of
the two pure types. A hybrid prehension is the
'Prehension by one subject of a conceptual prehension,
or of an "impure" prehension, belonging to the men-

conceptual prehension of X. In addition,
eternal object Y is also enacted in the
new occasion. This means that God has
been objectified by Y. Presumably the
objectification of God by Y was triggered
by the prehension of X derived from the
past actual occasion. The dynamic by
which this triggering occurs is not explained. Perhaps the objectification of
a past occasion by X leads to the objectifi-
ication also of God by X and this in turn
leads to the objectification of God by
Y because of the close association of X
and Y in God. Already this seems somewhat
farfetched.[1]

Cobb's detailed analysis of Whitehead is presented here because Cobb views this position--which "seems
somewhat farfetched"--as giving rise to two further
problems. These problems, even as the previous ones,
arise in so far as God, as actual entity, functions
in a manner different from that of other actual entities. The first problem may be stated thus: While
all actual occasions, other than God, function as
causally efficacious only in the initial phase of a
new occasion, God's causal efficacy functions also in
subsequent phases.[2] The second problem arises when

---

tality of another subject.' (PR 163) A positive prehension (also termed feeling) includes its datum as
part of the synthesis of the subject occasion, but
negative prehensions exclude their data from the
synthesis." (Sherburne, op. cit., p. 235.).

[1]Cobb, A Christian Natural Theology, p. 200.

[2]In Cobb's words: "Whereas in other actual occasions their causal efficacy for the new occasion
functions only in the initial phase, this interpretation of the rise of novelty requires that God's causal
efficacy function also in subsequent phases since
'conceptual reversion' occurs after the initial phase
of the occasion." Ibid., pp. 200-201; Cf. Process
and Reality, p. 378. Perhaps a brief comment regarding
"conceptual reversion" is requisite at this point.
Conceptual reversion occurs at the second phase of
concrescence, the phase of conceptual prehensions.
Conceptual reversion is one of the two subphases of
the phase of conceptual prehensions. The other sub-

it is noted that the prehension of the novel eternal
object is a hybrid prehension of God. If this is the
case, then, the novel occasion should appropriate it
as it does other hybrid prehensions. But to grant
this, would entail that the occasion not only reenact
the novel eternal object, but that it also entertain
the possibility of "secondary origination of conceptual feeling" which introduces new novelty. Such an
admission, Cobb maintains, would "lead to a regress
that is clearly vicious and completely unintended by
Whitehead."[1]

To alleviate these problems, Cobb proposes a
simpler, more coherent theory. His theory proposes
that the becoming occasion entertains only one hybrid
prehension of God and that included in this prehension
is the feeling of God's aim for the new occasion. This
aim includes both God's ideal for the occasion and the
possible alternative modes of self-actualization graded
in reference to the ideal.[2] This alleviates the necessity of any new hybrid prehension of God, while, at the
same time, it indicates that no possibility not included in the initial hybrid prehension will be rele-

---

phase is that of conceptual reiteration. While reiteration is always a factor in the concrescence of an
entity, conceptual reversion may or may not occur.
The meaning of conceptual reversion is summed up by
Sherburne in the following: "Conceptual reversion is
'secondary origination of conceptual feelings with data
which are partially identical with, and partially diverse from, the eternal objects forming the data in
the primary (subphase of phase two of concrescence)'
(PR 380). As a result of conceptual reversion 'the
proximate novelties are conceptually felt. This is
the process by which the subsequent enrichment of
subjective forms, both in qualitative pattern, and in
intensity through contrast, is made possible by the
positive conceptual prehension of relevant alternatives....(Conceptual reversion) is the category by
which novelty enters the world; so that even amid
stability there is never undifferentiated endurance'
(PR 381)." Sherburne, A Key to Whitehead's Process
and Reality, pp. 211-212.

[1]Cobb, A Christian Natural Theology, p. 201.

[2]Ibid.

vant for the becoming actual occasion. Cobb feels
that this interpretation allows us to hold that although there is a difference between God's function
of providing novelty and that of other occasions'
provision of novelty this difference need not be a
total one. It is possible for temporal occasions to
be responsible for some ordering of eternal objects,
and, in principle, this may be effective for future
occasions. The difference is that while God orders
all eternal objects, temporal occasions can order only
an infinitesimal selection. This difference does not
entail the incoherence to which Whitehead's position
lends itself.[1]

The second problem mentioned above, however, has
not yet been met. This problem is that of the relation
of God's prehension of the eternal objects and the
prehensions of the eternal objects by temporal occasions. Or as Cobb asks: "Is God's envisagement of
eternal objects totally discontinuous with the conceptual prehensions of temporal occasions?"[2] The problem
may be viewed from the standpoint of the ontological
principle. According to this principle, eternal
objects cannot be effective for a becoming occasion
except by the decision of some actual entity. In the
case of God, however, there seems to be an exception.
God envisages and orders, and hence makes effective,
all eternal objects without the activity of any prior
actual entity. This situation may offer two possible
interpretations. We may affirm that the ontological
principle is inapplicable as far as the relation of
God to the eternal objects is concerned, and thereby
admit incoherence in our position. The other alternative is to admit that the effectiveness of the
eternal objects for God is to be attributed to God's
primordial decision.[3] Cobb adopts the latter position
and then, asserts that, in principle,[4] it is possible

---

[1]In Cobb's words: "The difference, the vast difference, is that God envisages and orders all eternal
objects, whereas temporal occasions can order only an
infinitesimal selection of eternal objects. But this
kind of difference threatens no incoherence." Ibid.,
p. 201.

[2]Ibid., p. 202.

[3]Ibid.

[4]As Cobb points out: "The question is not wheth-

to affirm that the ontological principle allows for the decisions of temporal occasions also to "be explanatory of conceptual prehensions not derived from physical prehensions."[1]

Hence, Cobb concludes that if Whitehead would assert the possibility in principle of a temporal occasion's having the same relation toward some eternal objects with God has toward all, then he would maintain coherence in his system and the forms would "'belong no more to God than to any one occasion.'"[2] In this manner the return to the position asserted in Religion in the Making would be accomplished.

---

er such decisions occur or even whether there are actually any occasions capable of making such decisions. The question is whether in principle the kind of decision by which eternal objects become relevant for God is categorically impossible for all other actual entities. I see no reason to insist upon this absolute difference, and could even suggest that at highest levels of their intellectual functioning human occasions may be able to conceive possibilities directly." (Ibid., pp. 202-203.).

[1]Ibid., p. 202.
[2]Ibid., p. 203.

5. God and Creativity

In his clarification and development of Whitehead's thought concerning the relation of God and
creativity, Cobb stresses that a clarification of
Whitehead's position entails the attribution to God of
a more decisive role in creation than Whitehead intended. The aim of the following is to delineate Cobb's
attempt at this reformulation.

It is not to be denied that in Whitehead's analysis God's role in creation is significant. God
functions as provider of the initial aim of each
occasion. This function is of such importance that,
in a sense, God may be conceived as the creator of all
temporal occasions. Without the initial aim there
would in fact be no temporal occasions, and the initial
aim is never causa sui. Whitehead asserts that the
initial aim and the initial data constitute the initial phase of the occasion. This implies that the two
are equally contributory to the initial phase. But
this is not the case. "The initial aim," notes Cobb,
"is in reality the initiating principle in the occasion."[1] Its importance is to be noted by the following considerations. The initial aim determines the
standpoint that the becoming occasion will occupy.
This includes also the determination of the occasion's
locus and extent in the extensive continuum.[2] This
determination entails, in turn, the determination of
what occasions will be in the past, present, and future
of the becoming occasion. In other words, the initial
aim determines the initial data of the new occasion.
Morever, the greater importance of the initial aim
over the initial data is seen in that "the initial data
are not a part of the becoming occasion in the same
sense as the initial aim."[3] The initial data are
occasions in the past of the becoming occasion. They
are taken up by the becoming occasion as it objectifies
them, but the way in which they are objectified is
determined by the initial aim. Hence, the unquestioned

---

[1] Ibid., p. 204
[2] Ibid.
[3] Ibid.

importance of the initial aim can be seen. Further-more, Whitehead, in attributing the provision of the initial aim solely to God's activity, has attributed to God the all decisive role in creation.[1]

Cobb points out, however, that Whitehead does place restrictions upon the creative role of God which deny his sole responsibility for creation. The first restriction is evidenced by the fact that God's provision of an initial aim is the offering of an aim which is the ideal for the becoming occasion given the situation.[2] This means that the aim for the be-coming occasion is not an aim given in abstraction from the context in which the occasion will be be-coming. Rather, in providing the aim, God takes into account the situation of the actual world. A second restriction on God's creative action is seen in the fact that although the initial aim profoundly influ-ences the outcome of the occasion, it is not wholly determinative. In subsequent phases of the occasion's becoming it may readjust its aim, a possibility which leads Whitehead to assert that the entity is causa sui.[3] Third, God does not create the eternal objects. These pure possibilities for becoming are given. "He presupposes them just as they, for their efficacy in the world, presuppose him."[4] Finally, Whitehead knows of no doctrine of creatio ex nihilo. There is always God and the world. At every moment God is confronted by a world of which he must take account, a world which has partly determined its own form and is free to reject the ideal possibilities which God offers it.[5]

---

[1]Ibid., pp. 204-205.

[2]Ibid., p. 205

[3]Ibid.

[4]Ibid.

[5]Ibid. That this internal relation between God and the world, a relationship which entails that God take account of the actual situation in the world even as the world must and can take account only of the possibilities offered it by God, is basically Cobb's stance, even though he immediately modifies it, is seen in the preface of his theological work, God And the World. He presents his thesis when he says: "This is not a book about God, nor is it a book about the world. It is a book about how God is in the world

These limitations serve to mitigate the attribution of sole responsibility in the role of creation to God. Yet given these limitations, Whitehead's doctrine of God is, nevertheless, a doctrine of God as creator. Having noted God's role as creator in Whitehead's philosophy, Cobb compares it with the role of God as creator in Aristotle's thought. Just as in Aristotle the creator functions to provide form to a reality given him so also in Whitehead. But Cobb's thesis is "that the role of the creator in Whitehead must be more drastic than in Aristotle, more drastic also that Whitehead recognized."[1] In supporting his thesis, he presents an analysis of the role of prime matter in Aristotle and the role of creativity in Whitehead.

Our concern here is to present Cobb's reformulation of Whitehead's doctrine of God. Hence, we will move immediately to his consideration of Whitehead's concept of creativity. We note only Cobb's conclusion that Aristotle's main concern was an explanation of what things are, and that they are. According to Cobb, Aristotle was not concerned to answer the question as to why there is anything at all. If the question of why were asked, the answer would have to be that "prime matter is eternal and demands some form,"[2] yet, "prime matter does not explain why there is prime matter."[3] But Aristotle asked "only for an explanation of what in fact is."[4] This stance is also true of Whitehead. He, too, does not ask the radical question regarding why there is anything at all.

One may think that the question is implicitly asked and an answer found in Whitehead's concept of "creativity," but this is not the case. To what does

---

and how the world is in and from God. The title points further to the major underlying thesis of the book. Against those who see us as being forced to choose God or the world, I am affirming that we must choose God and the world. To choose one against the other is in the end to reject both." (Cobb, God and the World, p. 9.)

[1]Cobb, A Christian Natural Theology, pp. 206-207.
[2]Ibid., p. 207.
[3]Ibid., p. 208.
[4]Ibid.

creativity refer? First, it must be noted that for
Whitehead creativity does not "exist." His concept
of creativity does not conform to the categories of
existence.[1] Hence, although at times creativity plays
a dominant role[2] in Whitehead's philosophy, it cannot
be said that God himself is created by creativity.
Creativity is not an actual entity, and, therefore,
cannot function as the efficient cause of anything.[3]
Moreover, creativity is not to be considered as an
eternal object. Rather, it is treated by Whitehead
under the category of the ultimate. Unlike eternal objects, which are pure possibilities for becoming, creativity expresses absolute necessity.[4] In Cobb's
words, creativity for Whitehead is:

> that apart from which nothing can be. It
> is not in the usual sense an abstraction,
> for whatever is is a unit of creativity.
> Creativity is the actuality of every actual
> entity. We may think of all the forms em-
> bodied in each instance of creativity as
> abstractable from it, since creativity
> might equally have taken any other form so
> far as its being creativity is concerned.
> But it is confusing to speak of creativity
> as being itself an abstraction from its
> expressions, since it is that in virtue of
> which they have concreteness. Nevertheless,
> creativity as such is not concrete or
> actual.[5]

---

[1]cf. Ibid., p. 209; Process and Reality, pp. 32-33

[2]For example, where God is spoken of as the accident or creature of creativity. (Cobb, A Christian
Natural Theology, p. 206; Process and Reality, p. 11,
135.).

[3]Cobb, A Christian Natural Theology, p. 206.

[4]Discussing "The Category of the Ultimate" Whitehead observes: "'Creativity,' 'many,' 'one' are the
ultimate notions involved in the meaning of the synonymous terms 'thing,' 'being' 'entity.' These three
notions complete the Category of the Ultimate and are
presupposed in all the more special categories."
(Process and Reality, p. 31.).

[5]Cobb, A Christian Natural Theology, p. 210.

Having presented this description of creativity, Cobb
concludes that the concept is fundamentally intelligible even though it can only be pointed at and hoped
that it will be intuitively grasped.[1]

The big question for Cobb, however, is the
question whether Whitehead's principle of creativity
can answer the question as to why there is anything at
all. Cobb's answer is that it cannot.[2] Had Aristotle
answered the question he would have done so in terms
of stressing the necessity of an eternally unchanging
entity operative as the ground of the flux. Yet,
Whitehead's principle of creativity is "another word
for the change itself," and Whitehead "constantly denies that there is any underlying substance which is
the subject of change.[3] Whitehead assumed that the
process of creativity is everlasting, always taking
on new forms. Cobb contends that the mere notion of
creativity does not offer grounds for the faith that
it will continue everlastingly. It may simply stop
and there will be nothing. Even though creativity
is an inescapable aspect of every new entity which
occurs, it does not answer the question concerning why
the occasion occurs. In Whitehead each new occasion is
a novel addition to the universe. It is not merely a
new form of some eternal stuff.[4] If the question "why"
is raised, the answer that there was creativity in the
preceding occasions and there is creativity in the present occasions is inadequate, for if occasions ceased
to occur, there would be no creativity. Hence,
"creativity can explain only ex post facto."[5]

If the question of why is asked, the only answer
admissable in the context of Whitehead's philosophy
must be given in terms of the decisions of actual

---

[1] Ibid.

[2] As Cobb asserts: "My contention is that
'creativity' can not go even so far in the direction
of an answer as did 'prime matter.'" (Ibid., p. 210.).

[3] Ibid., p. 210.

[4] Ibid., p. 211.

[5] Ibid.

entities. According to the ontological principle the
only reasons are to be found in actual entities.[1]
Yet, the decisive element in any actual entity is its
initial aim, and this aim is derived from God. Hence,
God must be considered to be the answer to the question
as to why things are and what they are. God must be
conceived as the reason that entities occur as well
as the one who determines the limits of their occurrence.[2]

In summation, we recall that the following has
been noted. In the first place, the only "reasons"
for occurrences are to be given in terms of the decisions of actual occasions. Secondly, the actual occasions themselves occur and find their limitation by
reason of God's establishment of their subjective aim.
Finally, "creativity," not being an actual entity, cannot be the "reason" for any occurrence.[3] These observations enable us to understand the passages which
seem to subordinate God to creativity. Explaining
this position Cobb maintains that:

> those passages that seem to subordinate
> God to creativity...fundamentally... mean
> that God also is an instance of creativity.

---

[1]The ontological principle affirms that "every
condition to which the process of becoming conforms in
any particular instance, has its reason either in the
character of some actual entity in the actual world of
that concrescence, or in the character of the subject
which is in process of concrescence...According to the
ontological principle there is nothing which floats
into the world from nowhere." Whitehead, Process and
Reality, pp. 37, 373.

[2]Cobb, A Christian Natural Theology, p. 211.

[3]What Christian has stressed regarding eternal
objects can also be said of creativity: "According to
the ontological principle, 'actual entities are the
only reasons' (PR 37.). This means that actual entities are the only agents. It would be contrary to
this principle to suggest that eternal objects are the
reasons why actual entities are mediated, interpreted,
conveyed, introduced, or connected with each other."
(William A. Christian, An Interpretation of Whitehead's
Metaphysics, p. 237.

84

For God to be at all is for him to be a
unit of creativity. In this respect his
relation to creativity is just the same
as that of all actual occasions. Creativity does not explain why they occur
or what form they take, but if they occur
at all and regardless of what form they
take, each will be an instance of creativity, a fresh unity formed as a new
togetherness of the antecedent many and
offering itself as a member of the multiplicity of which any subsequent occasion
must take account.[1]

Hence, God is "subordinate to creativity only to the
extent that he, just as all other entities, instan-
tiates creativity merely by the fact that he is.
Creativity itself provides no reason. God, however,
is the reason for the being as well as the form of
actual entities.[2] Thus, the conclusion of Cobb's
argument is well summed up when he says:

...we may say in summary that God always
(and some temporal occasions sometimes) is
the reason that each new occasion becomes.
God, past occasions, and the new occasion
are conjointly the reason for what it becomes. Whatever it becomes, it will always,
necessarily, be a new embodiment of creativity.[3]

---

[1]Cobb, A Christian Natural Theology, p. 212.
[2]Ibid.
[3]Ibid., p. 214.

D. Critique and Analysis of Cobb's Whiteheadian
Doctrine of God

In the foregoing, Cobb's understanding of Whitehead's philosophy has been considered in some detail.
This consideration has been necessary because of
Cobb's close adherence to and dependence upon Whitehead's philosophy.[1] His attempt is that of understanding God's being and relationship to the world entirely in terms of the principles characterizing Whitehead's own system. As has been noted, Cobb asserts
that "Whitehead's philosophical reasons for affirming
God and his attempt to show that God is not an exception to all the categories[2] appears to me philosophically responsible and even necessary."[3] Yet, Cobb's
thesis is that Whitehead was not successful in his

---

[1]This is true not only of his major work, A
Christian Natural Theology, of which he said: "In
most of this book I have identified myself fully with
the position I have expounded on Whitehead's authority.
... Whitehead's philosophical reasons for affirming
God and his attempt to show that God is not an exception to all the categories appear to me philosophically
responsible and even necessary." (Cobb, A Christian
Natural Theology, p. 176); but also his theological
treatise God and the World, his essay "The Possibility
of Theism Today," and many other of his articles, e.g.:
"A Whiteheadian Christology;" "The Finality of Christ
in a Whiteheadian Perspective," (Kirkpatrick, op. cit.,
pp. 122-154); "Whitehead's Philosophy and a Christian
View of Man," (Journal of Bible and Religion, Vol. 32,
July, 1964, pp. 209-220); "Affirming God in a Non-
theistic Age," "Nihilism, Existentialism and Whitehead," (Religion in Life, Vol. 30, Autumn, 1961,
pp. 521-533); "Can Natural Theology Be Christian?"
(Theology Today, Vol. 23, April, 1966, pp. 140-142);
"Christian Natural Theology and Christian Existence"
(Christian Century, Vol. 82, March 3, 1965, pp. 265-267).

[2]Moreover, as Whitehead would say of God, "but
their chief exemplification."

[3]Cobb, A Christian Natural Theology, p. 176.

attempt to show that God is not an exception to the
categories descriptive of reality. According to
Cobb, Whitehead's God, conceived as an actual entity,
does not always act in a way characteristic of the
activity of other actual entities. He becomes an exception, and incoherence is thereby introduced. Moreover, according to Cobb, Whitehead's doctrine does not
entail that God be an actual entity, for, as he contends, Whitehead's doctrines about God "compel us to
assimilate God more closely to the conception of a
living person than to that of an actual entity."[1]
Finding points of incoherence in Whitehead's philosophy, therefore, Cobb undertakes "to develop a doctrine
of God more coherent with Whitehead's general cosmology and metaphysics than are some aspects of his own
doctrine."[2] In this attempt, Cobb recognizes that
"Whitehead moved far toward overcoming such incoherence," yet he also asserts that "one can go, and therefore should go, further yet."[3]

In Section C., therefore, Cobb's attempt to overcome the incoherence which he sees in Whitehead's
system was considered. An analysis of this attempt is
now in order. It will be remembered that Cobb's
attempt focused around five areas of concern, namely:
God as Actual Entity, God and Time, God and Space, God
and Eternal Objects, and God and Creativity.

Consider in the first place, Cobb's criticism of
Whitehead's development of God as an actual entity. It
is Cobb's contention that Whitehead deals too often
with the consequent and primordial nature of God as if
they were genuinely separable entities,[4] or as if God
were merely an addition of these two natures. But is
this in fact the case with Whitehead? Whitehead himself seemed to realize the danger of God's being so
considered that he would appear to be an instance of
two dichotomized natures. He cautioned time and again
that God is an actual entity, and as such, is a unity
any one aspect of which cannot be "actual" in and of
itself. That is to say, Whitehead's insistence that

---

[1]Cobb, A Christian Natural Theology, p. 188.

[2]Ibid., p. 176.

[3]Ibid., p. 177.

[4]Cf. above, p.

God is an actual entity is an insistence on the unity
of God. No one aspect of God considered alone is
actual, for only actual entities are fully actual and
"there is no going behind actual entities to find anything more real."[1] That Whitehead emphasized the
unity of God as actual entity is clearly seen in several important passages. In the following Whitehead
emphasizes that the primordial nature of God is an
abstraction:

> To sum up: God's 'primordial nature' is
> abstracted from his commerce with 'partic-
> ulars,' and is therefore devoid of those
> 'impure' intellectual cogitations which
> involve propositions. It is God in ab-
> straction, alone with himself. As such it
> is a mere factor in God, deficient in actual-
> ity.[2]

It is well to note that this observation comes early in
Process and Reality, so that one who reads of the primordial nature of God subsequently, regardless of how
many pages are expended in such a delineation,[3] will
know that he is reading about an abstracted aspect of
one unitary entity. Of this observation, Professor
Leclerc, in his introduction to Whitehead's metaphysics
has emphasized the importance of Whitehead's cautionary
statement. He says: "The last point in the previous
quotation is highly important. God is not to be identified with his 'primordial nature'; that is, God is
not to be conceived as wholly constituted by a primordial conceptual valuation of pure abstract eternal objects."[4] Or another of Leclerc's observations regarding Whitehead's doctrine may be helpful. Of White-

---

[1]Whitehead, Process and Reality, pp. 27-28.

[2]Ibid., p. 50.

[3]Cf. p. 64 Part of Cobb's contention that Whitehead treats the primordial and consequent natures of
God as if they were genuinely seqarable entities is
that in the doctrine of God developed in Process and
Reality, most of the references to God are references
to the primordial nature.

[4]Leclerc, Whitehead's Metaphysics: An Introductory Exposition, p. 203.

head's view he says: "The primordial nature is only
one aspect of God. We must be clear that in considering the primordial nature we are making an abstraction from God's complete actuality."[1] That Whitehead
does not intend for God to be viewed as two dichotomized natures, is also to be seen when he emphasizes
that God, considered in this abstraction "as primordial" is deficiently actual in two ways:

> Viewed as primordial, he is the unlimited
> conceptual realization of the absolute
> wealth of potentiality. In this aspect, he
> is not before all creation, but with all
> creation. But, as primordial, so far is he
> from 'eminent reality,' that in this abstrac-
> tion he is 'deficiently actual'--and this in
> two ways. His feelings are only conceptual
> and so lack the fullness of actuality. Sec-
> ondly conceptual feelings, apart from com-
> plex integration with physical feelings,
> are devoid of consciousness in their sub-
> jective forms.[2]

It is to be noted that in this quotation Whitehead not
only speaks of the primordial nature of God as an abstraction but also that he talks of this aspect as
being 'deficiently actual.' Such caution should be
adequate to convince one that the primordial nature
of God is not a genuinely separable entity. This
point is likewise emphasized in Sherburne's interpretation of Whitehead's doctrine. Of the primordial
nature of God he says: "...when we make a distinction
of reason, and consider God in the abstraction of a
primordial actuality, we must ascribe to him neither
fulness of feelings, nor consciousness."[3] Noteworthy
in this passage are the phrases with reference to the
primordial nature as "a distinction of reason" and an
"abstraction." Sherburne's point is emphasized when
he elaborates on his own interpretation in a footnote:

> The point is, of course, that we do ascribe
> to God 'eminent realtiy,' 'fulness of feel-
> ing,' 'consciousness,' and concern for 'what

---

[1]Ibid.
[2]Whitehead, Process and Reality, p. 521.
[3]Sherburne, op. cit., p. 180.

in fact comes to pass.' ...In his total
being, primordial, consequent, and superjective, he is all these. But considered
by an abstraction of reason as primordial,
and primordial only, God is none of these.
These are aspects of God dependent upon
his consequent and superjective natures...[1]

Schubert Ogden, too, in his review of Cobb's A Christian Natural Theology observes that Cobb's criticism
of Whitehead's dichotomizing God's primordial and consequent natures is unwarranted. Of Cobb's position he
says,

> His claim...that Whitehead associates
> God's aim 'exclusively with the primor-
> dial nature' (p. 183) ignores Whitehead's
> statement that 'the process of finite
> history is essential for the ordering of
> the basic vision, otherwise mere confusion!
> (Essays in Science and Philosophy, pp.
> 89ff.).[2]

Finally, not unimportant is Cobb's observation that "It
is always the actual entity that acts, not one of its
poles as such, although in many of its functions one
pole or another may be primarily relevant."[3] Of importance with reference to this observation of Cobb,
is Cobb's concession that Whitehead "must certainly
have meant to say this also about God."[4] It has been
observed that there are instances in which Whitehead
himself explicitly did say this about God, and it has
been noted that three of his interpreters viewed his
thought as exemplifying this unitary view. Add to
these considerations Cobb's own recognition that this
was in fact what Whitehead "meant to say," and it
seems reasonable to assume that this is in fact what
he did say, thus leaving unwarranted Cobb's criticism

---

[1]Ibid.

[2]Schubert Ogden, "Book Review of John Cobb's
A Christian Natural Theology," The Christian Advocate
Vol. IX., Number 18, (Sept. 23, 1965), p. 12.

[3]Cobb, A Christian Natural Theology, p. 178; Cf.
above p. 64.

[4]Ibid.

that Whitehead dichotomizes the two natures of God in
such a way that they are presented as genuinely separable entities.

Yet, Cobb assumes that this criticism is warranted, and retaining this assumption, he views Whitehead's
system as incoherent insofar as it entails "arbitrary
disconnection of first principles."[1] That is to say,
the four ultimate elements of his system, actual entities, God, eternal objects and creativity are arbitrarily disconnected. Cobb stresses that any such dichotomizing results in arbitrary disconnection, for any
attempt to analyze an actual entity merely in terms of
the addition of the analyzation of the two poles taken
individually omits the subjective unity, concrete
satisfaction, the power of decision and self-creation
requisite of an actual entity.[2] Hence, since Cobb
finds the dichotomizing of God's nature in Whitehead,
he feels it necessary to explain, more adequately than
did Whitehead, how God is related to actual occasions,
eternal objects and creativity. Yet, if one accepts--
as Whitehead himself, Leclerc, Sherburne, and Ogden
maintain--Whitehead's dilineation as being that of
presenting God as a unified actual entity, then the
disconnection of which Cobb speaks is not present, and
Whitehead's system is adequate, in this respect at
least, without Cobb's proposed alternative. That is
to say, if the criticism that Whitehead dichotomizes
God's two natures is not warranted, then Cobb's re-
vision of Whitehead's system to explain "how the
eternally unchanging primordial nature of God can provide different initial aims to every occasion"[3] is unwarranted or at least unnecessary.

Previously it has been noted that with his discussion of God and time, Cobb introduces the thesis
that the simplest way to understand Whitehead's description of God--the nontemporal, everlasting actual
entity--is "to regard God, like human persons, as a
living person."[4] In the previous section his reasoning

---

[1]Ibid., p. 177; Cf. Process and Reality, p. 9;
Also, above, p. 64.
[2]Cobb, A Christian Natural Theology, p. 178; Cf.
also above, p. 64.
[3]Ibid., pp. 179-180.
[4]A Christian Natural Theology, p. 188; Cf. above,
pp. 75-77.

regarding this thesis has been delineated. It should
be remembered that Cobb advances the thesis in an effort to make the Whiteheadian doctrine more coherent
that did Whitehead himself. Two areas of concern must
be dealt with here. In the first place it must be considered whether regarding God as a living person is
warranted by the Whiteheadian system. A second necessary consideration is Cobb's contention that "the view
that God is a living person...makes the doctrine of
God more coherent, and no serious new difficulties are
raised."[1]

As has been previously noted, Cobb observes that
for Whitehead God as actual entity differs from all
other actual entities in that he is nontemporal and
everlasting.[2] Yet, God's being non-temporal does not
entail the absence of process in God. Cobb contends
that Whitehead has made the difference between God and
other actual entities a radical difference, and that a
consideration of God as a person would make the system
more coherent. As has been previously observed, Cobb
argues that Whitehead's attribution to God of mere
internal process[3] raises several problems. First, if
the process attributed to God is merely internal process, as Cobb maintains that Whitehead's view entails,
then God cannot directly affect the world. Secondly,
internal process alone cannot account for the fact
that God provides the initial aim for each occasion.
Thirdly, mere internal process raises problems regarding God's satisfaction. If God is a single entity never to be completed, he can never know satisfaction;
yet, Whitehead explicitly refers to God's satisfaction.[4]

---

[1]Ibid., p. 192.

[2]Cf. pp. 75-76.

[3]Cf. above, pp. 77-78.

[4]Sherburne, too, sees problems in Whitehead's
doctrine of God as an actual entity. Noting that contemporary occasions do not prehend each other, he
argues that this eliminates the possibility of God's--
who is an actual entity in process of becoming--being
able to prehend any other contemporary occasion or of
any becoming occasion's ability to prehend God. (Cf.
Donald Sherburne, "Whitehead Without God," The Christian Scholar, Vol. L., Fall, 1967, pp. 251-273, esp.
p. 255.). Cf. also, A Christian Natural Theology, p.
189; Process and Reality, pp. 48, 135.

To overcome these problems, Cobb suggests that God be considered as a person rather than an actual entity.

The alternative which Cobb suggests at this point may serve to settle the problem of the possibility of satisfaction on the part of God and the problem of God's ability to prehend other occasions, but even if this is granted, doesn't the alternative also offer grave problems? In his consideration of God as a person, Cobb agrees with the Whiteheadian understanding of person when he says: "A living person is a succession of moments of experience with special continuity."[1] As long as one is speaking of temporal persons this definition of a person offers no great problems. One may ask the question regarding the ground of the succession of the moments of experience. That is, the question of the unifying agency could be asked,[2] for there is no purely internal reason why the various

---

[1]A Christian Natural Theology, p. 188. Cf. Whitehead: "An enduring personality in the temporal world is a route of occasions in which the successors with some peculiar completeness sum up their predecessors." (Process and Reality, p. 531.). Cf. also a discussion of the difference between what is called the traditional view of the self as "an absolute unity of the individual self--certainly from birth to death and perhaps beyond these extremes," and the view of process philosophy which views the self as "a succession of events or a plurality of selves...within what is apparently the one self" in Kenneth D. Freeman, "Self-identity and Responsibility in Process and Philosophy," pp. 2-3.

[2]In a review of Cobb's A Christian Natural Theology, Langdon Gilkey considers both the question of continuity and the answer given within the Whiteheadian system when he says: "In a system where each entity has the freedom in part to form itself, no "special continuity" with its own past would be possible unless each new occasion received from some consistent, permanent, unchanging and universal source an initial aim in congruence with what had gone before and what is still to come. Only with such structured freedom provided by the unchanging envisagement of possibility which is the primordial nature of God, are both novelty and order possible and compatible. Only thus are these enduring societies made up of occasions

moments of experience should constitute "special continuity"[1] or "with some peculiar completeness sum up their predecessors."[2] But with the Whiteheadian system, the answer is forthcoming in terms of prehensions which can be traced to the initial aim whose origin is traceable to God.[3] However, if God is considered to be a person, that is, if God is viewed as a route of successive occasions in which the successors with some completeness--except in God's case the "some completeness" would be absolute completeness--sum up their predecessors then the question of the ground of the unity of succession is also applicable to God. So long as God is considered an actual entity, then the question of unity is not raised. If, however, God becomes a series of ontologically discrete units of actualization, the question of the ground of his unity cannot be answered within the system.[4]

---

inwardly free from both their own past and the cosmos as a whole. Thus does Whitehead with great subtlety reverse the usual proofs of God, and make the cosmological argument depend upon the teleological: there is a world because there is order, and God is essential as the eternal ground of this order among possibility." (Langdon Gilkey, "Book Review: A Christian Natural Theology, by John B. Cobb, Jr.: Theology Today, Vol. 22, No. 4, January, 1966, p. 542.

[1]Cobb, A Christian Natural Theology, p. 188.

[2]Whitehead, Process and Reality, p. 531.

[3]Cf. Christian, An Interpretation of Whitehead's Metaphysics, pp. 322-330, 334-336.

[4]Both Langdon Gilkey and Fritz Guy have made this observation regarding Cobb's attempt to make the Whiteheadian system more coherent by considering God to be a person rather than an actual entity. In Guy's words: "What is a 'person?' For Whitehead 'an enduring personality' is 'a route of occasions in which the successors with some completeness sum up their predecessors.' (PR 531); Cobb applies this description to God, appropriately revising 'some completeness' to 'absolute completeness.' But he neglects to seek for the ground of the route of occasions. In the temporal world, that ground is God, whose unitary primordial nature provides the initial aim for each occasion and thus furnishes order in successive occasions, in enduring objects, in living persons, and in the totality of the universe. As long as God is an actual entity there is no problem, for everything is held together by the unity of that

95

Cobb notes further that there are systematic reasons why Whitehead prefers to speak of God as an actual
entity rather than a person. While persons experience
lack of self-identity through time and loss of what is
past, Whitehead wants to deny both these limitations of
God. Cobb contends that both self-identity through time
and no loss of what is past can be maintained of God
even if God is considered as a living person rather than
an actual entity. Yet, such a person would have to be
a unique person indeed. This leads to a consideration
of the systematic advantages accrued when God is considered as a person rather than an actual entity. In
the case of a human person there was a time when he was
not, and he faces a time when he will be no more. This
is true of temporal actual entities also. But God, considered by Whitehead as the nontemporal actual entity
and by Cobb as a person, is different insofar as he is
eternal--there never was a time when he was not--and

one non-temporal, transepochal entity. If, however, God
is not an entity but a series of ontologically discrete
actualizations, the question of the ground of his unity
becomes impossible to answer within the system." (Fritz
Guy, "Comments on a Recent Whiteheadian Doctrine of
God," Andrews University Seminary Studies, Vol. 4, July,
1966, p. 9.). Gilkey likewise rejects Cobb's attempts
when he says: "In a system where each entity has the
freedom in part to form itself, no 'special continuity'
with its own past would be possible unless each occasion
received from some consistent, permanent, unchanging
and universal source an aim in congruence with what had
gone before and what is still to come....In other words
PN /God in his primordial nature/ is the necessary presupposition for any route or sucession of occasions
which make up any society or object and even more any
'person.' Without the permanent structure provided over
time and passage by PN, such personal beings are incon-
ceivable in this categorial system. It follows, therefore, that God as PN cannot himself be conceived univocally as such a series. For one essential element of
that notion of a society is that it is dependent beyond
itself upon a structuring that transcends it--like
Thomas' contingent creatures, the societies of process
thought point beyond themselves to a further ground for
their actuality. If they do not, then all proof of God
and so all rationality to his conception in this system
vanishes. But if PN (as a univocally conceived society
of successive entities) points beyond itself for its

everlasting--there never will be a time when he will
not be. This can be said neither of ordinary actual
entities[1] nor of ordinary persons. Moreover, in both
ordinary actual entities and in ordinary persons, the
passage of time entails loss. Yet, this is not so with
God, who, according to Cobb, "vividly and consciously
remembers in every new occasion all the occasions of
the past. His experience grows by addition to the past,
but loses nothing."[2] There is no loss in God either
through his facing of a time when he will be no more or
through fragmentary re-enactment of the past in the
present. Yet, all other persons experience this loss.
That is to say, Cobb's God, who is a person, is indeed
a unique person, even as is Whitehead's God as an actual entity a unique actual entity. Cobb's contention
is that Whitehead's system which calls for a nontemporal, everlasting actual entity is incoherent. Yet,
does Cobb's alternative which calls for a non-temporal,
everlasting person who experiences no loss through time
any more coherent? This is not to agree with Cobb and
say that Whitehead's system is incoherent. It is
merely to assert that if Whitehead's system is incoherent, Cobb's alternative is likewise incoherent. In
other words, even if Cobb can say that in his consideration of God as person "no serious new difficulties
are raised," he cannot say that he has alleviated the
old difficulties which he sees[3] in Whitehead's delineation.

---

continuity of structure, then all is chaos: does it
thus presuppose itself, which is contradictory, or is
there another God beyond God, and so on ad infinitum?"
(Gilkey, op. cit., p. 542.).

[1]Processor Leclerc clarifies Whitehead's doctrine
by referring to God as a "unique actual entity" and
other actual entities as "ordinary actual entities."
Cf. Leclerc, op. cit., pp. 192-193.

[2]Cobb, A Christian Natural Theology, p. 191.

[3]Whether or not the incoherence which Cobb attributes to Whitehead is indeed present in Whitehead is
not the question here. The point is that if Whitehead's
system is incoherent at this point, Cobb has done nothing to alleviate such incoherence. Christian maintains
that Whitehead has successfully maintained coherence in
his doctrine that reality is to be understood in terms
of actual entities. At the conclusion of his chapter
on "God and the Categories" Christian observes: "I con-
clude that Whitehead's attempt to state a set of first
principles which apply both to God and to actual

97

Whitehead's reluctance to speak of God as a person is discussed by Christian in An Interpretation of Whitehead's Metaphysics. He notes that personality is not one of Whitehead's systematic categories. In fact, it is a presystematic term which is to be interpreted by means of the categoreal scheme, the categories of existence, explanation, and obligation.[1] Christian observes that in Whitehead's system human persons are interpreted as highly complex societies of actual occasions, and that God, being an actual entity, "clearly...is not a person in this systematic sense."[2] In an effort to avoid ambiguities, Whitehead is reluctant to speak of God as a person even in a presystematic way. His reluctance stems from the fact that traditional views of God as a person are related too easily with unreflective supernaturalism, a position which Whitehead wants to avoid.[3]

While attempting to avoid the simple attribution of personality to God, Whitehead also wants to avoid the opposite exteme of conceiving God as "sheer infinity"[4] or as "the impersonal order of the universe."[5] Hence, "he proposes his theory as a view that avoids both these extremes."[6] Even when, in more interpretative passages, he uses personal images[7] in reference to God, he stresses that such images are

---

occasions has been reasonably successful. (Christian, op. cit., pp. 300-301.).

[1]Christian, An Interpretation of Whitehead's Metaphysics,pp. 409-410.

[2]Ibid., p. 410.

[3]Ibid.

[4]Ibid., Quoted from "Mathematics and the Good," in Paul A. Schilpp, ed. The Philosophy of Alfred North Whitehead. (New York: Tudor Publishing Company, for the Library of Living Philosophers, 1951), p. 675.

[5]Ibid., Quoted from Religion in the Making, p. 150.

[6]Christian, op. cit., p. 410.

[7]For example, he speaks of God's wisdom (Process and Reality, pp. 525, 527, his patience (Ibid., p. 525) love (p. 532), tender care (p. 525).

symbolic, interpretative and unsystematic.[1]

That some theologians prefer to speak of God as
person in order to maintain the concept of the mystery of the divine entity is understandable, but Whitehead's system does not negate the mystery of the divine
actuality, but rather allows a place for such mystery.
As Christian notes:

> The systematic development of a categoreal
> scheme need not dispel mystery from that to
> which it applies, unless a sense of mystery
> is nothing more than a state of intellectual
> confusion. Indeed perhaps it is just when
> we think most clearly and coherently about
> reality that we see how 'mysterious' it is.[2]

Christian further recalls the following remarks from
Whitehead which indicate that Whitehead recognized the
element of mystery in the being of God: "'The depths
of his existence lie beyond the vulgarities of praise
or of power' (RM 154)." "'Of course we are unable to
conceive the experience of the Supreme Unity of Existence' (Imm /i.e. "Immortality," in Schilpp, ed. op.
cit./ 698.)"[3] Other factors in Whitehead's interpretation of God also support the intention of "mystery,"
for example, Whitehead's interpretation of the freedom
of God; the fact that his primordial aim is not conditioned; his power of conceptual supplementation is
unlimited; his power of initiating novel becomings is
unbounded, though conditioned; he never fails to a-
chieve satisfactions; and he is the supreme instance
of creativity.[4] Whitehead's realization of the concept
of the mystery of the divine nature, however, is to be
understood in relation to his concern for rationality.
As he notes: "Faith in reason is the trust that the
ultimate natures of things lie together in a harmony
which excludes mere arbitrariness. It is the faith
that at the base of things we shall not find mere arbitrary mystery."[5] Hence, Whitehead's concept of God

---

[1]Chrisitan, op. cit., p. 410.
[2]Ibid.
[3]Ibid., p. 411.
[4]Christian, op. cit., p. 411.
[5]Whitehead, Science and the Modern World, p. 24.

allows neither for attribution of arbitrary freedom to God nor of arbitrary mystery. As Christian observes: "It seems that if by divine freedom a power of absolutely unconditioned action is meant, then to speak of God as also 'a person' is to use the term in a symbolic way or to invite confusion, or both."[1] Two other considerations may help to clarify the matter. In the first place, according to Whitehead's theory, God-- who is an actuality which enjoys everlasting existence with no loss of immediacy--has a unity which is a continuing unity within an individual immediacy, rather than a unity characterized by a persistent pattern of definiteness with a continuity between individual immediacies.[2] Although this does not characterize a person in terms of Whitehead's understanding, it nevertheless "fits our common-sense notion of personal existence better than actual occasions and nexus do."[3] Secondly, Whitehead's notion of actual entity itself rises from an analysis of human experience.

The basic problem which Cobb faces here is a perennial one for philosophical theology. On the one hand, the philosopher-theologian can only prove the adequacy of his system by showing that no entity contradicts the basic categories of his system. On the other hand, the entity which is regarded as the source of all others, the ground of their being, the principle of the whole, cannot be an ordinary entity. That is to say, the sole ground for philosophical-theology is the uniqueness of God as the principle of the whole.[4] Yet, the philosophical-theological system cannot introduce a unique entity which does not conform to the categories applicable to all other actualities. If Whitehead's "unique actual entity" introduces incoherence into the system, no less does Cobb's unique person. Yet, perhaps Cobb could profitably take a word of caution from Whitehead at this point. The word of caution comes from Whitehead's understanding of the limits of philosophical speculation on the one hand, and his understanding of coherence on the other.

---

[1]Christian, op. cit., p. 411.
[2]Ibid.
[3]Ibid.
[4]Cf. Gilkey, op. cit., p. 540.

Although he wrote in defense of speculative philosophy,[1] Whitehead nevertheless stressed the limitations
of rationalism, a stress which led Christian to speak
of Whitehead's "humility about the enterprise of
speculative philosophy as such,"[2] a humility, nevertheless, which gives "no encouragement to intellectual
timidity."[3] His writings include warnings against
dogmatic rationalism or philosophical dogmatism. For
example, in Religion in the Making, Whitehead notes
"there never has been any exact complete system of
philosophic thought."[4] Later, what he says of religious dogmatism is applicable to his understanding of
philosophical dogmatism: "Idolatry is the necessary
product of static dogmas."[5] Showing that the proper
test" of the speculative system "is not that of finality, but of progress,"[6] Whitehead observes that "metaphysical categories are not dogmatic statements of
the obvious; they are tentative formulations of the
ultimate generalities."[7] Along with these--especially
when one is considering the place of God in Whitehead's
philosophy--two other passages are noteworthy. Concerning first principles, Whitehead observes:

> Philosophers can never hope finally to
> formulate these metaphysical first prin-
> ciples. Weakness of insight and defi-

---

[1]Process and Reality, pp. 4-26. Let it be noted
that the following is not meant to imply that Whitehead would question the importance of speculative philosophy. Rather, the explication is only meant to
serve as indicative of Whitehead's realization of the
limits of the speculative endeavor, a realization which
"kept him relatively free from that pride of intellect
from which some rationalistic philosophers have suf-
fered." (Christian, op. cit., p. 367.).

[2]Christian, op. cit., pp. 366-367.

[3]Ibid., p. 367.

[4]Whitehead, Religion in the Making, p. 139.

[5]Ibid., p. 142.

[6]Whitehead, Process and Reality, p. 21.

[7]Ibid., p. 12; Cf. also similar statements on
pp. 5, 6, 7, 12, 14, 20, 21, 519; Science and the
Modern World, pp. 160-161.

ciencies of language stand in the way
inexorably. Words and phrases must be
stretched towards a generality foreign
to their ordinary usage; and however such
elements of language be stabilized as
technicalities, they remain metaphors
mutely appealing for an imaginative leap.[1]

Closely related to this is a statement by Whitehead
which points to the limitations of man's reason while
at the same time demanding speculative boldness:

In a sense all explanation must end in an
ultimate arbitrariness. My demand is, that
the ultimate arbitrariness of matter of fact
from which our formulation starts should
disclose the same general principles of reality which we dimly discern as stretching
away into regions beyond our explicit powers
of discernment.[2]

In these passages Whitehead has spoken of "metaphors,"
"an imaginative leap," an "ultimate arbitrariness" and
of "dimly discerning" a reality "stretching beyond our
explicit powers of discernment." He realizes that the
God, who is an actual entity, is a unique actual entity, but his contention is that the facts of our experience require such a unique entity.[3] By the fact
that God is unique one cannot expect all statements
about God to be univocally applicable both to God and
to other actual entities. Yet, Cobb seems to feel
that coherence demands this. However, can statements
about God who is a unique person be univocally made
in reference to other persons? Does coherence demand
such univocity? Or rather, is Whitehead's system, and
Cobb's, coherent insofar as God, whether conceived as
an actual entity or a person, does not negate, sup-
plant or supersede the activity of other actual entities, but rather supplements and enhances the real
individuality and the influence of actual occasions?[4]

---

[1]Process and Reality, p. 6.

[2]Whitehead, Science and the Modern World, pp.
134-135.

[3]Cf. Leclerc, Whitehead's Metaphysics, pp. 192-
195.

[4]Cf. Christian, op. cit., pp. 301, 336, 381.

Moreover, Whitehead stressed that the really real was to be understood as an actual entity. He found that an adequate description of the really real required the admission of a unique actual entity, God, who was to be the chief exemplification of all the categories, not a principle invoked to save their collapse.[1] Cobb accepts this approach, too, as being the only adequate way in which God is admissable. Yet, he maintains that the Whiteheadian system is coherent only if God is considered as a person rather than an actual entity. However, if one has accepted the principle that God cannot be an exception to all the categories but rather is to be their chief exemplification, is the insistence that God is a person not tantamount to saying that all reality is to be understood in terms of "persons?" If so, would not the question of the maintenance of coherence require one to consider whether God as a person functioned in a way not unlike that of all other actualities themselves considered as persons? Yet, all of Cobb's alterations of Whitehead's system are concerned with the similarity or dissimilarity of the function of the actual entity God and other actual entities. Given Cobb's assertion that God is a person, should not Cobb reconstruct Whitehead's philosophy by describing how God as a person is related to all other actualities which themselves are to be considered as essentially personal. That is to say, Whitehead's requirement is that the ultimate "should disclose the same general principles of reality which we dimly discern as stretching away into regions beyond our explicit powers of discernment."[2] Cobb contends that the ultimate should be considered as a person. Yet, his suggestions for alteration of the Whiteheadian system are always considerations of God as actual entity in relation to other actual entities is merely to engage in a discussion utilizing the concept of God which has been rejected. The problem should be considered on the basis of how God as a person relates to all other actualities. This, too, offers problems however, for Whitehead's demand is that God "should disclose the same general principles of reality" as all other entities. Does this not entail that if God is considered to be a person rather than an actual entity, then all other

---

[1]Process and Reality, p. 521.
[2]Science and the Modern World, p. 135.

103

actualities are to be considered somehow as individual persons rather than individual actual entities. Consequently, the relationship which Cobb should describe is not the relationship between God, a person, and other actual entities, but rather between God as a person and other actualitites who themselves are considered as individual persons.

Already it has been noted that another area in which Cobb understands Whitehead's system to involve incoherence is Whitehead's doctrine of God's relation to the eternal objects. As has been shown[1] Cobb's contention is that Whitehead's doctrine affirms that God alone is to be responsible for the ordering of eternal objects. However, the doctrine can be coherent, he maintains, only if the possibility of temporal occasions' responsibility for some ordering of eternal objects is admitted. Cobb's altered Whiteheadian doctrine would assert that while God orders all eternal objects, it is also possible for temporal occasions to order an infinitesimal selection of eternal objects.[2] It is to be noted that Cobb alters the role of God with regard to his relation to the eternal objects, just as he alters it with regard to his function as sole provider of the initial aim. He rejects God's role as that of being solely responsible for ordering the eternal objects, just as he rejects God's function as sole provider of the initial aim. He makes God more like other occasions by admitting that other actual entities contribute to the initial aim of a becoming entity and also have the ability of ordering eternal objects. These considerations serve to indicate that Cobb's alterations in both cases have imposed limitations upon God which Whitehead himself does not impose. When Cobb turns to Whitehead's doctrine of creativity, however, he takes a different stand and demands that Whitehead must give to God a more radical role in creation.[3]

As has been shown, part of Cobb's rendering of the Whiteheadian system more coherent consisted of his attempt to show that God functioned in a way not

---

[1]Cf. above, pp. 86-93.

[2]Cf. Cobb, A Christian Natural Theology, p. 201.

[3]Cf. above, pp. 93-120.

radically different from that of other actual entities. The difference was to be alleviated by rejecting Whitehead's doctrine that God was unique in that he was solely responsible for the provision of the initial aim. Secondly, Cobb rejected attribution of uniqueness to God insofar as God alone is purported to have an unmediated relation to eternal objects while all other actual entities have a mediated relation.[1] His contention was that God should not be unique in the sense that he alone envisaged directly the eternal objects and that "Whitehead should not preclude in principle the possibility that a temporal occasion may have toward some eternal objects the kind of relation God has toward all."[2] It is to be noted that the initial aim and the eternal objects as pure possibilities for becoming are fundamental in the role of creation. Whitehead has found it necessary to attribute to God a role unique from that of all other actual entities in relation to both the initial aim and the envisagement of the eternal objects. Cobb, as has been shown, has questioned this attribution of uniqueness to God and has taken steps to make God function in a way not radically different from that of other actual entities. He has made God's function in relation to the initial aim and the eternal objects--both of which are fundamental in God's role in relation to creativity--less radical. Yet, he criticizes Whitehead for failing to have a radical doctrine of creation, and attempts "the attribution to God of a more decisive role in creation than Whitehead himself intended."[3]

In his attempt to give God a more radical role in creation than did Whitehead, of what does Cobb's proposed reconstruction of the Whiteheadian system consist? As we have noted, Cobb showed that Whitehead did have a doctrine of creation in that God functioned to establish the initial aim of each occasion and that God also envisaged all the eternal objects, the pure possibilities for becoming.[4] However, Cobb pointed out that even though God's role in creation was significant in Whitehead's thought, Whitehead nevertheless placed restrictions upon his creative role.[5] These

---

[1]Cobb, A Christian Natural Theology, p. 197.
[2]Ibid., p. 203.
[3]Ibid., p. 204.
[4]Cf. above, pp. 93-95.
[5]Cf. above, pp. 95-96.

limitations may be summarized as follows: First, although God is the sole initiator of the initial aim, this aim must always be given in consideration of the actual situation of the world. Second, although the initial aim profoundly influences the outcome of an actual entity, it is not wholly determinative. Third, God does not create the eternal objects, the pure possibilities for becoming. Finally, Whitehead has no doctrine of creatio ex nihilo.

In the foregoing[1] Cobb's proposed alteration has been considered. In that consideration it was noted that Cobb concluded that Whitehead's concept of creativity is fundamentally intelligible even though it can only be pointed at and hoped that it will be intuitively grasped.[2] Yet, Cobb considered the big question to be whether Whitehead's principle of creativity can answer the question as to why there is anything at all. Cobb's answer is that it cannot.[3] Therefore, his alteration consists in an explanation of the limitations of Whitehead's concept of creativity insofar as it cannot answer the question why. He says: "My contention is that 'creativity' can not go even as far in the direction of an answer as did 'prime matter.'"[4] However, Cobb should have no quarrel with Whitehead at this point for Whitehead's ontological principle affirms that the only "reasons" for occurrences are to be given in terms of actual entities.[5]

---

[1]Cf. above, pp. 93-102.

[2]Cf. above, p. 99. Also, A Christian Natural Theology, p. 210.

[3]Cobb fails to see that this is likewise--on the basis of the ontological principle--Whitehead's answer.

[4]A Christian Natural Theology, p. 210.

[5]Whitehead sums up the ontological principle and its significance when he says: "...the reasons for things are always to be found in the composite nature of definite actual entities--in the nature of God for reasons of the highest absoluteness, and in the nature of definite temporal actual entities for reasons which refer to a particular environment. The ontological principle can be summarized as: no actual entity, then no reason." (Whitehead, Process and Reality, p. 28.).

Cobb has viewed his task as that of giving God a more radical role in creation than did Whitehead himself. The results of Cobb's proposed alteration may be summarized as follows: First, the only "reasons" for occurrences are to be given in terms of the decisions of actual occasions. Second, the actual occasions occur and find their limitation by reason of God's establishment of their subjective aim. Finally, "creativity," not being as actual entity, cannot be the reason for their occurrence. Creativity itself provides no reason, while God is the reason for the being as well as the form of actual entities.[1]

This doctrine, Cobb alleges, is a more radical doctrine of creation than that which Whitehead himself espouses. Yet, how does it differ from that of Whitehead, or how is it more radical? Whitehead sums up his whole philosophy by pointing out that there are four creative phases in which the universe accomplishes its actuality. It will be noted that God is central in this accomplishment. First, there is the phase of conceptual origination, which is deficient in actuality, "but infinite in its adjustment of valuation."[2] This is God's primordial nature. Second, there is the temporal phase of physical origination giving rise to the multiplicity of actualities. This is directed by God's establishing subjective aims. Third, is the phase of perfected actuality, "in which the many are one everlastingly, without the qualification of any loss either of individual identity or of completeness of unity."[3] God functions as the ground of this phase, as the principle of limitation and concretion which directs by his lure for feeling. In the fourth phase of creativity the creative action completes itself. This is accomplished by God's "infinite patience" and "tender care that nothing be lost."[4]

Moreover, it must be noted that Cobb's "radical" doctrine of creation entails the incorporation of elements in Whitehead's system which Cobb has already

---

[1]A Christian Natural Theology, p. 214.

[2]Process and Reality, p. 532.

[3]Process and Reality, p. 532.

[4]Ibid., p. 525.

rejected or at least mitigated. This "radical" doctrine of creation includes affirmations that God is
the provider of the subjective aim and the reason for
the being as well as the form of actual entities.
Previously, however, Cobb had wanted to attribute
these functions in some respects to actual entities
other than God.[1]

What has the foregoing noted? On the one hand,
Cobb has been interested in making God function in a
way precisely like that of all other actual entities.
He has done this by making other actual entities to
function in their relation to creativity in a way not
different from the way in which God functions. Hence,
God is not to have a unique function as provider of
the initial aim and envisager of the eternal objects.
In this manner, Cobb contends, coherence is maintained.
On the other hand, Cobb contends that God must have a
more decisive role in creation than that assigned by
Whitehead's system. Two questions immediately arise.
First, does not the maintenance of coherence require
that God function in his creative role in a way not
radically different from that of other actual entities?
Yet, Cobb, who has argued for the similarity, suddenly
wants the difference stressed. Second, if Cobb wants
to maintain for God a more decisive role in creation
than Whitehead's system allows, why did he attempt to
alleviate God's unique function as establisher of the
initial aim and the envisager of eternal objects?
That is to say, Cobb, in the defense of his understanding of coherence has rejected the points in Whitehead's system in which God plays a decisive creative
role. He has attempted to show that other actual
entities can function in the provision of the initial
aim and the envisagement of the eternal objects. It
is true that Cobb stresses that God entertains all
possibilities of becoming while other actual occasions
entertain only an infinitesimal number. However, a
particular becoming actual entity does not require more
than the actualization of an infinitesimal number of
eternal objects in order for it to become. If entities
other than God in a particular becoming entity's past

---

[1]Which in fact Whitehead in a sense does insofar
as he places what Cobb sees to be limitations upon
God's creative role. (Cf. above, pp. 95-96.).

can provide for that entity its initial aim, and if
the entity in concrescence can envisage the number of
eternal objects requisite for its becoming--however
infinitesimal that number may be--then God need not
have any role in that entity's becoming. Hence, the
thesis emerges: Instead of making God's role in
creation more radical,[1] Cobb has rather presented a
situation in which God need not be considered as necessary at all-even though he may at one time have been
necessary--in the role of creation. Although he may
still function in the creative role, the possibility
that he need not do so has been introduced. An entity
could become, independent of God's activity, a possbil-
ity which Whitehead's "non-radical" doctrine would
never admit. Instead of making God's role in creation
more radical, Cobb has at least taken a step in the
opposite direction toward a deistic position or the
position of Sherburne's "Whitehead Without God."

---

[1]And therefore evidently more compatible with a
Christian doctrine of creatio ex nihilo.

II.   The Meaning and Reality of God In The
      Theology of Schubert Ogden

      A.   Introduction: The Problem of God

     Schubert Ogden readily recognizes that although
the reality of God has not always been one of the great
themes of theology,[1] it is today "the central theological problem."[2]   In fact, he would assert that "rightly understood, the problem of God is not one problem
among several others; it is the only problem there
is."[3]   The approach Ogden will take regarding this
central theological problem is indicated by his rejection on the one hand of any attempt to do theology
without God, and his acceptance on the other hand of
the Whiteheadian-Hartshornian affirmation of the reality of God.   Of the attempts to do theology without
God, Ogden simply says: "The claim currently made by
certain Protestant advocates of a theology post mortem
Dei--namely, that Christian faith does not require a
theistic explication--is so widely implausible as

---

     [1]"...for much of the theology of the first half
of our century, the reality of God was not its one
great theme."   (Schubert Ogden, The Reality of God,
p. 1.).

     [2]Ibid.

     [3]Ogden, The Reality of God, p. 1.   Noting Charles
Hartshorne's affirmation that "the theistic question
is entirely of a piece with the question of metaphysics generally," Ogden agrees with Hartshorne's more
radical contention that "the theistic question...is
not one more question, even the most important one.
It is, on the fundamental level, and when all its
implications are taken into account, the sole question.
(Ogden, "Theology and Philosophy: A New Phase of the
Discussion," The Journal of Religion, Volume XLIV,
Number 1, January 1964, pp. 4-5; Quoted from Hartshorne, The Logic of Perfection: Essays in Neoclassical Metaphysics, p. 131.).

scarcely to merit consideration."[1] "...all talk of a Christianity post mortem dei, is in the last analysis, neither hyperbole nor evidence of originality but merely nonsense."[2] "However absurd talking about God might be, it could never be so obviously absurd as talking of Christian faith without God."[3] Ogden contends against the theology post mortem dei, that if theology is possible only without God, then theology is not possible. Having rejected any attempt to do theology without God, Ogden asserts that theology must affirm the reality of God. The position he will take is summed up in his acceptance of Charles Hartshorne's words:

> In its early stages religion means certainty about many things. But we now see that he is most religious who is certain of but one thing, the world-embracing love of God. Everything else we can take our chances on; everything else, including man's relative significance in the world, is mere probability.[4]

This assertion is Ogden's way of emphasizing his contention that the theme of the reality of God is "in the last analysis, the sole theme of all valid Christian theology, even as it is the one essential point to all authentic Christian faith and witness."[5]

Ogden's stance, then, will be that of affirming the reality of God in the face of current denials of

---

[1]Ogden, "The Christian Proclamation of God to Men of the So-Called 'Atheistic Age,' Concilium, Volume 16: Is God Dead, p. 96.

[2]Ogden, The Reality of God and Other Essays, p. 15.

[3]Ogden, "Toward a New Theism," Theology in Crisis: A Colloquim on the Credibility of 'God', p. 5.

[4]Charles Hartshorne, Beyond Humanism: Essays in the New Philosophy of Nature, p. 44; Cf. Ogden, The Reality of God, p. x.

[5]Ogden, The Reality of God, p. x.

such reality. Yet, at the outset, he notes that an
immense problem is involved in such an affirmation.
He observes: "I am convinced that the usual ways of
approaching the problem of God today make an adequate
solution of it impossible..."[1] But, having offered
this observation, he takes a further step, and notes:
"...this is doubly tragic because the resources of our
situation, largely neglected though they are, offer
perhaps unparalleled opportunity for adequately solv-
ing it."[2] Our task, then, is to consider, in the
first place, Ogden's understanding of the "usual ways
of approaching the problem of God which makes an
adequate solution of it impossible," and, in the second place, his understanding of the resources available
for the solution of the problem.

     Consider in the first place Ogden's understanding
of the problem of God for today.[3] In an essay en-

---

[1]Ibid., p. ix.

[2]Ibid.

[3]That Ogden takes with great seriousness his contention that the problem of God for today is the central theological problem is evidenced by the fact that
inadequate attempts to solve the problem is the theme
of most of his published essays. Cf. e.g. "Beyond
Supernaturalism," (Religion in Life, Volume XXXIII,
1963-1964, pp. 7-18.) a theological appraisal of Honest
to God in which Ogden suggests that the problem of God
is not amenable to solution on the basis of Tillichian
categories or any other attempt in which God is considered from a monopolar perspective, but that Hartshorne's dipolar theism offers possibilities for
solution to the problem. The problem is delineated
more specifically, with some indications toward
solution in the following: "Toward a New Theism,"
(Theology in Crisis: A Colloquim on the Credibility
of 'God,' pp. 3-18.); "Bultmann's Demythologizing and
Hartshorne's Dipolar Theism," (Process and Divinity,
pp. 493-513); "The Christian Proclamation of God to
Men of the So-Called 'Atheistic Age,'" (Consilium:
Theology in the Age of Renewal, Volume 16: Is God
Dead, pp. 89-98.); "Love Unbounded: The Doctrine of
God," (The Perkins School of Theology Journal, Volume
XIX, Number 3, Spring, 1968, pp. 5-17.); "God and Phi-
losophy: A New Phase of the Discussion," (The Journal
of Religion, XLVIII, Number 2, April, 1968, pp. 161-

titled "The Christian Proclamation of God to Men of
the So-Called 'Atheistic Age,'" Ogden notes that "what
distinguishes Western humanity today is not a greater
degree of existential distrust of God but an ever more
wide-spread dissent from the assertions of classical
theism."[1] The dissent against God today is not a rejection of all forms of theism even though the formulations presented typically advance this claim. Such
a claim of total rejection of all theism is only "an
acoustic illusion"[2] which is, in reality, merely the
rejection "of the claim of classical theism itself to
be the only form of theism there is."[3] The predominance of "atheism"[4] today has derived its force from

---

180.); "Faith and Truth," (Frontline Theology, Dean
Peerman, ed. Richmond: John Knox Press, 1967, pp.
126-133.).

[1]Ogden, "The Christian Proclamation of God to Men
of the So-Called 'Atheistic Age,'" p. 93.

[2]Ibid.; Also, "Toward a New Theism," p. 7.

[3]Ibid. As Ogden notes in another article: "...
current announcements of the death of God are as widely
received as they are largely because the God who is
said to be dead is quite clearly the God conceived by
a form of theism which has long since ceased to be
reasonable to a vast number of contemporary minds."
(Ogden, "Love Unbounded: The Doctrine of God," p.7.).

[4]Explaining the ambiguity of the word "atheism,"
Ogden observes that although the term may be a referent to "persons who in one way or another actually
share in the atheism of our time, it may still refer
either to those whose existential self-understanding
is 'atheistic' in the scriptural sense of the word--
i.e. idolatrous--or else to those who withhold their
assent from that form of reflective theism traditionally presented in the preaching and teaching of the
church." ("The Christian Proclamation of God to Men of
the So-Called 'Atheistic Age,'" pp. 92-93.). The word
may designate both of these referents, but they are to
some extent independent and may or may not be present
at the same time.

theology's virtually complete acceptance of the classical form of theistic belief accompanied by the re-
fusal to entertain any other alternative.[1] If theology
has accepted classical theism as the only form of
theism, then a rejection of classical theism will seem
to entail a rejection of all theism. Ogden's task is
to inquire whether classical theism is, in fact, the
only form of theism,[2] but he first offers an account of
the widespread rejection of classical theism. He sees
two main reasons why men of today find the traditional
form of belief in God unacceptable. These may be
viewed as the atheist's two principal objections to
Christian theism.[3] First, those who have rejected the
traditional belief in God have done so because it seems
that they "can accept this traditional theism only by
affirming statements to be scientifically or historically true without the requisite backing and warrants."[4] For them acceptance of Christian theism en-

---

[1]Ogden, "The Christian Proclamation of God to Men
of the So-Called 'Atheistic Age,'" p. 93. Cf. also
Ogden's statement: "...there are many today who make
the...sweeping claim that theism as such has been
shown to be an unreasonable belief. But analysis dis-
closes that the claim usually owes its plausibility to
the tacit assumption by both sides of the traditional
theistic discussion that the classical form of Christian theism is the only form of such theism there is."
(Ogden, "Love Unbounded: The Doctrine of God," p. 7.).
Cf. also "Faith and Truth," pp. 131, 132 and "Theology
and Philosophy: A New Phase of the Discussion," in
which Ogden states that this is Flew's assumption, and
that Flew's argument is valid only if this assumption
holds.

[2]Whether this assumption is valid, or whether the
question of theism is more complex than theists and
atheists alike conventionally assume, we will presently
want to ask." ("Love Unbounded: The Doctrine of God,"
p. 7.).

[3]Cf. Ogden, "The Christian Proclamation of God to
Men of the So-Called 'Atheistic Age,'" pp. 93-94;"Love
Unbounded: The Doctrine of God," pp. 7-9; "Toward a
New Theism," pp. 7-9.

[4]Ogden, "Love Unbounded: The Doctrine of God,"
p. 7.; "The Christian Proclamation of God to Men of
the So-Called 'Atheistic Age,'" pp. 93-94; "Toward a
New Theism," p. 7.

tails acceptance of beliefs now widely regarded as false. Man is asked to regard as fact that which usual principles for determining fact would require him to regard as false.[1] For example, those who reject Christianity do so because they feel its acceptance requires them to believe that men and animals were created as a fixed species in no way related through the evolutionary process, or that the creation of the world took place at one definite time.[2] Moreover, even when one admits that the Scriptural material is to be viewed mythologically and hence lends itself to demythologization, there are still those who would reject Christian theism on the grounds that: "Christian belief means accepting the resurrection of Christ, and therefore it seems to involve believing in at least one miracle."[3]

The first problem, then, is that Christian theism is so widely rejected today because it seems to require--even when presented by some of its more sophisticated spokesmen[4] --acceptance of certain statements concerning the origin and end of the world, along with certain occurrences within the world, that are not warranted by our knowledge of science and history. To accept any statement as true in contradiction to the

---

[1]"When one is asked to believe, for example, that statements about creation and the last things refer to actual events in the past and future of world history, or that language about God's action in Christ denotes miraculous happenings contra naturam, he is asked, in effect, to suspend the warrants whereby he otherwise abjudicates historical or scientific claims to truth. He is asked to believe as statements of fact (albeit extraordinary statements of fact) what generally accepted canons for determining fact require him to regard either as false or as linguistic expressions of a quite different logical type." (Ogden, "The Christian Proclamation of God to Men of the So-Called 'Atheistic Age,'" p. 94; Cf. also, "Toward A New Theism," pp. 7-9; "Love Unbounded: The Doctrine of God," pp. 7-8.).

[2]Say, e.g. 4004 B. C.

[3]"Love Unbounded: The Doctrine of God," p. 8; quoted from Ninian Smart, Philosophers and Religious Truth, p. 26.

[4]Ibid.

scientific or historical data, or to accept any statement as true without the proper historical or scientific warrants, is to question the autonomy of science
and history within their own proper spheres. It is
this questioning "which makes classical theism so
widely unacceptable to contemporary men."[1]

A second reason for the rejection of classical
theism is that one can accept it only if he accepts
the classical metaphysical position of which it is an
integral part.[2] But this whole classical metaphysical
outlook is itself "contrary to all our experience and
thought as contemporary men."[3] On what ground does
Ogden make this assertion? What is his understanding
of classical metaphysics?[4] The essential point at
which modern man rejects classical metaphysics is that

---

[1]Ibid., pp. 8-9.

[2]Ogden, "Love Unbounded: The Doctrine of God,"
p. 9; "Toward a New Theism," p. 9.

[3]Ogden, "The Christian Proclamation of God to Men
of the So-Called 'Atheistic Age,'" p. 94. As Ogden
noted already in 1959: "...virtually all of the classical formulations which somehow constitute the basis
for any new theological statements are expressed in a
conceptuality which is decidedly pre-modern and therefore are radically called in question by our distinctively modern understanding of ourselves and our
world." ("The Situation in Contemporary Protestant
Theology: Systematic Theology," The Perkins School of
Theology Journal, Volume XII, Number 2, Winter, 1959,
p. 14.).

[4]His summary and, as he himself notes, simplified
view of classical metaphysics may be found in the following previously mentioned essays: "Toward a New
Theism," "Beyond Supernaturalism," "Love Unbounded:
The Doctrine of God," "Faith and Truth," and "Theology
and Philosophy: A New Phase of the Discussion." More
detailed treatment of the subject is to be found in
The Reality of God and Other Essays, especially pp. 1-
70. The topic is treated to a lesser extent in "God
and Philosophy," The Journal of Religion, Volume
XLVIII, Number 2, April, 1968, pp. 161-181, and the previously mentioned "The Situation in Contemporary
Protestant Theology: Systematic Theology."

of classical understanding of reality. As Ogden notes:
"the understanding of reality expressed in this kind
of metaphysics is one for which all our distinctive
experience and thought as modern secular men is negative evidence."[1] The essential point of rejection,
then, has to do with the classical understanding of
reality, and the defining characteristic of this understanding of reality is, according to Ogden, that there
are two kinds of reality.[2] This bifurcation of reality is evidenced, on the one hand, by the world of
becoming, the world of time, change, and real relation-
ships, the world of which each of us is immediately and
observably a part.[3] On the other hand, there is the
world of the changeless, timeless, imperishable, and
unrelated. This world alone is real in the full sense
of the word, and to this world alone may be attributed
the designation of divinity. It is the world of "the
absolute and eternal and immutable."[4] Although the
relation of these two worlds has always been a problem
of classical metaphysics to which various solutions
have been offered, there has been "complete consensus"
on one point, namely that "the relations between the
two worlds are one-way only."[5] The world of time and
change, the world of ordinary beings, is indeed related
to God as their "formal cause which they somehow exemplify or as the final cause toward which they move in
their several processes of self-development."[6] The
divine world of pure being, however, can be "in no
sense really related"[7] to the ordinary world of change

---

[1]Ogden, "Toward a New Theism," p. 9.

[2]Ogden observes: "From its first great formulations by Plato and Aristotle, the chief defining
characteristic of classical metaphysics has been its
separation of what is given in our experience into two
quite different kinds of reality." (Ogden, "Toward
a New Theism," p. 9; "Love Unbounded: The Doctrine of
God," p.8.).

[3]Ogden, "Toward a New Theism," p. 9; "Love Unbounded," p. 9.

[4]Ogden, "Toward a New Theism," p. 9.

[5]Ibid.

[6]Ogden, "Love Unbounded: The Doctrine of God,"
p. 9.

[7]Ibid.

and becoming. Any relation of God to beings-in-becom-
ing would involve his dependence upon others and his
participation in time and change which is the very
antithesis of his timeless and changeless being.

This classical metaphysical understanding was be-
queathed to the Western world by Greek antiquity, and
came to serve as the basis for the conceptualization of
the Christian faith. From the time of the church Fathers, attempts were made to identify the God of the
Christian faith with the absolute Being of the philosophers. Ogden observes that the difficulty, if not the
impossibility, of such an attempt was early recognized
by Philo of Alexandria, who, while having the "best
claim to be the founder of classical theism," nevertheless leaves "no question that the God of Israel, whose
very being is involvement in the creatures of his love,
can in no wise be simply identified with the Absolute
of classical metaphysics."[1] Yet, most of "christian
philosophy" has been attempts to make the identification, and the influence of such attempts has been so
great that most Western men have conceived of God in
terms of concepts derived from the Greek metaphysics
of being.[2]

This attempt to wed "the God of Abraham, Isaac and
Jacob" with the deus philosophorum, the identification
of the dynamic, related God of the Bible with the static, unrelated God of the philosophers, reveals the major stumbling block within classical theism, the presence of which leads contemporary men to reject traditional theism. Not only this, but insofar as classical
theism is assumed to be the only theism there is, then
the stumbling block leads to a rejection of all theism.
This attempted identification stands as a barrier to
acceptance of theistic claims in two ways. In the
first place, contemporary man has long been convinced
of the essential incoherence of the classical theistic
stance in its attempt to combine Greek secular wisdom
with the Scriptural religious insights. In the second
place, the central affirmation of Greek wisdom that the
world of time and change is inferior or not fully real
likewise leads to the rejection of classical theism.[3]
The rejection of classical theism's claim that the

---

[1]Ogden, "Toward a New Theism," p. 10.
[2]Ogden, "Love Unbounded: The Doctrine of God,"
p. 9.
[3]Ogden, "Love Unbounded: The Doctrine of God,"

world is somehow not fully real is indicated by the
words of one of the radical or death-of-God theologians
when he says:

> in this world...there is no need for religion
> no need for God. This means that we refuse
> to consent to that traditional interpretation
> of the world as a shadow-screen of unreality,
> masking or concealing the eternal which is the
> only true reality...The world of experience is
> real, and it is necessary and right to be ac-
> tively engaged in changing its patterns and
> structures.[1]

Ogden quotes Hamilton's words because he sees them as
being especially revealing in three ways. First, these
words indicate the ease with which one can move from
the words "God" and "religion" to a traditional interpretation of the world in relation to which these words
are to be understood. Second, Hamilton's words reveal
the confusion of "God" and "religion" with the "traditional interpretaion of reality." What Hamilton actually calls for is not the acknowledgment of the death
of God, but the acknowledgment of the demise of the
classical interpretation of reality. Third, Hamilton's
words point to the real reason why contemporary man
finds it necessary to reject the traditional form of
theism. "Man today," says Ogden, "finds this form of
faith so objectionable because it directly contradicts
his deep conviction of the reality and significance of
this world of time and change and of his own life within it."[2] The classical theist's understanding of God
as the Absolute of traditional metaphysics entails the
acceptance of a God who is external to man and the
world and totally unaffected by man. What man does or
does not do makes--in the final analysis--no difference,
for God is complete and utterly independent of anything
beyond himself. To be affected by or be in internal
relation to anything other than himself would demean
his perfection. In the last analysis, the world is
neither real nor of any consequence. Contemporary man
denies this understanding of reality.

---

pp. 9-10; "Toward a New Theism," p. 10.

[1]"Toward a New Theism," p. 10, from William Hamilton, "The Death of God Theology," The Christian
Scholar, Spring, 1965, pp. 45ff.

[2]Ogden, "Love Unbounded: The Doctrine of God,"
p. 10.

Realizing that "whatever is real and important must somehow include the present world of becoming," contemporary man finds "the classical form of Christian theism simply incredible."[1]

We have considered Ogden's understanding of two of the main reasons for the rejection of traditional Christian belief. These are, in the first place, that traditional Christian belief requires one to accept as history or science what one can accept responsibly only as myth; and in the second place, one is required to accept a classical metaphysical outlook which not only entails incoherence if identified with the Christian understanding of God, but also is contrary to all man's experience.[2] Given these two objections to Christian belief, what is Ogden's response? He asserts:

> So far as I understand the matter, the conditions of reasonableness in our situation demand the unqualified acceptance both of the method and world picture of modern science and critical history and of the reality of this world of time and change, which is the context of our lives as secular man.[3]

Such an acceptance of the method and world-picture of modern science and critical history along with the affirmation of the reality and significance of this world, clearly entails for Ogden a rejection of classical theism. Hence, Ogden outlines the task before him:

> I hold that if one is to continue to affirm with the Christian tradition that faith in God is both indispensible and reasonable, it is incumbent on him to show that such faith may be explicated in other terms than

---

[1]Ibid.; "Toward a New Theism," p. 11.

[2]Ogden, "The Christian Proclamation of God to Men of the So-Called 'Atheistic Age,'" pp. 93-94; "Love Unbounded: The Doctrine of God," pp. 7 and 9; "Toward a New Theism," pp. 7 and 9.

[3]Ogden, "Love Unbounded: The Doctrine of God," p. 10.

those of classical Christian theism.[1]

Having offered these two observations for initial consideration in attempting to answer the question of why the reality of God has now become the central theological concern, we now turn to Ogden's appraisal of the question in his collected essays. Theology has turned from the christological and anthropological concentration on which it focused between the two wars. The turn is symbolized by John A. T. Robinson's Honest to God the "all-controlling concern" of which is "the possibility and meaning of an honest faith in God in our time."[2] In considering the possibilities offered by Bonhoeffer, Bultmann and Tillich, Robinson recognizes that the one common demand of these three thinkers is that theology must be in the strict sense post-liberal.[3] In its driving concern for the meaning and truth of the Christian faith, nineteenth century liberalism attempted to consider the legitimate theological criticisms of the Enlightenment while at the same time presenting an appropriate formulation of the Christian faith.[4] Moreover, in affirming the proper autonomy and validity of secular methods of knowledge, liberalism reaffirmed the fundamental Protestant contention expressed in the phrase sola gratia -- sola fide.[5] Yet, liberalism was on the whole unsuccessful in implementing its concern, for in attempting to articulate a formulation of the Christian faith which would respect man's self-understanding of himself in the world, it was often uncritical, thus failing to respect the distinctive claims of faith.[6]

We are indebted to the theological movement of the first half of the twentieth century for its reaction against liberal theology's uncritical acceptance of modern man's self-understanding, a reaction which was not concerned merely to restore the status quo ante liberal theology, but rather attempted self-

---

[1]Ogden, "Toward a New Theism," p. 11.

[2]Ogden, The Reality of God, p. 2.

[3]Ibid., pp. 2-3.

[4]Ibid., p. 3.

[5]Ibid., p. 4.

[6]Ibid.

criticism from within the ranks of liberal theology. This movement succeeded in breaking the hold of liberal theology, but not so much by providing a more adequate solution than by exposing the inadequacy of liberal theology's achievements.[1] "Neo-orthodoxy's" understanding of the theological task as entailing a radical separation of Christian faith and modern culture presented a questioning of the meaning and truth of the Christian claims for men living in the modern secular world.[2] Since the Second World War, however, with the rising prominence of Tillich, Bultmann and Bonhoeffer,[3] the question of the applicability of the Christian faith to the modern situation has once more come to demand serious consideration, so that theologians have again become aware of their inescapable apologetic[4] task. The apologetic approach as-

---

[1]Ogden, The Reality of God, p. 5.

[2]Ibid., pp. 4-5.

[3]Ogden presents a brief critique of Tillich, Bultmann and Bonhoeffer, offering what he thinks to be the limitations of each man's theology vis a vis the contemporary situation, in his review of John A. T. Robinson's Honest to God, "Beyond Supernaturalism." His detailed study of Bultmann is to be found in Christ Without Myth, New York: Harper and Row, 1961, and in his introduction to Existence and Faith: Shorter Writings of Rudolf Bultmann, New York: Meridian Books, 1960.

[4]Ogden notes the ambiguity of and the negative connotations often associated with the word "apologetics," yet he believes this still to be the best word descriptive of the theological task of relating faith and culture. In using "apologetics" he notes: "Here, too, there are dangers of misunderstanding, since the word 'apologetic' is likewise ambiguous. Moreover, while Tillich expressly designates his theology as 'apologetic,' Bultmann generally resists the designation and understands the word only in a pejorative sense. Yet, despite this obvious difference, both thinkers, together with Bonhoeffer, so conceive the theologian's responsibility as to include the task for which 'apologetic' would still appear to be the best word. They insist that the terms of theological adequacy are always set not only by the faith which the theologian must seek to express appropriately, but also by the existence of man himself, to whom

123

sumes that any presentation of the Christian faith has
to take into account both the content of faith itself
and the existence of man. It assumes that the Christian faith is not completely alien to man, but can be
understood by man if it is so expressed that it takes
into account man's existential situation.[1]

The renewed emphasis on apologetic, however, does
not account for the fact that the central problem
facing contemporary theology is God rather than some
other theological emphasis. The reason that the doctrine of God has become of central significance has to
do with what Ogden views as "a fundamental change that
has become ever more apparent in our larger cultural
situation."[2] This change is evidenced by the fact
that contemporary man's outlook regarding his "more
creative self-expressions" "no longer seems merely
secular, but appears to have become increasingly
secularistic."[3] This assertion, of course, entails a
differentiation between the terms "secular" and
"secularistic," terms which, in ordinary parlance, are
assumed to be synonymous. Ogden suggests a refinement
of our ordinary usage similar to the way in which he
understands Gogarten's distinguishing between the two.
Ogden understands Gogarten to be speaking of two different kinds of secularization only one of which is to
be designated "secularism."[4] We now turn to a consideration of Ogden's differentiation.

Ogden views this "fundamental change" as a change
from a secular to a secularistic outlook, or, as he
would prefer, the change is one from secularity to
secularism. Illustrative of this change is the fact
that most men today are deeply influenced by the scientific world picture. Since the seventeenth century
men have increasingly accepted the scientific method
as that by which an adequate picture of the world and
knowledge of the world could be defined. The pursuit

---

the theologian must try to express that faith understandably." (The Reality of God, pp. 5-6.).

[1]Ibid., p. 6.
[2]Ibid.
[3]Ibid.
[4]Ibid., p. 7.

of knowledge of the world became a wholly "secular" affair not to be questioned by criteria heteronomously imposed by ecclesiastical or religious authority.[1] Insofar as traditional theological assertions appeared to make scientific claims, they were subjected to the scrutiny of scientific methodology thus revealing their inadequacies and inconsistencies.[2] In Ogden's words, then, "modern man long ago opted for the scientific method of science and therewith decided irrevocably for secularity."[3] Ogden views this decision for secularity as both a necessary and positive option.

Accompanying this irrevocable decision for secularity, however, is another more thoroughgoing application of the scientific method. Instead of merely claiming that the scientific method is the only means for obtaining information about the world as disclosed by our senses, some would further assert that the scientific method obtains the only knowledge there is.[4] This positivistic stance has come to be shared by many people who are by no means professional philosophers. For those who adopt this positivistic standpoint that scientific knowledge is the only knowledge there is, the question put before theology is no longer whether theology and science conflict, but the question whether theologians can make any meaningful statements at all. If knowledge is attainable only by the scientific method, then, theological statements, insofar as they are empirically unverifiable, cannot be said to be meaningful. Ogden calls this positivistic approach--the approach that knowledge gained by the scientific method is the only knowledge there is--a "secularistic" outlook. The secularistic outlook, then, is one which absolutizes the scientific method and world-view derived from the application of that method. True secularity, on the one hand, legitimately affirms the validity and autonomy of the scientific method in its own field. Secularism, on the other hand, asserts that the scientific method is the only valid means to any knowledge. It is this secularistic world-view which has "become

---

[1]Ogden, The Reality of God, p. 7.
[2]Ibid., p. 8.
[3]Ibid.
[4]Ibid.

ever more widely prevalent among contemporary Western men,"[1] and which accounts for much of the widespread rejection of theism in the contemporary world.

The movement from secularity to secularism is also evidenced in the field of ethics and morality. This area, too, has become thoroughly secularistic. Finding Kant's "autonomy of the will as the supreme principle of morality"[2]--an autonomy which nevertheless "leads ineluctably to religion"[3]--hopelessly unconvincing,"[4] many postmodern ethicists present their insights in a completely secularistic form. Denying any transcendent element, the secularistic ethicist presents his insights as the wholly immanent possibilities of man's self-understanding.[5] Hence, Ogden's conclusion is: "In their understanding of action, as in their view of knowledge, numbers of men today are no longer content merely to affirm the autonomy and importance of their life in this world, but deny unequivocally that this world in any way points beyond itself."[6] It is this secularistic outlook which has made the problem of God the central problem for Protestant theology. The denial of God is so often heard that any theologian cannot fail to find his whole endeavor concentrated on this single point.[7] This is indeed the "age of atheism."[8] If any theologian is to show that the word "God" as Christians use it has any meaning at all, he must show that "the sentences in which it occurs somehow express assertions capable of being true."[9] The theologian must now affirm the reality of God--if such reality is to be affirmed--in a situation in which this reality is expressly denied.

---

[1]Ogden, The Reality of God, p. 10.
[2]Ibid.
[3]Ogden, The Reality of God, p. 10.
[4]Ibid., p. 11.
[5]Ibid. Ogden offers Sartre and Camus as examples of such post-modern writers whose outlook is avowedly atheistic.
[6]Ibid., p. 12.
[7]Ibid.
[8]Ibid., p. 13.
[9]Ibid., p. 12.

In the foregoing, we have considered Ogden's understanding of the central problem confronting contemporary theology, that of the problem of affirming the reality of God. We have noted that, according to Ogden, the problem has become central for several reasons. In the first place, the reality of God is questioned because of the false assumption that in order to affirm the reality of God one must accept as fact that which critical history and the scientific method require him to reject as mythical or even false. In the second place, the reality of God is denied because of the illegitimate assumption that an affirmation of such a reality requires the acceptance of a classical metaphysics which no longer adequately describes modern man's understanding of himself and his world. Finally, and closely connected with the former reasons, the reality of God is denied because of the secularistic world view of a large majority of men. The secularistic world view affirms that there is only one way to knowledge, that of the scientific method of empirical verification, and that only that is real which can be verified by this means. Insofar as theologians cannot prove the reality of God by such an empirical methodology, the denial of his reality is warranted.

How is the theologian to confront these seemingly adequate reasons for the rejection of theism? He can either continue to affirm the reality of God and thus deny the atheistic assumptions, or he can accept these assumptions and surrender the primary claim of the historic Christian faith.[1] Ogden refuses to accept conclusions such as those of Paul M. van Buren in his The Secular Meaning of the Gospel, the thesis of which is that the reality of God can be completely denied without doing violence to the meaning of the Christian witness.[2] His reply to any attempt to do "theology without God" is simply stated:

> However absurd talking about God might
> be, it could never be so obviously absurd
> as talking of Christian faith without
> God. If theology is possible today only

---

[1]Ogden, The Reality of God, p. 13.
[2]Ogden, The Reality of God, p. 14.

on secularistic terms, the more candid
way to say this is to admit that theology
is not possible today at all....Faith in
God of a certain kind is not merely an
element in Christian faith along with
several others; it simply is Christian
faith, the heart of the matter itself.
Therefore, the very thing about the expressions of faith in Scripture and tradition
which makes a properly secular interpretation of them possible and even necessary
also makes a secularistic theology impossible. The issue here is indeed either/or,
and all talk of Christianity post mortem dei
is, in the last analysis, neither hyperbole
nor evidence of originality but merely
nonsense.[1]

In these words we recognize Ogden's intention to
approach the central theological problem of today by
insisting that an acceptance of the secularistic
attempt to base theology on the premise that God is
dead is a premature closure, for one cannot assume
that "secularism is an essentially unified and inter-
nally consistent outlook."[2] His contention is that
upon examination this assumption proves to be illegitimate, thus clearing the way for the affirmation of
the reality of God.

In examining the secularist claim, Ogden notes
that epistemologically the secularist is a positivist.
The secularist not only affirms the validity of the
scientific method for attaining knowledge, but rather
asserts that scientific statements along with the
purely analytic truths of mathematics and science are
the only kind which can validate their cognitive
claims. Ogden's immediate rejoinder to such a claim is
that this claim itself is "wholly unjustified in terms
of the only criteria it itself admits as possible" for
it can neither be empirically falsified nor is it an
analytic statement.[3] This alone, of course, does not

---

[1]Ibid., pp. 14-15.
[2]Ibid., p. 15.
[3]Ogden, The Reality of God, pp. 15-16.

establish the validity of metaphysical and theological usage, but it does caution against arbitrary denial of such validity.

Secularism has enjoyed such widespread acceptance because it serves as "the most extreme expression of a centuries-long reaction against the classical meta-physical-theological tradition of the Western world."[1] Our culture has been almost completely dominated by a total metaphysical-theological outlook which is today sharply opposed by our experience and thought as modern men. The secularists' denial of this outlook lends itself to ready acceptance. Assuming that the traditional philosophis perennis or "Christian philosophy," which weds classical Greek metaphysics and the Hebraic religious insights into a supernaturalistic theism, to be the only theism, both the secularist and the classical theist assume that any valid rejection of this kind of theism is tantamount to overcoming theism altogether.[2] The irreconcilable opposition between supernaturalistic theism[3] and our everyday experience as men living in a dynamic world of change makes the secularist's claim seem all the more valid. While true secularity entails the acceptance of logical consistency as a necessary condition of truth, acceptance of the classical theist position entails a denial of the necessity of self-consistency. On the other hand, the classical theist speaks of God's creation of the world as a free act, while at the same time, through the influence of classical metaphysics, the classical theist speaks of God's act of creation as one with his eternal essence which is in every way free from contingency. Moreover, classical theists

---

[1] Ibid., p. 16.

[2] Ibid., pp. 16-17.

[3] Ogden considers in some detail the problem of supernaturalistic theism along with a critical consideration of the attempts of Bonhoeffer, Bultmann, and Tillich to deal with the problems it poses in "Beyond Supernaturalism," (Religion in Life, Volume XXXIII, 1963-64, p. 7-18.) a theological appraisal of Robinson's Honest To God.

assert that man's end is to serve and glorify God by
doing his will. Yet, the God whom they ask man to
serve is conceived as a statically complete perfection
who could be no more affected by man's best actions as
by his worst.[1] If God is wholly indifferent to man's
thought and action in the world, then one's relation
to God is totally irrelevant. Hence, classical theism
is unacceptable to modern man not only because of its
theoretical incoherence but also because of its existential irrelevancy.[2]

Yet, the reality of God does not stand or fall
with the acceptance or rejection of the classical
metaphysical-theological scheme. We are indeed justified in rejecting the supernaturalistic conception of
God "which is in fact untenable, given our typical experience and thought as secular men,"[3] argues Ogden,
but rather than declaring the death of God, we must
merely assert the demise of a particular cast of
thought and "seek a conception of God's reality in
which the inadequacies of this traditional theism can
be overcome."[4]

---

[1]Ogden, The Reality of God, p. 17.

[2]Ibid., p. 18.

[3]Ogden, The Reality of God, p. 19.

[4]Ibid.

B. The Reality of Faith

In the preceding we have considered Ogden's
analysis of the central problem of contemporary theology. He has rejected any attempt at doing theology
without God as nonsense, and has instead opted to
attempt to construct a new theism while admitting the
demise of classical theism and rejecting any attempt
to return to its supernaturalistic stance. Bonhoeffer,
Bultmann and Tillich[1] have made important contribu-
tions, but neither of them has been able to take advantage of the resources made available by contemporary
philosophy. Some contemporary philosophers contribute
to the possibility of a solution to the current theistic problem, on the one hand, by showing us that
supernaturalistic theism is not the only viable theistic position. On the other hand, they also show that
God can be so conceived that the inconsistencies of
traditional theism can be avoided while still affirming the legitimate insights of our religious herit-
age.[2]

Ogden contends that no theistic scheme alone can
solve the problem of God. Our concepts of God remain
a mere idea having nothing to do with reality unless it
is exhibited "as the most adequate reflective account
we can give of certain experiences in which we all in-
escapably share."[3] Ogden's attempt, then, will be not
merely to offer a theistic scheme that is logically

---

[1]Cf. Schubert M. Ogden, "Beyond Supernaturalism,"
op. cit. for Ogden's comments regarding the place of
Bonhoeffer, Bultmann and Tillich in contemporary theology's position regarding the doctrine of God, and his
book Christ Without Myth, (New York: Harper and Row
Publishers, 1961.), and a later essay "Bultmann's
Demythologizing and Hartshorne's Dipolar Theism," in
Reese and Freeman, eds., Process and Divinity, LaSalle,
Illinois: The Open Court Publishing Company, 1964, pp.
493-513, for his understanding of the possibilities for
contemporary theology of Bultmann's thought.

[2]Ogden, The Reality of God, p. 20.

[3]The Reality of God, p. 20.

consistent, but also one that is warranted by man's common experience.

Having advanced these two necessary conditions for an adequate theology--i.e. that any adequate theological scheme must be both logically consistent and warranted by man's common experience--Ogden immediately begins consideration of the one thing in which all men today share. This one thing is, as Ogden views it, man's "affirmation of life here and now in the world in all its aspects and in its proper autonomy and significance."[1] Elaborating on secular man's affirmation of life, Ogden offers the direction he will take in reliance upon this common experience of men:

> My conviction is that it is in this secular
> affirmation that we must discover the real-
> ity of God in our time. The adequate re-
> sponse to secularistic negations will not be
> made by a supernaturalism that is no longer
> tenable or by a naturalism that uncritically
> accepts the same negations. It will be made,
> rather, by an integral secularity--a secu-
> larity which has become fully self-conscious
> and which therefore makes explicit the faith
> in God already implied in what it itself
> affirms.[2]

According to Ogden, then, the affirmation of life here and now in the world contains an implicit faith in God which only needs to be made explicit by its self-conscious expression. His task is to test this conviction and to make explicit the claim of the reality of God, as he asserts: "I now wish to claim that for secular man of today, as surely as for any other man, faith in God cannot but be real because it is in the final analysis unavoidable." For many, any attempt to

---

[1]Ibid.

[2]Ibid., Cf. also "Beyond Supernaturalism," op. cit.

[3]The Reality of God, p. 21. In "The Possibility and Task of Philosophical Theology," (Union Seminary Quarterly Review, Volume 20, pp. 271-279.). Ogden rejects the attempts which Bultmann seems at times to make, to provide a criterion for theology solely on the basis of existential analysis as offering no clear

substantiate this claim would seem doomed from the start. Great numbers of contemporary men seem to get along quite well with no belief in God whatsoever, and others, those designated "secularistic" by Ogden, expressly deny belief in God. Ogden's assertion that even these men believe in God implies that they are mistaken about their own beliefs. Although Ogden realizes these difficulties involved in affirming that belief in God is unavoidable, he nevertheless maintains that such a claim has merit for the theologian. The merit of claiming that belief in God is unavoidable is, according to Ogden, that "it is the only claim completely consistent with Christian faith in God itself. By its very character Christian faith so understands God that everyone must in some sense believe in him and no one can in every sense deny him."[1] To put this contention another way: "Unless God is somehow real for every man, he is not genuinely real for any man."[2]

Does such a claim eliminate, in principle, the claim of atheism? Ogden insists that his claim does not entail the proposition "There are no atheists" as a corollary. Rather, it merely entails that one uti-

---

alternative to a wholly subjectivistic approach to Christian faith. Calling for a less restricted view than that of Bultmann, he reaffirms the same point made above when he says: "The notion that human existence is in any instance the primary or exclusive reality of knowledge--even of philosophical knowledge--I regard as mistaken. Against it, I would set the dictum of Thomas Aquinas, 'Omnia cognoscentia cognoscunt implicite Deum in quolibet cognito (De veritate, 22, 2 ad 1) or (what is not different) Hartshorne's statement....that the reality of God is 'inherent in all basic secular conceptions and only intellectual inhibitions can keep it from being formulated.' In both cases, we are reminded that philosophical theology is possible because the original encounter in which all our knowledge has its basis is an encounter not merely with ourselves or our fellow creatures, but also with our infinite ground and end." (p. 275.).

[1]The Reality of God, p. 21.
[2]Ibid., p. 22.

133

lize extreme caution in interpreting the word atheism.[1]
In order to understand "atheism" one must distinguish
carefully the difference between faith and unfaith.[2]

Ogden points out that unfaith, like faith, occurs
at two essentially different levels of human life. He
designates these two different levels of unfaith as
"godlessness of the heart"[3] and "godlessness of the
mind."[4] The deepest level of unfaith is that of godlessness of the heart. This level, Ogden notes "is
not a matter of self-conscious disbelief, but is a more
or less conscious misunderstanding of one's own existence as a person."[5] The level of unfaith is an atheism
"in the bottom of the heart" rather than "in the top
of the mind."[6] It is the existential denial of God,
and is far more serious than the mere denial in the
mind. The existential denial may be accompanied by a
strict orthodoxy in one's professed beliefs. Or as
Ogden observes: "One may affirm God's reality with
one's mind as well as one's lips, and yet deny his
reality by actually existing as a godless man."[7]

Yet, Ogden does not understand this existential
godlessness to be completely negative and empty. This
level of unfaith does not imply the complete absence
of God. Such unfaith is not the absence of faith, but
rather "the presence of faith in a deficient or distor-

---

[1]Cf. also the following articles in which Ogden
discusses the problem of atheism: "The Christian
Proclamation of God to Men of the So-Called 'Atheistic
Age,' op. cit.; "Toward a New Theism," op. cit.; "Love
Unbounded: The Doctrine of God," op. cit.

[2]A discussion of Ogden's understanding of the two
levels of faith and of unfaith may also be found in
"The Christian Proclamation of God to Men of the So-
Called 'Atheistic Age,'" op. cit., pp. 89-93.

[3]The Reality of God, p. 23.
[4]Ibid., p. 24.
[5]The Reality of God, p. 23.
[6]Ibid.
[7]Ibid.

ed mode."[1] This distorted mode of faith is referred to
by Scripture as idolatry. Idolatry is not to be seen
merely as the diversion of one's ultimate concern from
God to some nondivine thing. It is also to be understood as one's regarding some nondivine thing as having
unique significance as a symbol or sacrament for the
Divine, the result of which is that one's faith is
divided between God and the nondivine entity purported
to bear the divine's presence in some unique way.[2] The
central issue, then, at the existential level is not
whether one is to believe in God or what God he is to
believe in, but how is one to believe in God. As Ogden
puts the question: "the issue is....how we are to
believe in the only God in whom anyone can believe and
in whom each of us somehow must believe."[3] There are
only two possibilities. Either one is to believe in
God alone, putting his trust solely in God, or one
believes in God in such a way that he divides his trust
between God and some idol alongside God.[4] It is with
reference to the second possibility that the term
"atheism" may be properly used. Hence, Ogden's contention is that at the existential level "faith in
God in some mode is unavoidable,"[5] but it may take the
perverted form of idolatry which lends itself to the
designation of atheism.

The second level of unfaith or atheism is "the
godlessness of the mind" or the self-conscious and

---

[1]Ibid. To amplify his description, Ogden refers
to H. Richard Niebuhr's contention that the negative
forms of faith "are to positive faith as minus 1, not
0, is to plus 1, or as error, not ignorance, is to
the life of reason." (The Reality of God, p. 23, from
H. R. Niebuhr, Radical Montheism and Western Culture,
p. 41.). Or again to Henri de Lubac: "The idea of
God cannot be uprooted because it is, in essence, the
Presence of God in man. One cannot rid oneself of that
Presence. Nor is the atheist a man who has succeeded
in doing so. He is only an idolater who, as Origen
said, 'refers his indestructable notion to God to anything rather than to God himself." (The Reality of
God, p. 23, from Henri de Lubac, The Discovery of God,
p. 180.).
[2]The Reality of God, p. 24.
[3]Ibid.   [5]Ibid.
[4]Ibid.

135

reflective denial of the reality of God. This is
atheism as commonly understood, in which one's explicit
expression of disbelief in God is taken as sufficient
evidence to support it as being the deeper level of
unfaith, the existential denial of God. Although this
reflective atheism may pervert the heart as well as the
mind, it is possible in any particular case that one
may explicitly deny God while affirming him in other
reflective affirmations or in his existential affirmations.[1] This is so because one may reject the particular conceptual scheme in which faith in God is expressed without negating belief in God as such.[2] It is
Ogden's contention that the secularistic denial of God
by contemporary men should be interpreted in this way.
The denial of God in our time is not the denial of
faith in God as such, but the denial of a particular
conceptualization of this faith.[3] Ogden's appraisal
is that the "Atheistic Age" of the death of God, the
age in which contemporary man finds himself, is merely
a "so-called atheistic age" for the contemporary denial
of God is not one which excludes faith in God altogether, but rather, in its widespread desemination, serves
"to make fully explicit the incompatibility between our
experience as secular men and the supernaturalistic
theism of our intellectual tradition."[4] Many try to

---

[1]The Reality of God, pp. 24-25.
[2]Ogden's interpretation is that much of the so-
called "atheism" throughout intellectual history has
not been a denial of God as such, but rather "a re-
fusal to accept some conceptual scheme in which faith
in God has found expression." (The Reality of God, p.
25.). Cf. also "The Strange Witness of Unbelief,"
The Reality of God, pp. 120-143, esp. 127-134.
[3]E.g. this is Ogden's contention in "The Christian
Proclamation of God to Men of the So-Called 'Atheistic
Age,'" op. cit.; "Beyond Supernaturalism," op. cit.;
and "Theology and Philosophy: A New Phase of the Discussion," op. cit.
[4]The Reality of God, p. 25. Cf. also "The Christian Proclamation of God to Men of the So-Called 'Atheistic Age,'" op. cit.

avoid reflective belief in God, and to the extent that
they succeed in completely denying him reflectively,
the distinction between faith and unfaith must be maintained at this second level. Yet, Ogden's thesis is
that all such attempts are "finally bound to fail."[1]
It now becomes his task to defend this thesis.

Ogden observes that the most convincing reason why
many feel successful in the denial of God at the reflective level is through reliance upon the argument
developed by the positivistically-minded linguistic
philosopher. The positivist not only challenges the
truth of statements about God, but faces the logically
prior question of whether theological statements have
any meaning. The positivist attempts to show that
religious language has no cognitive meaning whatsoever,
since it involves neither the use of the tautologies of
mathematics and logic nor statements of fact that are
empirically falsifiable. According to Ogden, the positivist case is formidable enough to effectively eliminate one important approach taken by the theologians
who attempt to validate the meaning of their statements
by appeal to special revelation.

> If the issue is whether assertions about
> God are even meaningful, argues Ogden,
> it will hardly do to reply--as many have
> done and are still doing--that such as-
> sertions rest solely on the basis of faith
> in a special revelation. Obviously, not
> even faith can assert something as true
> which is in principle lacking in any
> genuine meaning.[2]

The positivist's criticism can be met only by showing
that religious assertions are meaningful, but the appeal merely to special revelation cannot accomplish
this.

Ogden views Stephen Toulmin as one philosopher who
not only refuses to confine his linguistic analysis to
the narrow positivistic framework of many linguistic
philosophers, but also has contributed toward clarify-
ing why the positivist's account of the use of language

---

[1]The Reality of God, p. 25.
[2]Ibid.

137

cannot be accepted without qualification. Since Toulmin's argument is compatible with and supportive of the position Ogden wants to maintain, he examines it in some detail.[1] In An Examination of the Place of Reason in Ethics Toulmin attempts to clarify the kind of argument and the logical principles inherent in our reasoning as moral agents. In his examination he makes three observations. In the first place, he argues against "too narrow a view of the uses of reasoning."[2] His stance denies "the positivistic assumption that 'a mathematical or logical proof or a scientific verification can be the only kind of "good reason" for any statement.'"[3] Speech is no single purpose tool. It is used in a variety of fields, such as science, mathematics, ethics, aesthetics, and theology, in all of which questions of truth, falsity and justification are relevant. "It is this 'full variety of purposes for which speech is used' that makes clear 'the versatility of reason,' and thus confutes, along with certain other views, the positivistic limit on the scope of cognition."[4]

In the second place, Toulmin argues that both our language and reasoning must be understood in relation to the larger reality of life to which they belong.[5] The different uses of language arise in an attempt to explain, describe or communicate something about the various situations and activities in man's world of experience. Scientific language, for example, arises when one attempts to explain a phenomenon occurring in his life situation that his previous experience did not lead him to anticipate. Or, as Toulmin asserts, scientific explanation functions "to bring our past experience to bear upon our present and future explanations in such a way as to 'save appearances' and turn the unexpected, as far as possible, into the expected."[6]

---

[1]Cf. Stephen Toulmin, An Examination of the Place of Reason in Ethics. Cambridge: Cambridge University Press, 1964.

[2]The Reality of God, p. 27.

[3]Ibid.

[4]Ibid., p. 28.

[5]The Reality of God, p. 28.

[6]Ibid.

Likewise, moral reasoning and language arise from man's
attempt to explain and understand the life activities
centered around the pursuit of his desires and inter-
ests in a social context.[1]

In the third place, Toulmin maintains that science
and ethics have their bases in the attempt to realize
specific human purposes, they are not self-contained.
They point beyond themselves. To describe this
"pointing beyond," Toulmin offers the evidence of what
he calls the "limiting question."[2] For example, in a
chain of moral reasoning one may reach a point at which
a question seems to be a moral question but clearly is
not because it does not lend itself to any answer that
a moral statement or argument is capable of providing.
The question may be asked, "Why should I do right at
all?" Such questioning regarding why one should do
anything moral at all cannot be answered by moral reasoning. It is clearly a limiting or boundary question.
Such limiting questions also arise at the boundaries
of scientific explanation, questions to which no
amount of scientific reasoning can offer adequate
answers. The important point in Toulmin's analysis
for Ogden is:

> that it is to the category of limiting
> questions that Toulmin proposes to assign
> questions properly regarded as religious.
> The purpose of 'religion'...and thus of the
> kind of language and reasoning that can be
> called 'religious' or 'theological,' is to
> give answers to the questions that naturally
> arise at the limits of man's activities as
> moral actor and scientific knower.[3]

Toulmin refers to these limiting questions as
"arising naturally" because, according to his view,
they, too, just as moral and scientific questions,
arise in the context of some actual situation of life.
His contention is that men are faced by problems much
more profound than those exemplified by scientific or
ethical concerns. Man's uncertainty about the future

---

[1]Ibid., p. 29.
[2]Ibid., p. 30.
[3]The Reality of God, p. 30.

is not resolved by his ability to predict certain
events. Rather, the very fact that man exists, entails
that he is faced by a total threat to his existence.[1]
Man's most serious problem is that of accepting himself in the world, pursuing scientific knowledge, and
assuming moral obligation in the midst of the pro-
foundest uncertainties about meaning and about what the
future finally holds. Men are so threatened by mean-
inglessness and uncertainty in their actual life situation that they have a deep "'desire for reassurance,
for a general confidence about the future.'"[2] From
this life situation arises the limiting questions to
which religion, in its various forms, attempts to give
answers,[3] thus providing the needed reassurance. Religion's relevance to science and ethics is indicated
when Toulmin observes the function of religion:

> 'Over those matters of fact which are not to be
> "explained" scientifically (like the deaths
> on their birthdays of three children in one
> family), the function of religion is to help
> us to resign ourselves to them--and so feel
> like accepting them. Likewise, over matters
> of duty which are not to be justified fur-
> ther in ethical terms, it is for religion
> to help us embrace them--and so feel like
> accepting them.'[4]

If this is the function of religion, then it is not
necessary to hold, as the positivist does, that all
religious statements are invalid or that there is no
criteria whereby they can be judged. Toulmin's con-

---

[1]Ogden shows his appreciation for Pascal's words
in quoting those in which Toulmin likewise finds meaning: "'When I consider the briefness of my life,
swallowed up in the eternity before and behind it, the
small space I fill, or even see, engulfed in the infinite immensity of spaces which I know not, and which
know not me, I am afraid....Who has set me here? By
whose order and arrangement have this place and this
time been allotted me?...'" (The Reality of God, p.
31.).

[2]Ibid., p. 31; An Examination of the Place of Reason in Ethics, p. 216.

[3]The Reality of God, p. 31.

[4]Ibid.

tention is that religious questions arise in a life
situation just as do scientific and ethical questions.
Religious language therefore, has its logic appropriate
to it just as science and ethics have the different
logics appropriate to them. Religious language has its
own logic, for religious questions are grounded in actual life, and they themselves prescribe the standard
by which their answers are to be validated. Religious
questions prescribe the standard that:

> a good religious answer 'will give us a
> reassurance which will not be disappointed;
> will allay our fear of "the eternity before
> and behind the brief span" of our lives,
> and of "the infinite immensity" of space;
> will provide comfort in the face of dis-
> tress; and will answer our questions in a
> way which will not seem in retrospect to
> have missed their point.'[1]

Ogden considers in some detail two of the central
points concerning the standard which Toulmin contends

---

[1]The Reality of God, p. 32. Toulmin notes that
"theological" and "religious" arguments, questions and
answers are on a logical footing quite different from
that of science and ethics. Hence, he offers a word
of caution: "But it is only if we suppose that religious arguments pretend (say) to provide exact knowledge of the future--so competing with science on its
own ground--that we can be justified in attempting to
apply to them the logical criteria appropriate to
scientific explanations; and only if we do this that
we have any grounds for concluding (with Ayer) that
'all utterances about the nature of God are nonsensi-
cal,' or (with Freud) that religion is 'an illusion.'
Provided that we remember that religion has functions
other than that of competing with science and ethics
on their own grounds, we shall understand that to reject all religious arguments for this reason is to
make a serious logical blunder--an error as great as
that of taking figurative phrases literally, or of
supposing that the mathematical theory of numbers (say)
has any deep, religious significance. There are two
such errors, as Pascal points out--'first, to take
everything literally; secondly, to take everything
spiritually'--and it is asking for trouble if one ig-
nores the difference between questions of science and

that religious questions provide for the establishment of their own validity. The first of these is the function of religious assertions for providing re-assurance.[1] The second is the relevance of religious assertions to both scientific explanations and moral thought and action.[2] In the first place, Ogden agrees with Toulmin's contention that providing reassurance is one function of religion. He observes that this reassurance is precisely that, a "re-assurance," an "assuring again." This indicates that "religious assertions can serve to reassure us only because they themselves are the re-presentation of a confidence somehow already present prior to their being made."[3] Ogden stresses that Toulmin's position allows this interpretation, for Toulmin has recognized the truly representative character of ethical and scientific as well as religious assertions.[4] All three are grounded in man's actual existence. All three arise as man attempts to answer basic questions coming out of life itself. All three rest on certain presuppositions that things are a certain way. For example, scientific questions take for granted that events are so ordered that our experience of them in the past and present warrants our making some conclusions concerning the future. Likewise, our moral questions rest on definite assumptions, for example, the assumption that some course of action ought to be adopted and that the adoption of a particular course is rationally justifiable.[5] The same presence of assumptions can be noted regarding religous questions. The religious question presupposes a "ground of confidence" that is "somehow real" which makes possible" 'a reassurance which will not be disappointed.'"[6]

---

ethics, which are matters of <u>reason</u>, and things like the existence of God, which are matters of faith." (Toulmin, <u>op</u>. <u>cit</u>., pp. 212-213.).

   [1]<u>The Reality of God</u>, pp. 32-**33**.

   [2]<u>Ibid</u>., pp. 34-37.

   [3]<u>Ibid</u>., p. 32.

   [4]<u>Ibid</u>., p. 33.

   [5]<u>The Reality of God</u>, p. 33.

   [6]<u>Ibid</u>. That for Toulmin and Ogden, both ethical and religious assertions have this same re-presentative character is evidenced by Ogden's summary interpretation: "...we do not ordinarily ask <u>whether</u> there are

If the presupposition of all religious questions is the assurance of a ground of confidence, religious assertions do function "re-presentatively" or "re-assuringly." Hence, contends Ogden, religious assertions "are not so much the cause of our general confidence that existence is meaningful as its effect,"[1] by which he means:

> that the various 'religions' or 'faiths'
> of mankind, including what may be called
> the 'Christian religion,' are one and all
> expressions or re-presentations of a yet
> deeper faith that precedes them. Logically
> prior to every particular religious assertion
> is an original confidence in the meaning and
> worth of life,[2] through which not simply

---

good actions or even what the standards are by which all our actions must be judged; we ask instead for a rational justification of what we are to actually think and do in deciding between the courses of action concretely open to us.

"So, too, with our religious question or questions. If Toulmin is right /and Ogden affirms that he is/, in religious inquiry also, the real issue is never the issue of whether--of whether there is some ground in reality for 'a general confidence about the future.' Nor, for the matter, is it the purpose of such inquiry to determine what, in principle, must be the nature of that ground. To the contrary, we cannot so much as ask the religious question without presupposing not only that a ground of confidence is somehow real, but also that it is such as, in Toulmin's words, to make possible 'a reassurance which will not be disappointed.'" (The Reality of God, p. 33.).

[1] The Reality of God, p. 33.

[2] The idea of religion as being at its very base a "confidence in the meaning and worth of life" is affirmed by Ogden repeatedly. Cf. e.g. Ogden's words: "Neither man's openness to error nor his lack of perfect trust precludes the possibility of an adequate philosophical theology; for to be human at all is to have some confidence in the meaningfulness of life, and thus some awareness of God that can be conceptually explicated, provided it is made the object of sufficient care," (Ogden, "Bultmann's Demythologizing and Hartshorne's Dipolar Theism," in Reese and Freeman,

all our religious answers, but even our
religious questions first become possible
or have any sense.[1]

All religions, then, represent attempts at a self-
conscious understanding of this original confidence.
All are to some extent _fides quaerens intellectum_.
The several religions represent attempts of "that
original faith itself in its search for a more fully
conscious understanding of its own nature."[2]   Hence,
Ogden argues in agreement with Toulmin that one function of religion is that of providing reassurance, for
as he says: "Because all religions are by their very
nature re-presentative, they never originate our faith
in life's meaning, but rather provide us with particular symbolic forms through which that faith may be
more or less adequately re-affirmed at the level of
self-conscious belief."[3]

---

eds., _Process_ and _Divinity_, p. 509.).
    "The driving motive...of inquiry, as, indeed,
indirectly of the whole of human existence, is what
can only be described as an elemental confidence in
the final worth of our life as men. We exist as the
selves we are only because of an inalienable assurance
that our lives are not merely different, but are somehow both real and of ultimate significance." (Ogden,
"Toward a New Theism," op. cit., pp. 12-13; "Love Unbounded: The Doctrine of God," op. cit., p. 11.).
    The importance of "confidence" in Ogden's under-
standing of religious life is seen also in his reference to faith as "the integral confidence" of the entire self in the 'pure unbounded love' to which all
theological assertions refer and which is decisively
promised to the world through Christ and his Church."
(Ogden, "The Christian Proclamation of God To Men of
the So-Called 'Atheistic Age,'" op. cit., p. 90.).
    [1]The _Reality_ of _God_, pp. 33-34.
    [2]_Ibid._, p. 34.
    [3]The _Reality_ of _God_, p. 34.

The second point which Toulmin makes regarding the function of religion, and closely related to the first, is that religious assertions in providing reassurance are relevant both to science and to moral thought and action. This is true because religious questions are limiting questions arising at the boundaries of science and morality, and, as such, they necessarily have a bearing on such dimensions of human life.[1] Religious assertions tell us "that because our existence as such is finally meaningful, we are free to pursue the right and investigate the mysteries of the universe without succumbing to cynicism or despair."[2]

It is Ogden's contention that if religious assertions have the function of explicating the basic confidence in life's meaning requisite for making moral decisions, then it follows that "the original confidence they re-present is itself the necessary condition of all our moral action."[3] Such confidence may not reach religious expression, or it may be admitted that no religion as such is necessary to moral action. Yet, although such confidence in life's meaning is not self-consciously expressed, its presence is requisite to any moral choice. Ogden holds it to be "both basic and inescapable" that "morality is unavoidable dependent on faith, regardless of its independence of the particular religions in which such faith finds expression."[4] Later, Ogden asserts that the fundamental

---

[1]The relevance of religion for ethics is at least indicated in Toulmin's words: "Ethics provides the reasons for choosing the 'right' course: religion helps us to put our hearts into it." (Toulmin, An Examination of the Place of Reason In Ethics, p. 219.).

[2]The Reality of God, p. 35.

[3]Ibid.

[4]The Reality of God, p. 36. This contention is presented repeatedly by Ogden, e.g.: "In any analysis which is in the least convincing, our moral life, like our science and all other undertakings, can never be represented as wholly self-contained. Always presupposed by even the most commonplace of moral decisions is the confidence that these decisions have an unconditional significance." (Ibid.) Or again, when he quotes Whitehead's words as verbalizing "a faith common to us all": "...the immediate facts of present action pass into permanent significance for the

point which he wishes to make is, namely, "that moral
thought and action are existentially possible only
because their roots reach down into an underlying confidence in the abiding worth of our life,"[1] for one
cannot rationally decide for "the eventual nullity of
his decisions."[2] This is true even of the suicide who,
in taking his own life, implicitly affirms the meaning
of his choice.[3] Ogden's own summary is thus expressed: "...to be moral at all is always to beg the basic
question to which the religions of mankind are more or
less adequate attempts to express the answer....it is
to just this question that we find ourselves driven
when we follow our moral reasoning to its final limits."[4]

     Ogden has considered Toulmin's analysis of reli-
gious language as supportive of his thesis that attempts to avoid explicit belief in God or to deny his
reality altogether are bound to fail.[5] The initial
phase of Ogden's conclusion is, as we have seen, "that
no reflective inventory of the existential beliefs by
which we actually live...can pretend to be successful
which fails to take account of our basic confidence in
the abiding worth of our life."[6] Having taken this
step, Ogden next turns to showing the "essential con-
nections" between this existential faith in the meaning of one's life and "what is properly meant by the
word 'God.'"[7] Once one understands the conditions
under which the word "God" is rightly used, argues
Ogden, then the "essential connection" will become
clear.

Universe. The insistent notion of Right and Wrong,
Achievement and Failure depends upon this background.
Otherwise every activity is merely a passing whiff of
insignificance." (Ibid., p. 37.).

[1]Ibid., p. 36.
[2]Ibid.
[3]Ibid.
[4]Ibid., p. 37.
[5]Ibid.
[6]Ibid.
[7]Ibid.

146

The "essential connection" which Ogden sees between our basic confidence in the worth of life and
the word "God" is described when Ogden affirms:

> I hold that the primary use or func-
> tion of "God" is to refer to the objective
> ground in reality itself of our ineradicable
> confidence in the final worth of our exis-
> tence. It lies in the nature of this basic
> confidence to affirm that the real whole of
> which we experience ourselves to be parts is
> such as to be worthy of, and thus itself to
> evoke, that very confidence. The word 'God,'
> then, provides the designation for whatever
> it is about this experienced whole that calls
> forth and justifies our original and inescap-
> able trust, thereby meaning existentially, as
> William James once said, "'You can dismiss cer-
> tain kinds of fear.'" From this it follows
> that to be free of such fear by existing in
> this trust is one and the same thing with af-
> firming the reality of God.[1]

Having presented this affirmation, Ogden considers
a possible criticism, namely, that such an analysis of
'God' in terms of trust in the significance of life
fails to establish that the word has any reference to
an objective reality. Ogden observes that such an
objection rests "on a failure to observe the peculiar
conditions that govern the use of the word 'real' and
the other terms related to it."[2] What is to be considered "real" must be understood as what is to be considered relevant for the particular mode of experience
under observation, while that which is irrelevant to
the particular context may be considered "mere appearance."[3] This means that the question of the "reality"

---

[1]The Reality of God, pp. 37-38.

[2]Ibid., p. 38.

[3]In this discussion, Ogden again finds Toulmin
enlightening. Cf. especially, Toulmin, An Examination
of the Place of Reason in Ethics, "Reason and Reality,"
pp. 102-117. Explaining that: "'Reality,' in any
particular mode of reasoning, must be understood as
'what (for the purposes of this kind of argument) is
relevant,' and 'mere appearance' as 'what (for these
purposes) is irrelevant.' And since these purposes
differ from case to case, that which is, say, 'aes-

of something is always accompanied by the presupposition of some mode of reasoning, such as the scientific mode or the aesthetic mode, and we must, therefore, employ the mode of reasoning that will take account of the questions and answers requisite for deciding the issue of a particular thing's reality.

The point Ogden immediately wants to make, on the basis of the preceding examination of the conditions that govern our use of the word "real," is that the question of the reality of God can only be adequately considered when we presuppose that mode of reasoning proper to religion. But, what is evidenced when we assume the mode of reasoning religion presupposes? According to Ogden:

> Once we presuppose the mode of reasoning proper to religion...--and not to presuppose it is to leave religious issues in principle undecided--the question whether God is real at once becomes pointless. This is because, as we explained above, 'God' is the very meaning of 'reality' when this word is defined in terms of our basic confidence in the significance of life and the kind of questions and answers such confidence makes possible.[1]

---

thetic reality' may yet be, for physics, 'mere appearance;' Toulmin concludes: "In consequence, there is simply no room for the question, 'The sky can't be both a deeper blue and not a deeper blue; so which is it?' In the situation described, there is no way of choosing, and no genuine opposition between the 'alternatives.' The form of words 'Which is it really?' ceases to express a genuine question at all: the most it can call for is a decision--'Which am I to treat as relevant, for these purposes; the scientific or the artistic criteria?' To suppose that it still expresses a question, to continue looking for the one and only really real meaning of 'reality,' is to enter upon a wild-goose chase of the most metaphorical kind--not just a literal wild-goose chase (for a wild-goose is a very solid object in spite of being so elusive), but the endless pursuit of an imaginary bird." (Toulmin, op. cit., pp. 114-115.).

[1]The Reality of God, p. 39.

One may inquire how this ground of confidence is best
to be conceived or whether any particular historical
religion is justified in claiming any decisiveness in
its representation, but once the religious mode of
reasoning is presupposed, the question of the objective
reality of God need not even be raised.[1]

To observe the implications of this conclusion,
Ogden turns once again to the example of morality.
Ogden has stressed that all moral choices presuppose a
basic confidence in the worth of life. He has further
identified the ground of this confidence with what we
mean by the word "God." If this be the case, all non-
theistic moral theories are essentially fragmentary in
that "they leave the final depth of morality itself
utterly unillumined."[2] They shed light on the fore-
ground of morality while leaving the background in
total obscurity. The nontheistic moral theorist finds
himself in a dilemma, for to do justice to all the
presuppositions of our moral questions and answers
entails making affirmations which conflict with atheistic denials, while to stress these denials leads
increasingly toward moral nihilism.[3]

Ogden's conclusion, therefore, is that faith in
God is finally unavoidable not only at the existential
level but also at the level of self-conscious belief.
To give a reflective account of our experience requires
either some form of theism "properly understood" or
merely "inventories of our beliefs that are either essentially fragmentary or else shot through with self-
contradiction."[4] Having described his understanding
of the way in which our moral reasoning leads us to
ask limiting questions the provision of answers to
which is the primary function of religion, Ogden as-

---

[1]The Reality of God, p. 39. In Ogden's words:
"...to question whether the word 'God' as here analyzed
refers to anything objectively real is not, I believe,
a sensible inquiry. If the religious mode of reasoning
is once assumed, there is no point in even raising this
question; and, if such reasoning is not assumed, we can
never hope to answer it." (Ibid.).

[2]Ibid., p. 40.

[3]Ibid., pp. 40-41.

[4]Ibid., p. 42.

serts that the same can also be shown of our scientific reasoning. Both presuppose "an original confidence in the ultimate significance of life"[1] the question of the ground of which finds its answer in the affirmation of the reality of God. Hence, Ogden affirms that not only our moral thought and action and our scientific endeavors, "but our existence as such in all its undertakings is a standing testimony to God's reality."[2]

---

[1]Ibid., pp. 42-43.

[2]Ibid., p. 43. Of this final assertion Ogden concludes: "This as I believe, is the only really essential 'proof of God's existence'--that we are selves at all only because of our existential faith in him and that, in consequence, such faith must also be affirmed self-consciously if the reflective inventory of our beliefs is to be both complete and consistent." (Ibid.).

C. The Objectivity of God

In the preceding Ogden's understanding of the problem of God for today, along with his assertion of the reality of faith, has been considered. In the former, Ogden objected to any concept of God which contradicted man's historical, scientific and existential knowledge of himself and his world. In the latter, Ogden asserted that faith is somehow "real" for every man. Implicit in both of these is the contention, which Ogden shares with Cobb through Whitehead and Hartshorne, that "God is not to be treated as an exception to all metaphysical principles, invoked to save their collapse. He is their chief exemplification."[1] Ogden remains consistent with this contention in his understanding of the way in which one can speak objectively about God. As the problem of the objectivity of God is considered, recall that Ogden's demand is that God is to be treated, not as an exception to all the metaphysical categories, nor merely as an example of them, but rather, he is to be treated as their chief exemplification.

In an essay entitled "Theology and Objectivity," Ogden examines the claim currently enjoying importance among theologians "that theological thinking and speaking are or (since the assertion is really normative) ought to be nonobjectifying."[2] His examination

---

[1]_Process and Reality_, p. 521; Cf. also, _The Reality of God_, p. 154.

[2]_The Reality of God_, p. 71. Ogden indicates the importance of this question by observing that the theme of the Second Consultation on Hermeneutics at Drew University in 1964 was "The Problem of Nonobjectifying Thinking and Speaking in Contemporary Theology." (Cf. _The Reality of God_, p. 71, note 1.). The problem of objectivity is also implicit in the essays "Faith and Truth" in Dean Peerman, ed. _Frontline Theology_. Richmond: John Knox Press, 1967, pp. 126-133; and "Myth and Truth," _McCormick Quarterly_, Volume 18, 1965, pp. 57-76. Cf. also Ogden's understanding of the problem in his essay "The Understanding of Theology in Ott and Bultmann," in John B. Cobb and James

151

consists of a consideration of four related yet distinct meanings of the term "nonobjectifying." An examination of these meanings will serve to indicate in what sense--if any--Ogden admits of speaking of the "objectivity" of God.

Before considering the possible meanings of theological thinking and speaking nonobjectively, Ogden first offers a tentative definition of "theological thinking and speaking," making clear that the "theology" of which he speaks is explicitly "Christian theology." His tentative definition, then, is: "theological thinking and speaking are a more or less distinguishable type or level of thinking and speaking about God as apprehended through the witness of faith of Jesus Christ."[1] Regarding this definition Ogden makes three observations. First, all theological thought and speech has as its object or referent the God of Jesus Christ.[2] Second, that God is somehow the object of all theological thought and speech does not mean that he is the only such object. Yet, that cannot properly be considered theology which fails to entertain the minimal intention of saying and thinking something meaningful about the God of Jesus Christ.[3] Third, the definition which Ogden proposes does not assume some particular concept of God as an essential element in theological thinking and speaking, for this

M. Robinson, eds. The Later Heidegger and Theology. New York: Harper and Row, 1963, pp. 157-173.

[1]Ibid., p. 72.

[2]Ibid., p. 72.

[3]Ibid., p. 73. As Ogden notes: "...far from obvious to me is that one could properly speak of 'theology' at all without assuming the minimal meaning suggested by the word as used historically and also re-expressed in the proposed definition--namely, a thinking whose primary object is God as disclosed through the witness of Christian faith and a speaking which, whatever its other uses, intends to assert something meaningful about the same divine object." (The Reality of God, p. 73.).

is to be determined by the actual intentional referent, God himself.[1]

Having advanced this tentative definition of theological thinking and speaking, Ogden then turns to a consideration of the claim that such speaking and thinking ought to be nonobjective. From existentialist philosophy and theology comes the claim that man's cognitive encounter with reality has a two-fold form. This consists on the one hand of man's own internal awareness and on the other hand in his awareness-- somehow grounded in his original existential aware- ness--of reality distinct from the self, the object of ordinary experience. This existential analysis of knowledge as "existential" and "objectifying" offers the first frame of reference through which the notion of nonobjectifying thinking and speaking is to be understood.[2] Ogden readily recognizes with many con- temporary Protestant theologians that theological thinking and speaking is nonobjective in this sense. To say that theological thinking and speaking is non- objectifying is to say that there is a difference in principle between the thinking and speaking of science and that of theology. Theological thinking and speaking is not of the same logical type as that of scientific statements.[3]

---

[1]Ibid., in Ogden's words: "...thought and speech are determined as theological by their actual inten- tional object or referent, God himself, not by any concept of God or the term expressing it....Whether the term be 'God' or 'the transcendent' or 'the uncon- ditioned' or 'being-itself,' or any number of other terms that readily come to mind, it can very well function as an instance of theological speaking in the sense of the definition. And the same is true, mutatis mutandis, of the various conceptualities of which all such terms are the linguistic expressions. If any conceptuality serves in a certain way or at a certain level to conceive God as understood by Christian faith, then it is, on my terms, a theological conceptuality, and the thinking it makes possible is theological thinking." (p. 73.).

[2]The Reality of God, pp. 74-75.

[3]Ibid., p. 75.

Some theologians, however, fear that to admit that theological language is nonobjective in this first sense is to affirm that theological language asserts nothing. These hold that there is no difference between scientific and theological statements, and they both are in principle falsifiable, even if, in the case of theological statements the device of "eschatological verification"[1] has to be employed. Ogden rejects the assertion that theological language is objectifying just as is language whose referents are objects of sense data. He objects on the ground that the affirmation that theological statements are in principle falsifiable implies "that theological assertions about the being and nature of God are somehow about an actual or potential object of ordinary sense perception."[2] Ogden rejects the "mythological" representations of God on the same ground that he rejects this manner of objectifying God. That is to say, he rejects mythological representations of God not because such representations conflict with the claims of modern science, but because mythological representations objectify God under the same conditions applicable to objects perceived by external perception. In both instances God is viewed in the manner of an object of our sense perception. Insofar as this is the case, God's transcendence, as apprehended by the Christian faith, is seriously misrepresented, and the "qualitative difference" between God and all entities other

------

[1]Cf. the view of one of the proponents of "eschatological verification" in John Hick, Philosophy of Religion. (New York: Prentice-Hall, Inc., pp. 100-103; also, John Hick, ed. The Existence of God.) (New York: The Macmillan Company, 1964). A critique is to be found in William Blackstone, The Problem of Religious Knowledge. (Englewood Cliffs: Prentice-Hall, Inc., 1963), pp. 112-116.

[2]The Reality of God, p. 76. Elaborating on this view, Ogden asserts: "If such assertions are even 'eschatologically' verifiable in the manner of scientific hypotheses, it is not clear to me why they should be considered properly theological assertions at all." (The Reality of God, p. 76.).

than himself is not recognized.[1] Hence, Ogden summarizes the main reason for demythologizing and for
denying the objectifying characteristic of science
when he says:

> ...the main reason for demythologizing and
> for seeking a theological conceptuality al-
> ternative to that of science as well as to
> myth is, as Bultmann says, 'faith itself'--
> by which he means not only faith's character
> as a mode of existential self-understanding,
> but also faith's distinctive apprehension,
> precisely as self-understanding, of the
> transcendent reality of God.[2]

Some existential philosophers and theologians,
who do not hold the twofold account of knowledge as
either existential or objective to be exhaustive, recognize a third form of knowledge disclosed in one's

---

[1]As Ogden emphasizes: "Like myth, science can
think and speak about reality only as the object of
our sense perceptions, and so could represent God only
by similarly misrepresenting the uniqueness of his
reality as God." (The Reality of God, p. 76.).

[2]The Reality of God, p. 76. Ogden realizes that
much of what has been traditionally accepted as theology is not nonobjectifying in the sense as here considered, and insofar as it has not been, it can no
longer pass for theology. Yet, it does have a different purpose from that of scientific and ordinary
objectifying thinking, and therefore, rather than cat-
egorize such theological formulations (e.g. myth) as
without theological significance, Ogden prefers to
designate them as pretheological "witness" which the
theologian is not to eliminate but to attempt to understand. (Cf. The Reality of God, pp. 76-77.). That
such an evaluation of myth is not totally negative is
to be seen in Ogden's essay "Myth and Truth" in which
he joins in "the attempt to clarify and defend the
claim that myth is somehow capable of truth." (The
Reality of God, p. 101.). He stresses that "an
identification of the true with what can be scientifically verified is an intolerable oversimplification,"
(p. 103) and he observes that the current consensus in
contemporary Protestant theology is "that myth can be
true, but that such truth as it can have is not that
of empirical science." (p. 103.).

being able to distinguish between the other two forms. This type of knowledge is neither existential nor objectifying (in the sense previously discussed), but rather consists of a phenomenological analysis of man's existence. Illustrative of this third approach, which is related to, but distinct from, the two forms of knowledge previously considered, is Heidegger's distinction between the "existential" (existenziell), as the "understanding uniquely present in each individual existence as its own personal encounter with reality,"[1] and the "existentialist" (existenzial), as "the understanding exemplified in a descriptive analysis of the phenomenon of existence in general."[2]

This distinction gives rise to a second meaning of the word "objectifying." Illustrative of this is Bultmann's use of the word. He considers not only scientific thinking and speaking to be objective but also the thinking and speaking of the existentialist analysis. The difference between existential and objectifying knowledge, notes Ogden, can be expressed by representing the existential as "concerned" or "involved," since it "has to do quite directly with the gain or loss of our authentic existence as selves,"[3] and the objective as "disinterested" or "detached."[4] Since existential knowledge "has to do quite directly with the gain or loss of our authentic existence," while existentialist analysis "is a reflective matter which has to do only indirectly with realizing our authentic existence and so is (relatively) disinterested instead of concerned, detached instead of involved," then existentialist analysis can also be regarded as "scientific" or "objectifying" in

---

[1]Ibid., p. 78.
[2]Ibid. Ogden notes that it is this phenomenological analysis which Heidegger views as constituting a first step toward "ontology."
[3]The Reality of God, p. 79.
[4]Ibid. Cf. Paul Tillich, Systematic Theology, Vol. II., p. 26, in which he distinguishes between "Existential and Existentialist Thinking."

character.[1]

This new and slightly different understanding
of "objective" leads once more to the question of
whether theological thinking and speaking are objective in this second sense. Bultmann holds, observes
Ogden, that theology is objectifying in this second
sense.[2] Even if one sees theology as "a movement of
faith itself"[3] or "the extreme contrast to objectifying
knowledge," one can nevertheless "distinguish between
faith, witness, and theology" only "by seeing them as
points along the continuum defined by the two poles of
existential self-understanding and objectifying knowledge"[4] in this second sense. While Ogden grants that
faith itself is the extreme contrast to objectifying
knowledge, he nevertheless stresses that insofar as it
is conscious faith, it is already evidenced as some
form of belief, albeit a belief in which personal concern and involvement are at a maximum.[5] That, for
Ogden, faith always entails objectifying in this sense
is evidenced when he observes that "it is doubtful

---

[1]Ogden notes that this is Bultmann's position
while other existentialists "have denied that a scientific analysis of human existence is possible," e.g.
Karl Jaspers. Cf. The Reality of God, pp. 79-80. But
cf. Ogden, "The Understanding of Theology in Ott and
Bultmann," in James M. Robinson and John B. Cobb, eds.
The Later Heidegger and Theology, pp. 157-176, esp.
p. 165, in which Ogden insists that Jaspers' "clarification of existence," insofar as it claims to be uni-
versally understandable must be "objectifying" in this
second sense.

[2]Ogden notes that Bultmann "includes under 'objectifying' all thinking and speaking sharing in a
reflective subjective form essentially like that of
modern science." (The Reality of God, p. 80.).

[3]As Ogden understands Heinrich Ott's position.
The Reality of God, pp. 80-81.

[4]Ibid., p. 81.

[5]Ibid.

whether one can speak of an unconscious faith."[1]
Examples of this thinking and speaking in the lowest
objectifying degree may be seen in spontaneous confession, preaching and prayer, in which the one involved speaks "in the lowest abstractions that language
is capable of."[2] Yet, even in speaking in the lowest
abstractions, one is nevertheless objectifying the
reality to which such speaking refers, for he, of necessity, speaks in a higher degree of generality, utilizing universal concepts and greater abstraction of
language. Stressing this contention, Ogden asserts:

> Just when theology is true to its her-
> meneutical task of critically interpreting
> the church's witness in an appropriate and
> understandable conceptuality, it cannot but
> involve a more reflective and so mere objec-
> tifying type of thinking and speaking than is
> represented either by the various forms of
> witness or by the still more existential
> phenomenon of faith itself.[3]

In stressing that theological thinking and speaking must always be objectifying in this second sense,
Ogden offers two objections to those who hold that:

> God is always Subject and never object, and
> so theology can be held to have a scientific
> character only by restricting it to the

---

[1]Ibid.

[2]Ogden refers to this thinking and speaking as
"witness" and considers it as basically non-reflective
and pre-theological. The character of such thinking
and speaking is well illustrated by Whitehead's description of Jesus' sayings: "The reported sayings of
Christ are not formularized thought. They are de-
scriptions of direct insight. The ideas are in his
mind as immediate pictures, and not as analyzed in
terms of abstract concepts. He sees intuitively the
relations between good men and bad men; his expressions
are not cast into the form of an analysis of the
goodness and badness of man. His sayings are actions
and not adjustments of concepts. He speaks in the
lowest abstractions that language is capable of, if
it is to be language at all and not the fact itself."
Religion in the Making, p. 56.

[3]The Reality of God, p. 82.

158

critical interpretation of Christian
faith or witness and by denying that it
is in any sense an objectifying thinking
and speaking about God to whom faith is
directed.[1]

In the first place, the assertion "God is always
Subject and never object," involves a self-contradiction, for it itself is an objectifying assertion. Second, the view begs the question to which only objectifying thought about God can provide the answer.[2]
Hence, Ogden concludes that "there is as much reason
for God to be the object of the objectifying thinking
and speaking of theology as for him to be the eminent
Subject whom I know as my God here and now only in my
own existential understanding of faith."[3]

A third sense of "nonobjectifying" must now be
considered. Certain modern analytic philosophers
hold that if theological statements are nonobjective
in the sense of being "nonscientific,"[4] then these
statements are also "noncognitive."[5] That is to say,
proponents of this view would hold that theological
utterances "cannot really be 'about' anything, much
less about some divine object called 'God.' Rather,
they can only have some function other than that of
making assertions, and the values 'true' and 'false'
simply have no application to them."[6] Theological

---

[1]Ibid. Ogden understands this to be the view of
Gustaf Aulen in The Faith of the Christian Church.
Philadelphia: Muhlenberg Press, 1960, p. 3.

[2]The Reality of God, p. 83. Ogden points out
Hartshorne's observation that the assertion "God is
always Subject and never objective" contains the hid-
den premise, entertained by classical natural theology,
that "God is so essentially 'simple' that one cannot
distinguish diverse aspects of his being." (p. 83.).

[3]Ibid.

[4]Cf. above, pp. 184-186.

[5]The Reality of God, p. 84.

[6]Ibid. Cf. this view as presented by R. M. Hare
in Anthony Flew and Alasdair Macintyre, eds. New
Essays in Philosophical Theology. New York: The
Macmillan Co., 1955, pp. 99-102; and R. B. Braithwaite.
An Empiricist's View of Nature of Religious Belief.
Cambridge: Cambridge University Press, 1955.

expression of this view is found in Paul van Buren's
The Secular Meaning of the Gospel in which van Buren
argues that theological statements are in no way to be
taken cognitively as assertions about a divine reality.
They assert nothing about God, but rather about man
and his perspective. Theological assertions about the
being and nature of God are really nothing more than
the reflection of the attitude or perspective of Christian man. They assert nothing in themselves, but
whether the person who makes the assertions has the
perspective expressed in the theological statement is
open to empirical falsification. Van Buren claims that
his thoroughly nonobjective interpretation of theological thinking and speaking is legitimatized by the
gospel itself.

Ogden objects to approaches similar to van Buren's
on two counts. In the first place, while agreeing
with van Buren that faith statements are indeed expressions of man's basic attitude toward the world,
Ogden disagrees with his contention that they are
nothing more than this.[1] While the language of faith
is in important respects like the language in which
one expresses his attitudes about the world, one
cannot assert that such expression is its only function. Moreover, while the language of faith is not
literally identical with the use of language by modern science, one cannot assert that it thereby is wholly noncognitive.[2] Ogden contends that the language
of theology is "in important respects sufficiently
like the language of science that to deny it any asser-
tive meaning whatever is seriously to misunderstand
it."[3] In the second place, Ogden rejects van Buren's
view on the basis that it entertains "too narrow a
view of the uses of reason."[4] There are various uses
of reason, Ogden observes, and van Buren errs in that

---

[1]As Ogden asserts: "...what Christians have
hardly ever recognized, I believe is that their witness
is nothing but this human decision, that it can be appropriately interpreted as making no reference whatever
to the objective reality of God, and that it asserts,
if anything, merely something about themselves and
their own subjective attitude toward life." (The Reality of God, p. 87.).

[2]Ibid., pp. 87-88.

[3]Ibid., p. 88.

[4]Ibid., p. 88.

"he assumes too readily that a mathematical or logical proof or a scientific verification can be the
only kind of 'good reason' for any statement."[1] Ogden
notes that Bultmann, too, insisted on the need for a
thoroughgoing existential interpretation, yet he re-
sisted the idea that such an interpretation meant a
reduction of theological statements to "a merely 'secular' content."[2] Ogden insists on the possibility of
some objective reference to God, and he sums up his
own position in the words of Bultmann: "If speaking
about God's act is to be meaningful, it must indeed be
not simply a figurative or 'symbolic' kind of speaking
/i.e., simply a way of designating man's own subjective
self-understanding/, but must rather intend a divine
act in the fully real and 'objective' sense."[3] In this
statement Ogden finds "at least token support" for his
view that "theology neither can nor must be nonobjectifying, if that means wholly noncognitive, and so
lacking in all direct objective references to God and
his gracious action."[4]

---

[1]Ibid.

[2]Ibid., p. 86, cf. also p. 89.

[3]Ibid., p. 90, Insertion is Ogden's.

[4]Ibid. Cf. also Ogden, "Beyond Supernaturalism,"
(op. cit.) pp. 7-18, and David L. Edwards, ed. The
Honest to God Debate in which Bishop Robinson expresses
a view in agreement with Bultmann's and with which
Ogden agrees: "What I believe is true is, as van Buren
says, that we live 'in an age in which statements about
"How things are" are expected to have some sort of relationship to man's experience of each other and of
things.' In other words, theology is not making affirmations about metaphysical realities per se, but
always describes an experienced relationship or en-
gagement to the truth. It is in this sense that I
would agree with Tillich's dictum...that 'all theological statements are existential.' They are not objective propositions about 'things in themselves;' but
neither are they simply affirmations of my outlook or
perspective on life. They are statements about the
reality at the level of 'ultimate concern' (as opposed
to proximate concern--the level at which scientific
statements, etc., are true.)." (David L. Edwards, ed.
The Honest to God Debate, pp. 252-253.).

Finally, Ogden considers a fourth meaning of the word "nonobjectifying" and asks whether theological thinking and speaking can be said to be nonobjectifying in this sense. He sums up the fourth sense of nonobjectifying when he points out that some theologians would hold that "although theological utterances do somehow have a genuinely cognitive meaning or use, they nevertheless cannot be referred to any generally applicable principle of verification, so that the issue of their truth or falsity cannot be rationally adjudicated."[1] Having noted this fourth sense in which objectivity is used, Ogden immediately denies that theology is nonobjective in this sense. Rather, he contends that if cognitive status is to be claimed for theological thinking and speaking, then such status "may be claimed for statements only if one is prepared to support the claim by clearly specifying the principle in accordance with which the truth of the statements can be rationally determined."[2] Elaborating on this contention, he observes: "If we neither can nor need deny that theological statements intend to assert something true about the objective reality and action of God, then we neither can nor need deny that these statements are somehow susceptible of rational justification."[3]

Having rejected consideration of theological thinking and speaking as nonobjective, in this fourth sense, Ogden considers three areas in which his affirmation that theological thinking and speaking must be objective (in this fourth sense) are often considered to be problematic. First, some theologians (Bultmann, for example) deny that theological statements can be verified. Ogden's response to this is that such an assumption belongs to the narrow positivistic view of the scope of cognition which assumes that the only meaning of verification is that of science, mathematics, and logic. He recalls that "the uses of argument are many" and stresses that affirming the necessity of rational justification of theological statements does not entail that "the relevant kind of ar-

---

[1]The Reality of God, p. 91. Ogden notes that this "seems" to be Bultmann's position. Cf. Ibid., p. 91, note 40; also, p. 92.

[2]Ibid., p. 92.

[3]Ibid.

162

gument is that either of mathematics or of the special
sciences."[1]

A second obstacle to the acceptance of the rational justifiability of theological assertions is the
confusion that such a demand entails that faith itself
must be held to be verifiable or demonstrable.[2]
Ogden's response to this problem is that it is a profound mistake to suppose that faith itself could be
directly verified. The problem arises only where one
fails to distinguish between faith, taken in the strict
sense as existential self-understanding, and theology,
the level at which the faith is explicated.[3] "If theological statements not only express faith, but also
assert something about the divine reality in which
faith understands itself to be based," contends Ogden,
"the question of how they are to be rationally justified is an altogether appropriate question."[4]

A third objection to the demand that theological
statements must be rationally justified is what Ogden
describes as "a profound skepticism about metaphysics."[5] Ogden's response is that if theological statements are to make assertions which in some sense are
meaningful, then the only kind of assertions they can
make are metaphysical assertions. By this, he means
that theological statements make assertions which on
the one hand have objective reference to "how things
are," while on the other hand, they are not empirically
falsifiable as are the assertions of the special sci-

---

[1]Ibid.

[2]Ibid.

[3]As Ogden observes: "...the level of our actual
existence, which is the level of faith as such, is
simply not the level at which the question of rational justification arises. Where it does properly arise
is at the level of thought and speech through which the
existential understanding of faith is theologically
explicated--provided, of course, that such thought and
speech are held to have some genuine cognitive import."
(The Reality of God, p. 93.).

[4]Ibid.

[5]Ibid.

163

ences.[1] The kind of falsifiability to which theological and metaphysical assertions are subject is that
of misrepresenting "the common structure of all of our
experiences, of which we are originally aware inter-
nally, and thus is falsified by any one of them we
choose to consider."[2] Ogden does not assert that theological statements merely are metaphysical assertions.
Rather, he merely affirms that insofar as they express
assertions, they "belong to the general class of metaphysical assertions and are therefore subject to the
kind of rational justification appropriate to this
class. But, with this knowledge of Ogden's position
one is reminded of the "profound skepticism about metaphysics,"[3] of which Ogden earlier spoke. His response
to this is that such skepticism "both reinforces and is
reinforced by a highly selective reading of philosophical development in the modern period."[4] This "highly
selective reading" has all but completely ignored the
fact that metaphysics itself has passed through one of
its most decisive transformations in its history, a
transformation which points to its having a future as
well as a past.[5] Exemplary of this transformation is
the philosophy of Whitehead in which "all the main
themes of the metaphysical tradition are given neoclassical expression" in an attempt to incorporate modern
philosophy's contribution while overcoming the weakness

---

[1]Ibid. He elaborates by observing: "Such assertions cannot be thus falsifiable because their specific
use or function is to represent not the variable details of our experience of reality, but its constant
structure--that which all states of experience, regardless of their empirical contents, necessarily have
in common." (Ibid.).

[2]Ibid.

[3]The Reality of God, p. 93.

[4]Ibid. As he contends: "The dominant movements
in the philosophy of our own century, whether on the
Continent or in the English-speaking countries, have
been un- or even anti- metaphysical, and it is from
them that most Protestant theologians have taken their
orientation. Thus to 'overcome metaphysics,' either
in Heidegger's way or in some other, has come to be
one of the most frequently expressed goals of the
Protestant theology of our time." (Ibid., p. 94.).

[5]Ibid.

of classical metaphysics.[1] Hence, Ogden concludes
that it is no longer the case--as is conventionally
assumed--that one must either accept traditional metaphysics altogether,[2] but, rather one can now take
advantage of neoclassical metaphysics as exemplified
by the philosophies of Whitehead and Hartshorne. Process philosophy is not--like some existentialism and
linguistic philosophy--a philosophical fragment which
"purchases a greater depth of phenomenological insight
or a higher degree of conceptual precision at the price
of abandoning philosophy's ancient quest for an integral secular wisdom."[3] Rather, process philosophy attempts a comprehensive philosophical outlook. It is
this philosophy, contends Ogden, that can provide
Protestant theology with a world view as comprehensive
and at the same time as Christian as the Thomistic.[4]
He summarizes his contention when he says:

> ...I am quite certain that, apart from
> the resources that some such philosophy
> is in a position to provide, the claim
> of theological statements to cognitive
> status cannot be responsibly made or
> supported. If theological thinking and
> speaking have to do properly and primarily
> with the God who discloses himself in
> Jesus Christ, then they involve claims to

---

[1]Ibid.

[2]Recall that this was Ogden's stance regarding the
assumption that traditional theism is the only theism,
the only alternative to which was merely rejection. Cf.
above pp. 133-144.

[3]The Reality of God, p. 96.

[4]This, Ogden contends is an answer to Jaroslav
Pelikan's question: "Can Protestantism provide its
adherents with a world view which is as comprehensive
and yet as Christian as the Thomistic? Or must Protestant thought choose between comprehensiveness and evan-
gelical loyalty?" (Jaroslav Pelikan, The Riddle of
Roman Catholicism. Nashville: The Abingdon Press,
1959, p. 227.). Cf. The Reality of God, p. 96.

truth that can be conceptually stated and justified solely in terms of an adequate metaphysics and philosophical theology. I wholly agree, therefore, that the challenge laid down by van Buren and others can be effectively met only by a theology that is frankly and fully metaphysical and thus is prepared to take responsibility for the meaning and truth of its assertions.[1]

In the foregoing Ogden's understanding of the question of nonobjectivity has been considered in some detail. Ogden has asserted that theology is nonobjective insofar as "theological thinking and speaking are different in principle from what goes on in modern science."[2] For Ogden this exhausts the sense in which "nonobjectivity" is applicable to theological statements. Having made this clear, Ogden's stance is that theology must maintain a three-fold objectivity. First, "theology in its own way is scientific."[3] Second, theological statements are primarily assertions about God and his action.[4] Third, the justification of theological statements, insofar as they are justifiable at all, can only be a metaphysical justification.[5] Ogden's position is well summed up when he makes the following observation regarding his conclusion: "As I see it, the problem of nonobjectifying thinking and speaking in contemporary theology is that this threefold objectivity, which is of the very essence of the theological enterprise, will be obscured rather than clarified, abandoned rather than forthrightly affirmed."[6]

---

[1]The Reality of God, p. 97. The way in which Ogden himself contributes to this adequate metaphysics and theology will be explicated in the two following sections of this study.

[2]Ibid., p. 98.

[3]Ibid.

[4]Ibid.

[5]Ibid.

[6]Ibid.

D. The Temporality of God

It has been shown that Ogden's understanding of the objectivity of God is consistent with his demand that God be treated as the chief exemplification of all metaphysical categories rather than an exception to them. This same contention is asserted again in Ogden's consideration of God's relation to time. Ogden objects to the traditional analogia entis which is caught in incoherence[1] insofar as it negates positive aspects of existentiality--such as temporality and real relatedness--to God rather than understanding God in such a way that he is the eminent exemplification of such characteristics. Ogden asserts that the analogical method must be applied to God in such a way that God be considered the chief exemplification of all categories requisite of any being. Hence, Ogden's rejection of the non-temporality of God and his understanding of God as the chief exemplification of temporality will now be considered.

The usual attempts by theologians today to form a doctrine of God take one of two general positions both of which still retain insurmountable difficulties blocking the way to a consistent and meaningful doctrine of God. The first of these positions is that of classical theism. This position, present in the church since the time of the Fathers, attempts to unite the faith witnessed to in Scripture, in which the reality and significance of time and history is stressed, and

---

[1]As he asserts: "The whole point of any analogia entis is to enable one to think and speak of God in meaningful concepts, while yet acknowledging that those concepts apply to him only in an eminent sense, which is in principle different from that intended in their other uses. All that a valid method of analogy requires is that the eminence attributed to God really follow from, rather than contradict, the positive meaning of our fundamental concepts as given by experience. Just this, of course,...the classical practice of analogy is unable to do. Because it rests on the premise that God can be in no sense really relative or temporal, it can say that he 'knows' or 'loves' only

the metaphysics of classical antiquity. Classical
theism has consistently followed "some form of the
traditional _via negationis et eminentiae_, and its most
characteristic assertions have always involved the
denial that God is in any literal sense temporal or
really related to the world."[1] The classical theistic
view, then, on the one hand, recognizes that the God
of Scripture is undeniable related to his creatures,
while on the other hand it attempts to unite this insight with classical metaphysics "the hallmark" of
which "has always been its denial that God is in any
sense structurally related to beings other than himself."[2] Attempting to avoid this dilemma, classical
theists have asserted that God's relation to the world
is to be considered analogically and not literally.
The difficulty of such a stance, notes Ogden, is that
"on conventional metaphysical premises, to say that
God is not literally related to the world could only
mean that he is literally not related to it; and so the
classical _analogia entis_, like traditional theism in
general, has been continually caught in incoherence
and self-contradiction."[3] Although Ogden realizes that
there have been attempts to delineate a doctrine of God
which takes into account postclassical influences--i.e.
the attempts of Paul Tillich and Ian Ramsey--he, nevertheless, contends that these attempts still bear the
characteristic features of classical theology and consequently affirm a nontemporalistic theism.[4]

---

by contradicting the meaning of those words as we
otherwise use them." (The Reality of God, p. 59.).
Cf. also, Ibid., pp. 151, 154, 183; and Charles Hartshorne's essay "The Standpoint of Panentheism," especially Section A. in which he discusses the Law of
Polarity, in Charles Hartshorne and William L. Reese,
editors, Philosophers Speak of God (Chicago: The
University of Chicago Press, Phoenix Books, 1953), pp.
1-25, esp. pp. 1-15.

[1]The Reality of God, p. 158.
[2]Ibid., pp. 150-151.
[3]Ibid., p. 151.
[4]Ibid., p. 158.

The second general position has variegated strands which make it difficult to describe. Yet, the unifying factor common to all these strands is "a sharp rejection of classical theism with its way of analogy and a deep conviction as to the reality and significance of time and history that can hardly be reconciled with classical metaphysics."[1] This position, entertaining a strong suspicion or even rejection of metaphysics and natural theology, asserts that all statements about God are to be understood, not as assertions but as statements primarily or wholly about human existence, or man's existential self-understanding.[2] This general position, then, attempts to overcome what it views as contradictory in the classical theistic position by affirming that theological statements say nothing about "how things are" but rather only function as expressive of a "blik" or "an intention to behave in a certain way."[3] The inevitable impasse which arises when these positions are considered as the only two alternatives in any consideration of a doctrine of God is described by Ogden when he observes:

> On the one hand, those who represent the position of classical theism can explicate Christian faith's reference to a transcendent God only by denying or seriously obscuring the reality and significance of temporality. On the other hand, the spokesmen for the more modern view succeed in doing justice to temporality, and thus to man and his historicity, only by denying or failing adequately to explicate the certainty of faith in its eternal ground.[4]

Having summarized these positions, Ogden notes that the impasse involved becomes obvious only in the most

---

[1]Ibid., pp. 158-159.

[2]Ibid., p. 159. Cf. above pp. 191-194 for Ogden's understanding of this position and its proponents, esp. Paul van Buren and R. B. Braithwaite. Cf. also The Reality of God, pp. 159-160.

[3]Ibid., p. 159.

[4]Ibid., p. 160.

extreme expressions of the two positions, but he stresses that neither position offers a real third alternative. One is left to "choose either the sacrifice
of time and man to God's eternity" on the one hand, or
"the abandonment of God and infinity for the temporality of man,"[1] on the other hand. Yet, these are not
the only two alternatives, asserts Ogden. The resources for settling the dilemma are available in the
neoclassical expressions of a dipolar theism in the
process thought of Whitehead and Hartshorne, or in
Heidegger's thesis of the temporality of God.[2] With
the consideration of Ogden's description of the contemporary theological dilemma one confronts in any
attempt to formulate a doctrine of God and his contention that the resources for avoiding an impasse are
now available, a consideration of his proposal of a
third alternative is now in order.

One possibility for overcoming the impasse in
which contemporary theology finds itself, contends
Ogden, is to be found in the work of Martin Heidegger
whose "work as a philosopher has been stimulated and
even determined by influences emanating from contemporary theology."[3] His studies of various theologians,
such as Augustine, Luther and Kierkegaard, convinced
him of the irreconcilability between the conceptuality
of the classical metaphysical tradition and the understanding of existence which these theologians attempted
to explicate by means of classical metaphysics.
Relying on the resources of the classical conceptual
tradition, one could do justice "neither to the 'actualization of factual existence' (or the historicity of

---

[1]Ibid.

[2]Cf. Ibid., p. 161, 163.

[3]The Reality of God, p. 144. In agreement with
Otto Poggeler's contention in Der Denkweg Martin
Heideggers, Ogden affirms of Heidegger that he was "a
thinker whose mediated encounter with the New Testament
and with theologians like Augustine, Luther, and
Kierkegaard had aroused 'the suspicion that the God
of philosophy is not the living God of faith and that
metaphysical theology is not the final answer to the
question of thinking.'" (Ibid., p. 145.).

man) nor to the 'godness of God' as Christian faith
understands them."[1] A proper understanding of these
would require a radical reorientation of traditional
metaphysical thinking. Ogden contends that the basis
for such a radical reorientation is to be found in
Heidegger's work. Consequently, he attempts to interpret one of the footnotes in Heidegger's Sein und Zeit
in order to show "that what he there proposes as a
philosophical interpretation of God's eternity has a
unique relevance for the attempts of Christian theologians to develop an adequate doctrine of God for our
time."[2] The footnote to be considered contains what
Ogden calls the following "remarkable sentences:"[3]

> It requires no extensive discussion to show
> that the traditional concept of eternity, in
> the sense of the 'stationary now' (nunc stans),
> is drawn from the vulgar understanding of time
> and is limited by an orientation to the idea
> of 'constant' presence-on-hand. If the eternity
> of God would admit of being 'construed' philo-
> sophically, it could be understood only as a
> more primal and 'infinite' temporality.

---

[1]Ibid., p. 145.

[2]Ibid., p. 147.

[3]The reasons for calling these sentences "remarkable" notes Ogden, are fourfold: "First, they constitute one among only a very few explicit references to
God or to theology in a work whose central purpose and
theme are quite different from those that properly
determine the task of the theologian. Second, this
passage is the only place in the book where Heidegger
at all makes explicit what his attempts to reorient
metaphysical thinking would mean for a philosophical
doctrine of God...Third, the philosophical theology
Heidegger here presents, as it were, in nuce involves
a radical departure from the classical philosophical-
theological tradition." Fourth, just as he has translated into formal ontological terms the understanding
of man presented in the New Testament, so also "his
proposal for a philosophical construction of God's
eternity as infinite temporality would seem to represent a similar 'ontologizing' of the primitive Christian understanding of God." (The Reality of God,
pp. 145-146.).

Whether the _via negationis et eminentiae_
could offer a possible way to this goal
would remain uncertain.[1]

Although he observes that Heidegger did not fully
develop the footnote,[2] nor admit the historical antecedents which he and Poggeler view as influential on
Heidegger at this point, Ogden nevertheless maintains
that Heidegger's proposal has meaning and "unique relevance for the attempts of Christian theologians to develop an adequate doctrine of God for our time."[3]
Hence, he is not so much interested in establishing the
historical antecedents as he is in explicating the
meaning and relevance of Heidegger's proposal.

To delineate the meaning and relevance of
Heidegger's proposal, Ogden begins by considering
Heidegger's understanding of the task of philosophy.
For Heidegger, the task of philosophy is that of formal
ontological analysis. That is to say, philosophy attempts to provide a completely general ontology or an
understanding of being as such. In so doing, philosophy makes as its object of analysis human existence,
not merely to provide an anthropology but more so "to

---

[1]_Ibid._, p. 145. Martin Heidegger, _Being and Time_
(English translation by John Macquarrie and Edward
Robinson. New York: Harper and Row, 1962, p. 499,
note xiii.).

[2]As Ogden remarks: "On the face of it, the footnote does nothing more than propose a philosophical
interpretation of God that is coherent with Heidegger's
analysis of human existence and that, like this analysis, thoroughly revolutionizes the conventional metaphysical wisdom. Nevertheless, I am persuaded we
are not far from the truth if we regard his proposal as
stimulated and perhaps even determined by the same theological influences that were otherwise so decisive for
this phase of his work. I regard it as highly probable
that here as in _Sein und Zeit_ generally, the historical
background of Heidegger's statements is the understanding of man and of God with which his encounter with
Christian theology served to acquaint him. (_The Reality of God_, p. 146.).

[3]_Ibid._, p. 147.

answer the ultimate question of the meaning of being itself."[1] This analysis is formal and ontological, not material and ontic. It provides an existentialist (existenzial) analysis, not an existential (existenziell) understanding.[2] Hence, contends Ogden, if the task of philosophy is that of providing a formal ontological analysis of being as such, then the task of philosophical theology based on Heidegger's principles could only be that of offering "a formal ontological analysis of the being of God."[3] Ogden summarizes the task of such a theology by observing:

> The question to be asked by such a theology would not be the 'existential' question of God, which every man must be supposed to ask in asking about his own 'authenticity' (Eigentlichkeit), but rather a more purely theoretical question about God, which would parallel in this inquiry the 'existentialist' question that philosophy properly addresses to human existence. This implies, in turn, that the object of philosophical theology would not be the divine 'existence' (Existenz), but, in some sense of the word, the divine 'existentiality' (Existenzialitat), the basic structure or essence that determines 'the godness of God,' even as existentiality in the human case is the ontological structure determining the manness of man.[4]

According to Ogden, there would be no incompatibility between such a philosophical construction and a confessional faith grounded in a special revelation. Rather, the philosophical construction would provide "a necessary complement to" confessional theology,[5]

---

[1]Ibid., p. 148.

[2]Ibid.

[3]Ibid.

[4]Ibid.

[5]Ibid, Elaborating on this Ogden contends: "Just as there can be, in principle, no opposition between a philosophical analysis of human existence and a theological explication of the particular self-understanding of Christian faith, so there also could be no

for faith as self-understanding is also an understanding of God and his action, and if this faith is to be properly explicated it can only be through an adequate, understandable philosophical theology.

Ogden immediately realizes that a possible objection to such an interpretation is that it presupposes a strict analogy between the being of man and the being of God.[1] Just as in man the distinction must be made between essential structure (existentiality) and the concrete actualization of that structure (existence), so also must the distinction be maintained with reference to God. Ogden affirms that it is this analogy which Heidegger means to assert, for his distinction between 'primal temporality' (ursprungliche Zeitlichkeit) and both the 'within-timeness' (Innerzeitigkeit) "which is the derived mode of being-temporal appropriate to mere objects or 'presence-on-hand,'" and the actual occurrence of 'primal time' which is the "temporalizing of temporality" is merely another way of asserting the difference between existentiality and existence.[2]

This strict analogy between the being of man and the being of God involves two main considerations. In the first place, God's being, like man's is in some sense a being in the world (In-der-Welt-sein). In the second place, the analogy affirms that God, like man has a past and a future as well as a present. What does God's being-in-the-world mean? If the eternity of God is to be interpreted as his more primal temporality, then real internal relatedness to others is not an accident of his being, but its essential structure. Moreover, God's relatedness to the world cannot be construed merely as theoretical knowledge. Just as "man's relation to his world is not primarily the disinterested registration of bare data in consciousness, but an active participation in others of an essentially

---

incompatibility between a proper philosphical construction of the being of God and a theological witness to God's concrete action as revealed in Jesus Christ." (Ibid., pp. 148-149.).

[1] Ibid., p. 149.

[2] Ibid.

practical and emotional kind" which can only be described in the "eminently nontheoretical term 'care,'"[1]
so also is God's relation to the world to be understood. The point to be noticed, stresses Ogden, is
that "Heidegger's concepts of 'temporality' and 'care'
are logically so related that God can be construed as
temporal only by also construing his being as care, and
thus as essentially as being-in-the-world with others,
in real internal relations to them."[2] In this view of
God considered essentially as a being in the world in
internal relation with others, one encounters a stance
radically different from that of the classical Western
tradition which denies that God is in any sense structurally related to beings other than himself.

The second consideration of Heidegger's affirmation that God's eternity is to be construed as primal
temporality is that God has a past and future as well
as a present. Recalling that this is to be understood
in analogy to man's experience of time, Ogden first
notes Heidegger's interpretation of the phenomenon of
time in relation to man's experience, and then applies
this experience analogously to God. Heidegger asserts
that our everyday experience of time is not original
but rather derived from a more primal temporality.
The primary time of our experience is not the "within-
timeness" whereby we order the objects of our everyday
experience, but "the time constituted by our experiencing itself."[3] This time constituted by our experience itself, this actual-occurrence time, has a relation to the being of others and to itself. By memory
it has a relation to its past, and by anticipation, to
its future. The ordered whole of significance is experienced as one continually projects himself toward
the future in terms of a specific range of possibilities inherited from one's past. · Consequently, the
present is to be considered not as an extensionless
moment in our experience, but rather "the decisive
'moment' (Augenblick) in which our experience itself

---

[1] Ibid., p. 150.
[2] Ibid.
[3] Ibid., p. 151.

occurs and is constituted."[1] Analogously, God, too, is
"an experiencing self who anticipates the future and
remembers the past and whose successive occasions of
present experience are themselves temporal occurrences."[2] Such an understanding of God's eternity
sharply diverges from the classical theological understanding in which God's eternity is "defined as the
'stationary now,' or as sheer nontemporality,"[3] a concept of eternity which "can only mean the literal
negation or exclusion of the distinctions that the concept of temporality entails."[4]

In summing up what he feels is the significance of
Heidegger's assertion that the eternity of God is to be
construed as a more primal temporality, Ogden contends
that:

> ...if the being of God is to be construed
> somehow as a more primal temporality, this
> can mean no less than that God, like man,
> essentially exists as being-in-the-world,
> with real internal relations to others,
> and that, as this kind of caring, experi-
> encing self, his successive occasions of
> present experience each involve the same
> kind of relations to the future and the
> past exhibited by our own occasions of
> experience as men.[5]

---

[1]Ibid., p. 152.

[2]Ibid.

[3]Ibid.

[4]Ibid. Elaborating on the classical theological
view, Ogden notes: "True, at this point also, their
absolute negation of a basic concept with reference to
God is more or less ambiguous. Analogically, at least,
God is conventionally conceived as having a will or
purpose and still other perfections that imply temporal
distinctions. And yet, once again, such analogical
speaking is completely emptied of meaning by the non-
analogical denial that the being of God is in any
sense temporal being." (Ibid.).

[5]Ibid., p. 153.

Having made this summary, however, Ogden emphasizes that to assert only the similarities between God
and man derived from Heidegger's analogical analysis
is to fail to do justice to the analogical relation
which Heidegger intends. Such an approach would fail
because an analogy implies differences as well as
similarities between the two analogues under consideration. Hence, the differences must also be considered,
for "if God's being is to be construed as analogous to
the being of man, this must mean that God's essential
structure is not only the same as man's but also, in
some significant respect, different from it."[1]

This significant difference is to be seen by the
fact that while God's eternity is to be construed in
terms of temporality, it is to be construed not merely
in these terms but rather in terms of "infinite" (un-
endlich) temporality.[2] While God's temporality is to
be understood as infinite, the distinguishing characteristic regarding man is not his temporality but his
finitude. While both God and man are characterized by
being-in-the-world in relation to others and to their
own future and past, only man, and not God, is a being-
in-the-world "circumscribed by definite limits and
therefore encompassed by what he is not."[3] Hence,
man's temporality is conditioned, determined, and
limited. He is not his own ground. He finds himself
"thrown" into the world. He comes from a source beyond himself. Man recalls a "precedent nothing," for
there was a time when he was not; but also he is determined by a "subsequent nothing," for he is a being-
toward-death. There will be a time when he will be no
more.[4] Hence, Ogden observes of man: "Because the
temporality that defines his being is itself in principle temporally finite and limited, he can be who he
truly is only in the full consciousness of this finitude and the deliberate acceptance of his temporal
limitations."[5]

---

[1]Ibid.
[2]Ibid.
[3]Ibid., p. 153.
[4]Ibid., pp. 153-154.
[5]Ibid., p. 154.

In God, however, there is a complete absence of such temporal finitude and limitations. "God's temporality is not itself temporally determined."[1] There never was a time when he was not, and there never will be a time when he will not be. He can, therefore, "experience nothing less than a literally limitless past and future."[2] In this understanding, Heidegger finds agreement with traditional theology; so his departure is not a complete denial of classical theology. Heidegger, too, maintains a qualitative difference between God and man, but the distinction is such that he does not deny temporality of God, but rather views God as its eminent exemplification.[3]

A second aspect of man's finitude is that he is radically limited in space. Man's world never coincides with the totality of beings. He is always restricted. For man to be at all entails that he be confined to some definite range of possibilities "inherited from his finite past and projected into his finite future."[4] He does not relate fully to others for his encounter with them is relative to "the perspec-

---

[1] Ibid.

[2] Ibid.

[3] The Reality of God, p. 154. Reference to God as the "eminent exemplification" of temporality rather than its negation recalls Whitehead's words that "God is not to be treated as an exception to all metaphysical principles, invoked to save their collapse. He is their chief exemplification." (Process and Reality, p. 521.). Elaborating on Heidegger's understanding of God as eminent exemplification of temporality Ogden says: "God's eternity is not sheer timelessness, but an infinite fullness of time, for which our own finite temporality provides a real but hardly univocal likeness. This means that Heidegger's implied reformulation of the analogia entis is not, like its classical precedent, involved in essential incoherence. Perfections entailing temporal distinctions may be predicated of God without being emptied of meaning by contradictory negations; and the assertion of God's qualitative distinction from finite beings does not exclude, but positively implies, the meaningfulness of such predication." (The Reality of God, p. 154.).

[4] Ibid., p. 155.

tives imposed by his own particular projects of self-understanding."[1] Yet, man, failing in his everyday life to realize these limitations and face their truth, treats others as mere "objects of his own finite appreciations" and, thus absolutizing finite limitations, he fails to be open to those whose being in themselves transcends their being objects for him in his world.[2]

Again, however, God whose temporality is infinite does not face these limitations. Hence, the qualitative difference between God and man is again revealed. Ogden considers this difference between God and man when he says:

> While God's being, like man's is being-in-the-world, in real relation to others, God's relatedenss to others is radically unlike man's in being itself not merely relative, but wholly absolute. That God is related to other beings is itself relative to nothing beyond God himself, but is grounded solely in his own complete openness to possibility or to the future simply as such. Consequently, God's world can comprise nothing less than the sum total of all beings other than himself, both present and past, and his only environment is the wholly internal environment encompassed by his not merely finite but infinite care. Moreover, the truth constituted by God's encounter with his world is not simply some relative truth, but the truth—truth in its absolute and definitive meaning. The final measure of all things as they are in themselves is precisely their being in and for God's infinite care; and the ordered whole of significance that in each present constitutes his actual world is the ultimate integrity of all the significance there is.[3]

This passage is quoted here in toto, not only because it well summarizes Ogden's understanding of the way in which God, like man, is temporally and spatially related to the world even though God's relation to the

---

[1] Ibid.
[2] Ibid.
[3] Ibid., pp. 155-156.

world is qualitatively different from that of man.
It also points to an emphasis in Ogden's theology as
a whole, namely, the contention that just as the human
self experiences both relation and transcendence to
its body, analogously God as a self experiences both
relation and transcendence to the world.[1]

The understanding of the qualitative difference
between God and man reveals once again that Heidegger's
break with traditional theology is not total. Yet,
the distinct difference between Heidegger and traditional theology is marked by the fact that whereas
traditional theology views God's absoluteness as a
denial of his real relation to others, for Heidegger
God's absoluteness is seen precisely in his eminent
relatedness to all.[2]

It is Ogden's contention, then, that whereas the
classical or traditional analogical method fails to
provide the resources for a valid theological method,
Heidegger's analogical method makes such provision.
The traditional analogical method, the via negationis
et eminentiae, often contained contradictions between
the two elements of which it was composed. The positive perfections predicated of God on the one hand
were emptied of any meaning by the denials of the via
negationis. For example, the traditional via negationis led to a denial of positive perfections inherent in the meaning of being itself, perfections such
as primal temporality and real internal relatedness.
In Heidegger's view, however, God's uniqueness is not
seen in denying temporality or internal relationality
to God but rather in applying temporality and internal
relationality to God while negating their limitations
as man--whose basic characteristic is that of fini-
tude--experiences them.

Ogden's contention, then, is that "the profound
truth of the temporality of God is something we as
theologians are all sooner or later going to have to
learn,"[3] and Heidegger's footnote is servicable in this

---

[1]Cf. The Reality of God, pp. 155, 178. 180.
[2]Ibid., p. 156.
[3]Ibid., p. 163.

regard. But, quoting Gogarten, he offers this reminder: "Needless to say, it does not have to be
Heidegger from whom one learns this. If one thinks
he can learn it better elsewhere, all well and good.
But, in one way or another, learned it must be."[1]

      E. The Relation Between God and the World

    In the preceding section the stance which Ogden
takes regarding the relation between God and the world
was indicated by his assertion of the temporality of
God. It was noted that this temporality entails that
God is a being-in-the-world with real internal relations to others, and that this being-in-the-world
further entails that God is a being who has a past,
from which he inherits possibilities through memory,
and a future, toward which through anticipation he
looks to the actualization of possibilities. Having
already thus been introduced to Ogden's stance regarding the problem of the relation between God and the
world, the task now is to explicate his position explicitly, in an attempt to delineate his answer to the
questions: "How does God function in human life?"[2]
and "What sense does it make to say, 'God acts in
history?'"[3]

    It is to be noted that Ogden's formulation of the
question in the form of "What sense does it make to
say, 'God acts in history?'" is not the same as the
question: "Can one make sense of the statement, 'God
acts in history?'", for the former formulation presupposes a positive answer to the latter. Ogden asks the
question in the former formulation--hence, presupposing

---

[1]Ibid.

[2]Schubert Ogden, "How Does God Function in Human
Life?" Christianity and Crisis, Volume 27, May 15,
1967, pp. 105-108.

[3]Ogden, "What Sense Does It Make To Say 'God
Acts In History?'" The Reality of God and Other Essays, pp. 164-187.

an affirmative answer--for two reasons. First, the
real issue for Ogden is not whether the statement "God
acts in history"makes sense, but what sense it makes.
That Ogden views the issue in this way is explained by
his contention that "it belongs to the very nature of
the theologian's work that the possibility of speaking
of God's action in history is not the question he
must consider."[1] Hence, it is Ogden's contention that
theologians must speak of the action of God in history,
for a theology without such an active God is impossible. As he noted earlier:

> If theology is possible today only on sec-
> ularistic terms, the more candid way to say
> this is to admit that theology is not pos-
> sible today at all....The issue here is in-
> deed either/or, and all talk of a Chris-
> tianity post mortem dei is, in the last
> analysis, neither hyperbole nor evidence
> of originality but merely nonsense.[2]

The theologian, then, according to Ogden, need not ask
the question "Can one speak of God's action in history?", for his very task presupposes an affirmative
answer. But, the theologian does ask "What does it
mean to say, 'God acts in history?'", for "he recognizes that not all the ways in which his fathers in the
faith have spoken of God's action are relevant possibilities for men today."[3]

Secondly, Ogden notes that the way in which he
formulates the question is important in that his formulation indicates his reliance upon the "functional
analysis" phase of linguistic philosophy rather than
the "verificational analysis" phase.[4] The question
of verificational analysis was whether theological
statements can make sense, and the answer to this ques-

---

[1]The Reality of God, p. 164.

[2]Ibid., pp. 14-15.

[3]Ibid., p. 164.

[4]Cf. Frederick Ferre, Language, Logic and God,
pp. 8-57 for a delineation of his understanding of
"verificational analysis," and pp. 58-66 for his description of "functional analysis."

tion was a firm negative response. But this answer
"was based less on a careful analysis of the actual
uses of religious and theological language than on certain a priori assumptions that reflected...'an extreme
respect for science and mathematics' and 'an extreme
distrust for metaphysics.'"[1] Hence, Ogden's approach
is to be that of "functional analysis," which consists
of an attempt "to determine what sense such statements
in fact do make by analyzing their function in actual
religious and theological speech."[2] Ogden's attempt
to do this consists of a twofold approach. First, he
attempts to clarify the problem and indicate what resources are available for its solution. Second, he
attempts to point the way to a constructive solution.

Consider, in the first, place, his understanding
of the problem and the possibilities for its solution.
Ogden agrees with Bultmann that the central elements
of Christian theology are presented in mythological
language. This means that the statements in which theology has ordinarily spoken of God have the same objectifying character[3] as the statements of empirical science, although their intention, use or function is
different from that of scientific statements. In
mythological language "God and his action are represented as though God were but one more secondary cause
in the chain of secondary causes and his action but
one more alongside those of other causal agents."[4]

---

[1] The Reality of God, p. 165.

[2] Ibid.

[3] That is, they represent the reality of which
they speak in terms of space, time, causality and
substance.

[4] The Reality of God, pp. 166-167. In excluding
mythological language as adequate for speaking about
God, Ogden is quick to note that by excluding "myth"
both he and Bultmann do not mean to exclude all analogical speaking about God. As will be discussed
later, Ogden himself utilizes a method of analogy in
his attempts to point to a solution of the problem
"What sense does it make to say, 'God acts in history?'" Therefore, of Bultmann's (and his own) understanding of myth, he cautions: "Bultmann does not so
define 'myth' (or 'mythology') as to make it inclusive
of all analogical discourse about God....he distinguishes a 'mythological' way of speaking of God and

The use of mythological statements, Ogden observes, entails two difficulties. First, mythological
statements, having the linguistic form of scientific
statements, are open to scientific criticism the results of which are devastating. The statement "God
acts in history," says Ogden, "certainly cannot make
scientific sense, since the logic of scientific discourse simply leaves no room for it in its traditional
mythological form."[1] The second difficulty is that it
is questionable whether mythological statements make
any theological sense. In objectifying God by representing him and his action in categories appropriate
to the empirical sciences, myth misrepresents God's
transcendence by depicting God merely as one more item
within the world. These two difficulties, indicating
the inappropriateness of mythological language to
express the Christian faith, give rise to the consideration of nonmythological ways in which the meaning
of the Christian affirmation "God acts in history" can
be expressed.

A solution to the search for a nonmythological
way to express theological statements is partially[2]
available through Bultmann's method of "existentialist
interpretation," which emphasizes that "the true meaning of theological statements is not scientific but
'existential.'"[3] The function of theological state-
ments--even of the mythological statements--according

---

his action from another way that he refers to as 'analogy;' and this distinction can be understood only if
the restricted scope of his definition of 'myth' is
carefully observed. The specific difference of myth
is not that it speaks of God in terms also applicable
to the nondivine, but that its terms are 'objectifying'
in a manner appropriate only to ordinary empirical
knowledge and its refinement by the various special
sciences." (p. 167.).

[1]Ibid., p. 167.

[2]"Partially" must be used here, for, as will be
shown later, Ogden sees inadequacies in Bultmann's
solution, namely: First, the one-sidely existentialist
character of his solution, (p. 170) and second, his
failure to carry out the existentialist interpretation
consistently. (p. 173.).

[3]The Reality of God, p. 168.

to Bultmann, is not to provide scientific information, but to express "an understanding of man's existence as a historical being who must continually decide how he is to understand himself in the world."[1] The theologian's task, then, is to realize that theological statements intend to be thoroughly existential, and therefore to give this intention meaningful expression.[2]

Ogden agrees with Bultmann's proposed solution, namely, that all theological statements are to be considered as existential statements, but he stresses that Bultmann's solution itself is problematic at at least two points. The first problem is that Bultmann's solution has a "one-sidedly existentialist character."[3] It has been noted that for Bultmann all theological statements are to be treated as statements about man and man's possibilities for understanding his existence. What Ogden sees to be the one-sidedness of this approach is illustrated by Bultmann's interpretation of Paul.[4] In this interpretation Bultmann recognizes that every assertion about God is likewise an assertion about man and conversely every assertion about man is

---

[1]Ibid., p. 169.

[2]Ibid. Two examples of Bultmann's rendering mythological statements meaningful by interpreting them existentially and hence according to their intention, are his interpretation of the statements that God is Creator and God is the Redeemer. Of the statement "God is Creator" he says that it is "in its fundamental intention not the statement of a cosmological theory that seeks to explain the origin of the world, but rather man's confession to God as his Lord--the Lord to whom the world belongs, whose power and care sustain and preserve it, and to whom man himself owes obedience." (Ibid., p. 169.). Statements about God as final redeemer function "to remind us that 'the fulfillment of life cannot be the result of human effort, but rather a gift from beyond, a gift of God's grace.' Hence, to affirm such statements is really to affirm an understanding of one's existence in which one renounces every attempt at self-contrived security and utterly opens himself to the security of God's love, wherein all things find ultimate acceptance." (Ibid., p. 169).

[3]The Reality of God, p. 170.

[4]Cf. Bultmann, Theology of the New Testament, Vol. I., pp. 185-352.

to be understood as an assertion about God, but he concludes that Paul's theology is to be treated as anthropology, a doctrine of man. Ogden questions this "one-sided" solution when he observes that if Bultmann's premise—that for Paul all statements about God are statements about man and vice versa—is correct then rather than concluding that Paul's theology is best to be understood anthropologically, one could with the same legitimacy understand Paul's theology as precisely that, a doctrine of God. Bultmann, however, does not entertain this second conclusion.[1]

While not entertaining the second conclusion, however, Bultmann mitigates the one-sideness of his existentialist stance by his theory of analogy.[2] Although Bultmann's theory of analogy is not developed, nevertheless, he makes clear that he does not intend to exclude a direct speaking of God and his action that is requisite of Christian faith. Hence, concludes Ogden, what Bultmann calls for instead of mythology is not an existentialist interpretation alone but "existentialist interpretation plus analogy."[3] To supplement Bultmann's fragmentary theory of analogy and his existentialist analysis of man, Ogden suggests the dipolar view of God espoused by Charles Hartshorne.[4] Ogden wants to make clear that he is calling for a thoroughgoing existentialist interpretation of theological

---

[1]Cf. Ogden's essay "Bultmann's Demythologizing and Hartshorne's Dipolar Theism," in William L. Reese and Eugene Freeman (eds.). Process and Divinity: The Hartshorne Festschrift. LaSalle, Illinois: Open Court, 1964, pp. 493-513.

[2]It is because of this theory of analogy that Ogden stresses that John Macquarrie "goes too far" in viewing Bultmann as so interpreting the "Christian faith that it is in danger of becoming indistinguishable from a merely human self-understanding utterly lacking in any divine basis or object." (The Reality of God, p. 171.). Contrary to Macquarrie, and because of his theory of analogy, Ogden maintains that "Both in practice and in theory, Bultmann makes clear that he has no intention of reducing faith simply to a human attitude or perspective." (Ibid.).

[3]Ibid.

[4]Ibid., p. 172.

statements while at the same time demanding that these statements also speak directly of God and his actions.[1] Agreeing with Hartshorne, he says: "self-knowledge and knowledge of God are inseparable," and "neither is clear unless both are somehow clear."[2]

The second problem which Ogden sees in Bultmann's proposed solution to the problem offered by mythological statements is that Bultmann fails "consistently to carry out"[3] the "existentialist interpretation" he intends. Ogden contends that Bultmann's claim "that authentic human existence is factually possible solely in consequence of God's unique act in Jesus Christ"[4] is itself mythological by Bultmann's own definition, and therefore requires existentialist interpretation. What the claim "only in Jesus Christ" means when submitted to existentialist interpretation is, according to Ogden, "not that God acts to redeem only in the history of Jesus and in no other history, but that the only God who redeems any history--although he in fact redeems every history--is the God whose redemptive action is decisively re-presented in the word that Jesus speaks and is."[5] But this interpretation, too, raises problems, the constructive solution of which lies in Ogden's attempt to develop a theory of analogy, one which takes into account the necessity of existentialist interpretation of theological statements.

Although Ogden agrees with Frederick Ferre that the logic of analogy as it has been normally interpreted is no longer tenable,[6] he nevertheless argues

---

[1] Ibid.

[2] Ibid., note 16, from "The Idea of God--Literal or or Analogical?" Christian Scholar, June, 1956, p. 136.

[3] The Reality of God, p. 173; Cf. also Christ Without Myth, pp. 111-126.

[4] The Reality of God, p. 173.

[5] Ibid.

[6] Cf. Frederick Ferre, Language, Logic and God. Cf. also Ferre's discussion of religious language in Part III. of his Basic Modern Philosophy of Religion, New York: Charles Scribner's Sons, 1967, pp. 301-451.

that this does not entail the assertion of the un-
tenability of theories of analogy. Noting that the
problems of the classical theory of analogy are one
and the same as those of classical theism, Ogden argues:

> Because classical theism in the impossible
> attempt to synthesize the personalistic
> view of God of Holy Scripture with the
> substance ontology of classical Greek phi-
> losophy, the theory of analogy it develops
> to rationalize its procedures cannot but be
> an inconsistent and untenable theory.[1]

Ogden's doctrine of analogy is a doctrine utilizing the neoclassical insights of Charles Hartshorne.
The crucial aspect of this analogical method is that
"God is to be conceived in strict analogy with the
human self or person."[2] By the word "strict" one is
reminded that some concepts referring to God are to be
taken literally. By "analogy," however, one is reminded that God is both like and unlike man. God is
not a self in univocally the same sense that man is a
self. To put this in a Whiteheadian context, strict
analogy means, on the one hand, that God is not an exception to all other metaphysical categories, while on
the other hand, it points to the fact that he is not
merely an exemplification of the categories but their
chief exemplification.[3] An example illustrative of the
fact that God is not an exception nor merely an exemplification but the chief exemplification of all metaphysical categories is seen by the fact that whereas
the human self is related only to a very few others,
the divine self is effectively related to all others.[4]
The same can be seen in considering God's dependence on
his world. Whereas man is dependent upon God and his

---

[1]The Reality of God, p. 174.

[2]Ibid., p. 175. Cf. also Process and Reality,
p. 521: "God is not to be treated as an exception to
all metaphysical principles invoked to save their
collapse, he is their chief exemplification."

[3]The Reality of God, p. 175.

[4]Ibid.

world both for his actuality and his existence, in the case of God there is no existential dependence.[1] God is partially dependent, however, in what he is. As Ogden explains: "What actual state of the literally infinite number of states possible for him," he is in, "depends both on his own contingent or free decisions and on the free decisions of the creatures who constitute his world."[2]

God, then, according to Ogden, is to be understood in strict analogy to the human self. Moreover, he affirms that God's action is to be conceived in strict analogy to that of the human self. But this affirmation requires a clarification of what is meant by man's action.[3] Whereas human action is ordinarily understood to be a specific word or deed by which the human self undertakes to accomplish some particular project or purpose, it is also to be considered in a more primary and fundamental sense as the action whereby the self constitutes itself as a self.[4] The decisions by which the human self constitutes itself as a self may take one of two basic forms. The self may open itself to its world and make its decisions on the basis of a consideration of all the factors that confront it. Or, it may close itself to part of its

---

[1]As Ogden stresses: "That God is in some actual state or other, or in relation to some actual world, is dependent on nothing whatever and is in the strictest sense necessary." (Ibid., p. 176.).

[2]Ibid. Ogden contends that this failure to distinguish between actuality and existence leads to an exaggerated fear of "anthropomorphism," Tillich, he feels, fails to make this distinction. Cf. Tillich, Systematic Theology, Vol. I., pp. 275f.

[3]The Reality of God, p. 176.

[4]Ibid., p. 177. As Ogden argues: "Indeed, it is only because the self first acts to constitute itself, to respond to its world, and to decide its own inner being that it 'acts' at all in the more ordinary meaning of the word; all its outer acts of word and deed are but ways of expressing and implementing the inner decisions whereby it constitutes itself as a self." (The Reality of God, p. 177.).

world and make the decisions which constitute itself
on the basis of a restricted sensitivity. These two
ways correspond to the self who loves, thus participating fully in the constitution of his own being and
in the being of others, and the self who hates, thus
becoming estranged from possibilities for himself and
others. In either case, one's outward acts will express the primal inner act of love or hate.[1]

Ogden asserts that God's action is to be understood by strict analogy to this understanding of man's
action. God's action is to be understood, first of
all, as the act whereby he as such is constituted and
constituted as a self who loves. God's being can be
described as that of "pure unbounded love."[2] Hence,
says Ogden, "the primary meaning of God's action is the
act whereby, in each new present, he constitutes himself as God by participating fully and completely in
the world of his creatures, thereby laying the ground
for the next stage of the creative process."[3] His love
differs from that of the human self, however, in that
it is "pure and unbounded"..."direct and immediate,"[4]
for his "power of participation in the being of others
is literally boundless."[5] If one accepts this theory
of strict analogy, then to assert that God is Creator
does not mean merely that all are dependent upon his
power and love and bound to do his will. This is only
the indirect meaning of the statement. The direct
meaning, however, is that "the ultimate ground of
every actual state of the world is not just the individual decisions of the creatures who constitute its
antecedent states, but rather these decisions as re-
sponded to by God's own decision of pure unbounded
love."[6] Moreover, to say that God is Redeemer does
not mean merely that the self has radical freedom and

---

[1]Ibid.

[2]Cf. Ogden, "Love Unbounded: The Doctrine of
God," op. cit., pp. 5-17.

[3]The Reality of God, p. 1-7.

[4]Ibid.

[5]Ibid., p. 178.

[6]Ibid., p. 178.

openness to the world, but what is more, it means
that:

> ...the final destiny of myself and of all
> my fellow creatures is to contribute our-
> selves not only to the self-creation of the
> subsequent worlds of creatures, but also
> to the self-creation of God, who accepts
> us without condition into his own ever-
> lasting life, where we have a final stand-
> ing or security that can nevermore be lost.[1]

Although Ogden does not explore the ramifications of
these interpretations further, he nevertheless notes
that these concepts demonstrate that theological
statements not only have an existential significance
but that some theological statements refer directly to
God and his action.[2]

In turning directly to the question, "What sense
does it make to say, 'God acts in history?'," Ogden
observes that his foregoing argument has stressed that
God's creative action as such is not "an action in
history, but an action that transcends it."[3] Moreover,
he asserts that "God's action as Redeemer cannot be
simply identified with any particular historical event
or events."[4] Yet, although God's action is always
his action and can never be simply identified with the
action of ordinary historical beings, there are two
senses in which God can be said to act in history.

First, if God's relation to the world is to be
understood in strict analogy to man's relation to his
body, then it can be said "that every creature is to
some extent God's act--just as, by analogy all our

---

[1]Ibid., pp. 178-179.

[2]Ibid., p. 179.

[3]Ibid.

[4]Ibid. He explains his position when he notes:
"As the act whereby he ever and again actualizes his
own divine essence by responding in love to all the
creatures in his world, it is an act that transcends
the world as the world's ultimate consequence."
(Ibid.).

191

bodily actions are to some extent our actions as
selves."[1] Although every creature has a certain freedom, such freedom has definite limits which are ultimately grounded in God's own freedom. Hence, in this
sense every creature has its basis in God's creative
action."[2]

A second sense in which God can be said to act in
history is through man's capacity of consciousness or
self-consciousness, the capacity by which man is
"uniquely the creature of meaning."[3] Because of his
capacity of self-consciousness, notes Ogden, man:

> ...is able to understand himself and his
> fellow creatures and the divine reality in
> which they have their origin and end and,
> through his thought and language, is able
> to bring all this to unique expression. As
> logos himself, he is able to grasp the
> logos of reality as such and to represent
> it through symbolic speech and action.[4]

Insofar as man can do this, he can "represent or speak
for the divine,"[5] an action by which "he re-presents
not only his own understanding of God's action, but,
through it, the reality of God's action itself,"[6] so
that "one may even say that, in this case, man's action
actually is God's action."[7]

---

[1]The Reality of God, p. 180.
[2]Ibid. Or, in Whitehead's terms, God functions
"in history" as the principle of limitation and concretion. God is "that actual entity from which each
temporal concrescence receives that initial aim from
which self-causation starts." (Whitehead, Process and
Reality, p. 374.).
[3]The Reality of God, p. 180.
[4]Ibid., pp. 180-181.
[5]Ibid., p. 181.
[6]The Reality of God, p. 181. Ogden continues:
"...just as, in our case, our outer acts of word and
deed may be said to be ours just because or insofar as
they give (or are understood to give) expression to the
inner actions whereby we constitute our existence as
selves." (Ibid.).
[7]Ibid.

Man's capacity of self-consciousness, whereby
he may ascertain meaning can enable him, at least in
principle, to "grasp and express the ultimate truth
about his life."[1] Hence, man's words and deeds always
carry the possibility of not re-presenting or only
fragmentarily re-presenting the divine logos.[2] Thus,
according to Ogden, what is meant by the statement
"God acts in history" is:

> ...primarily that there are certain dis-
> tinctively human words and deeds in which
> his characteristic action as Creator and
> Redeemer is appropriately re-presented or
> revealed...Because through them /i.e. the
> human words and deeds/ nothing less than
> the transcendent action of God himself is
> re-presented, they are also acts of God,
> that is, they are acts of God analogously
> to the way in which our outer acts are our
> acts insofar as they re-present our own
> characteristic decisions as selves or
> persons.[3]

However, if Ogden is to carry out consistently
Bultmann's method of existential interpretation, he
must not only explain what he means by the statement
"God acts in history," but also he must explain what is
meant by the statement "God acts decisively in history
in Jesus Christ."[4] Insofar as Bultmann claims that
God acts decisively only in the history of Jesus Christ,
he is remaining within the very mythological framework

---

[1]Ibid., p. 182.

[2]As Ogden notes: "The existence of the several
historical religions is a constant reminder that this
possibility is in fact actualized; for given the quite
different and conflicting understandings of existence
expressed in these religions, they cannot all be true
and so cannot all be genuine revelations or acts of
God." (Ibid., p. 183.).

[3]Ibid., p. 184.

[4]Note that it was in Bultmann's explanation of
this "event" that Ogden criticized him of returning to
the mythological framework he was attempting to overcome. Cf. The Reality of God, p. 173 and above, pp.
226-228.

which he demands must be overcome. The claim, stresses Ogden, is not that God acts "only in Jesus Christ," but rather that the only God who redeems any history is re-presented in Jesus Christ. To say that any event is the "decisive" act of God "can only mean that, in it, in distinction from all other historical events, the ultimate truth about our existence before God is normatively re-presented or revealed."[1] To say that such an event is decisive is not to say that it is the only event, but rather to assert that it is the event in terms of which all other claims to revelation are to be adjudicated. It is the "revelation of revelations" or the "final revelation."[2] Such final revelation, however does not occur in isolation from man. In order for an event to become a decisive act of God it must be received and understood by someone as having decisive revelatory meaning in his life. The final revelation is not only "a revelation of something," but also "a revelation to somebody,"[3] for, as Ogden stresses, the "'subjective' component in the revelatory correlation is existentially fundamental."[4]

To say that Jesus is the decisive act of God is to affirm that in him is expressed that understanding of human existence which is the ultimate truth about our life before God.[5] His acts witness to the truth that all things have their ground and end solely in God's unbounded love.[6] Moreover, he shows that authentic life is to be found only when one gives himself wholly to the keeping of that love, rejecting all other alleged securities.[7] If this understanding of existence which Jesus reveals is true, if indeed man is

---

[1]The Reality of God, p. 184.

[2]Cf. Tillich, Systematic Theology, Vol. I, pp. 132-137 for a discussion of "final revelation."

[3]The Reality of God, p. 185. Cf. Tillich's discussion of "Event, Fact and Reception," Systematic Theology, Vol. II, pp. 98-99.

[4]The Reality of God, p. 185.

[5]Ibid., pp. 185-186.

[6]Ibid., p. 186.

[7]Ibid., p. 186.

created and redeemed by God's unbounded love, then
Jesus himself _is_ God's decisive act in the way in which
God's action in history has been described above.
Hence, Ogden concludes:

> ...if Jesus is God's decisive act, the
> ultimate truth about our existence--indeed
> about every man's existence--is that we are
> created and redeemed by God's love, and
> that in abandoning ourselves wholly to him
> we realize our true life. It is the nature
> of the Christian faith that it resolves this
> hypothetical statement into a categorical
> confession by affirming its antecedent and
> thus also affirming its consequent.[1]

Ogden summarizes his understanding of the way in
which God's act is to be understood as both transcendent to history and in history when he says:

> the two statements that God's act is, in one
> sense, not a historical act at all, while,
> in another sense, it is precisely the act of
> Jesus' history, mutally require and support
> one another. Just when we take with complete
> seriousness the utter transcendence of God's
> action as sovereign Creator and Redeemer, the
> historical event of Jesus' life and ministry
> is seen to be God's decisive act in human
> history.[2]

In this way, Ogden answers the question: "What sense
does it make to say, 'God acts in history?'"

-----

[1]_Ibid._, pp. 186-187.
[2]_Ibid._, p. 187.

195

F. Critique and Analysis of Ogden's Doctrine of God

In the consideration of the reality of God in the thought of Ogden, it was immediately indicated that Ogden views the problem of God as the central contemporary theological problem.[1] With this contention, he finds ready agreement, not only in John Cobb's theology[2] but also in that of Macquarrie and Herzog, both of whom view the problem of God as the central problem of theology today, and in so doing draw support from Langdon Gilkey, Martin Marty, Dean Peerman, Robert Funk and others.[3] If one agrees that the problem of God is indeed the central theological problem today, then the question immediately arises: "How does one attempt to solve the problem?" As has been shown, Ogden's initial attempt toward solution of the problem consists of his analysis of "the reality of faith," a reality to be affirmed in the midst of a "so-called"[4] atheistic age. That Ogden refers to the "atheistic age" as "so-called" gives some indication of the direction in which his attempted solution is to go--the age is really not atheistic after all--and this, in turn, demands some analysis of Ogden's argument.

In his discussion of "the reality of faith," Ogden's thesis is: "I now wish to claim that for secular man of today, as surely as for any other man,

---

[1]Cf. above, pp. 133-135; Ogden contends: ".... rightly understood, the problem of God is not one problem among others, it is the only problem there is." (The Reality of God, p. 1.).

[2]Cf. above, p. 9; Cobb, A Christian Natural Theology, pp. 14-15.

[3]Cf. above, pp. 1-10; Also, Herzog, Understanding God: The Key Issue in Present-Day Protestant Thought, pp. 11-16, p. 145, note 2.

[4]Cf. Ogden, "The Christian Proclamation of God to Men of the So-Called 'Atheistic Age,'" op. cit., pp. 89-98.

faith in God cannot but be real because it is in the
final analysis unavoidable."[1] Ogden's understanding
of faith and unfaith, by which he intends to establish
that faith in God is unavoidable, has been explicated
above. In this explication it was noted that Ogden's
insistence that faith is unavoidable is accompanied by
his stress that such an insistence does not entail an
affirmation of the impossibility of atheism or unfaith.
To assert the avoidability of faith, however, implies
that those who deny God are somehow mistaken in their
beliefs. Nevertheless, Ogden stresses that the claim
of the avoidability of faith is "the only claim completely consistent with Christian faith in God itself."[2] Elaborating on this contention he remarks:
"By its very character Christian faith so understands
God that everyone must in some sense believe in him
and no one can in every sense deny him."[3] Such an
understanding of God may well be consistent with the
claims of the Christian faith. Yet, several questions
come to mind. What meaning does such a claim have for
secularistic "modern" man, the man to whom Ogden intends to speak? Moreover, does the fact that an assertion of this unavoidability of faith is made by the
Christian man in reference to all other men assure that
the man referred to will affirm such a faith? What
relation does Ogden's broad understanding of faith--of
which "the various 'religions' or 'faiths'...are one
and all expressions"[4] -- have to the specifically
Christian faith? The point is, that Ogden is attempting to speak meaningfully to "the modern, secular man"
whose tendency is to deny, not only the validity or
meaningfulness of the Christian faith, but also the
meaningfulness of faith in God. Hence, the mere
assertion that Christian faith so understands God that
everyone must in some sense believe in him and no one
can in every sense deny him can hardly serve to establish dialogue with Ogden's "modern man."

---

[1]The Reality of God, p. 21.
[2]Ibid.
[3]Ibid.; Cf. above, p. 161.
[4]Ibid., p. 33.

Yet, as has been shown, Ogden still attempts to
retain a place for unfaith or atheism. The question
is, however, does he succeed in his attempt? As has
been noted above, Ogden understands unfaith to
occur at two levels. First, is the "godlessness of
the heart," the deepest level of unfaith, which is the
existential denial of God when one exists as a godless
man.[1] The second level of unfaith, Ogden designates
as "godlessness of the mind." This level of atheism
is evidenced by one's self-conscious and reflective
denial of the reality of God. Ogden notes that one
may be an atheist in either one or both of these
senses. Yet, he contends, that neither of these levels
or both together constitute a godlessness which is completely negative and empty. As Ogden understands
atheism it may include a denial of God with the mind
accompanied by an affirmation of him existentially, or
a denial of God existentially accompanied by an intellectual affirmation of his reality. Yet, such unfaith
or atheism, contends Ogden, is never the complete absence of faith in God. Rather, it is "the presence
of faith in a deficient or distorted mode."[2] Hence,
Ogden's admission of unfaith is not an understanding of
unfaith as the complete opposite of faith, not unfaith
as the negative or absence of faith. His understanding
of unfaith is merely faith exhibited in a distorted or
fragmentary way. By unfaith he means merely a defi-
ciency of faith, or an idolatrous faith, a faith directed toward some nondivine thing or a faith which
regards some nondivine as having unique significance as
a symbol of the divine, so that one's loyalty is directed between God and the nondivine thing. Ogden
asserts, therefore, that even the atheist has faith in
some sense. For Ogden there is no absolute unfaith.
Yet, one wonders just what is the meaning of an unfaith which is not really unfaith. Ogden, it will be
remembered, is attempting to speak to "modern secular
man." If he is to do so, he must take secular man's
denial of faith in God more seriously. Merely to define unfaith as distorted faith either does not speak
to those who consider themselves to be denying faith,

---

[1]Cf. above, pp. 160-162; The Reality of God, p.
23.

[2]The Reality of God, p. 23.

199

or else the definition of faith must be considered in order to ascertain just what it means. This is especially necessary since Ogden admits no real polar contrary in contrast to which one could understand faith.

Ogden's understanding of faith has been delineated above, therefore, it is not necessary to describe it again in detail. At this point, a brief recapitulation of his understanding of faith will be considered in order to raise some questions regarding it. For Ogden, faith is exemplified in "our basic confidence in the abiding worth of our life."[1] In stressing that any adequate theological scheme must be warranted by man's common experience, Ogden asserts that the one thing which all men share today is an "affirmation of life here and now in the world in all its aspects and in its proper autonomy and significance."[2] As has been shown, Ogden asserts that all men exemplify this confidence, and that "what is properly meant by the word 'God'"[3] has an "essential connection" with this confidence. Ogden has argued that even the atheist has such confidence in the abiding worth of life, and insofar as he does, he can be said to have faith in God. Ogden's argument has already been delineated above, but it may be summarized as follows: Man, by the very fact that he is, makes decisions. A choice between alternatives entails an assertion of meaning and value regarding the choice made. An affirmation of meaning and value in life situations is an affirmation of confidence or faith in life's abiding meaning and worth. This confidence must have a ground. The ground of this confidence is properly what one means when one speaks of God. Therefore, all men somehow have faith in God, or, faith in God is somehow real for all men.[4]

To what extent Ogden pushes his contention that any human decision presupposes "a basic confidence in the abiding worth of our life"[5] is exemplified by his treatment of Albert Camus' understanding of the absurd

---

[1]The Reality of God, p. 37; Cf. above, p. 178.
[2]The Reality of God, p. 20.
[3]Ibid., p. 37.
[4]Cf. above, pp. 158-182.
[5]The Reality of God, p. 37.

hero. Of those who deny the reality of God--and Camus
is an example whom Ogden considers--Ogden notes that
"the essential inadequacy of the position is nothing
less than outright antinomy or contradiction."[1] His
understanding of this antinomy or self-contradiction is
noted when he says:

> If all our moral thought and action rest on
> an underlying confidence in the final meaning
> of life, then we are implicitly affirming such
> confidence, together with its transcendent
> ground in all that we think and do. Therefore,
> it is logically impossible utterly to deny
> this ground of confidence without explicitly
> contradicting the implications of morality
> itself.[2]

Yet, in this critique, Ogden has made a subtle but
important change in the wording of his conditional
clause. Earlier, he asserted that the one thing which
all men share today is an "affirmation of life here
and now in the world in all its aspects."[3] One could
readily agree with Ogden at this point, even as Camus
does. However, when he discusses this common element,
he shifts from speaking exclusively of "life here and
now in the world" and talks rather of "basic confidence
in the abiding worth of life" or, as in his conditional
clause quoted above, he speaks of "the final meaning
of life."[4]

Admittedly Camus does have a place in his thought
for confidence and hope, but such is not final and
abiding, but rather "here and now in the world" or
"nowhere."[5] Numerous passages throughout Camus's work

---

[1]Ibid., p. 40.

[2]Ibid., p. 40.

[3]Ibid., p. 20; Cf. above, p. 242.

[4]Ibid., p. 40.

[5]As Thomas Hanna sums up Camus's thought: "For
the honest man, a reality, no matter how bitter, can
never be traded for an illusion or hope, no matter how
redemptive." (Hanna, The Lyrical Existentialists.
New York: Atheneum, 1962, p. 263.).

confirm this. Consider only several examples. "Not
to believe in the profound meaning of things belongs to
the absurd man."[1] "Yes, man is his own end. And he is
his only end. If he aims to do something, it is in
this life."[2] "The rebel...demonstrates that in reality, he prefers the 'We are' to the 'We shall be.'"[3]
"Man is mortal, that may be; but let us die resisting;
and if our lot is complete annihilation, let us not
behave in such a way that it seems justice!"[4] These
examples point to the fact that Camus does assert some
meaning and hope, but only in a preliminary fashion,
only in this life. There is no hope for final, abiding
meaning. His stance is well described in the title of
an essay summarizing his philosophy: "The World of the
Man Condemned To Death."[5] That he at no point considers the condemnation to be revoked or overcome is
realized when he says: "I don't know whether this
world has a meaning that transcends it. But I know
that I do not know that meaning and that it is impossible for me just now to know it. What can a meaning
outside my condition mean to me? I can understand
only in human terms."[6]

The stance is reinforced by his criticism of the
existentialist philosophers.[7] Camus understands that
the absurd results "from the conflict between our

---

[1]Albert Camus, The Myth of Sisyphus and Other Essays. (Justin O'Brien, trans.). New York: Vintage
Books, 1955, p. 54.

[2]Camus, The Myth of Sisyphus, p. 65.

[3]Camus, The Rebel: An Essay on Man in Revolt.
(Anthony Bower, trans.). New York: Vintage Books,
1956, p. 282.

[4]Camus, Resistance, Rebellion, and Death. (Justin
O'Brien, trans.). New York: Alfred A. Knopf, 1961,
p. 26.

[5]Rachel Bespaloff, "The World of Man Condemned to
Death," Camus: A Collection of Critical Essays.
(Germaine Bree, ed.). Englewood Cliffs, New Jersey:
Prentice-Hall, Inc., 1962, p. 92.

[6]Camus, The Myth of Sisyphus, p. 38.

[7]Cf. Thomas Hanna's discussion of Camus's relation
to existentialism in the introduction to his work on
Camus: The Thought and Art of Albert Camus. Chicago:

awareness of death and our desire for eternity, from
the clash between our demand for explanation and the
essential mystery of all existence."[1] He notes that
the existentialist philosophers have realized the
absurdity which links man and the world, but he stresses that "all of them without exception suggest escape."[2] He rejects Chestov's "stopgap" theory of God
which views God as functioning to solve problems which
for man are insoluable,[3] while at the same time he asserts that Jasper's affirmation of transcendence is an
unwarranted leap.[4] In contrast to these two views
Camus maintains that one must begin with what he experiences and remain within this arena, living "without
appeal" to anything beyond human experience. Hence,
he says, "The leap in all its forms, rushing into the
divine or the eternal, surrendering to the illusions
of the everyday or of the idea--all these screens
hide the absurd."[5]

Thomas Hanna sums up the courses of action which
Camus sees available to the one who admits the certainty of the absurd. He says:

> There are two courses of action: We may escape
> this certainty, whether through suicide, through
> this 'leap' or through a tailor made world of
> hope; or we may take upon ourselves the agoniz-
> ing burden of the Absurd in which we unlearn

Henry Regnery Company, Gateway Editions, 1958, pp.
xv-xxi.

[1]Philip Thody, Albert Camus. London: Hamish
Hamilton, 1957, p. 4; Cf. also, The Myth of Sisyphus,
pp. 3-37; The Rebel, pp. 13-25.

[2]The Myth of Sisyphus, p. 24.

[3]Ibid., p. 25. Camus notes that Chestov's philosophy "is altogether summed up" in the following
Chestovian remark: "The only true solution is precisely where human judgment sees no solution. Otherwise, what need would we have of God? We turn toward
God only to obtain the impossible. As for the possible, men suffice." (The Myth of Sisyphus, p. 25.).

[4]Ibid., pp. 24-25.

[5]Ibid., p. 67.

to hope, cling to our lucidity, and remain
in continual revolt against the world.[1]

This summary of Camus's understanding of the courses of
action open to "man in the world condemned to death" is
worthy of consideration at this point because it indicates the point at which Camus would criticize Ogden
while at the same time, it serves to indicate the point
at which Ogden misinterprets Camus and attributes to
Camus what Camus would consider an unwarranted leap.
Camus would probably consider Ogden's position to be a
leap to "a tailor made world of hope," hence involving
what Camus calls "philosophical suicide."[2] But the
important consideration is Ogden's criticism of Camus.
His criticism of Camus will be quoted in full because
it contains the same questionable presupposition that
his argument that "all men somehow have faith in God"
contains. Ogden argues:

> According to Camus, the whole character of
> human life is determined by its essential
> absurdity, by the unclosable gap between
> our demand for rationality, practical as
> well as theoretical and 'the unreasonable
> silence of the world.' Thus we must live
> without any guarantee that our own actions
> or the human enterprise as such are finally
> worth while. Nevertheless, Camus insists
> that the only fitting response to this
> absurdity is heroic resistance against it,
> which includes an absolute lucidity about
> our condition, together with an affirmation
> of our life in spite of its ultimate mean-
> inglessness. Indeed, in Camus' later writings,
> this response of resistance comes to embrace
> a profoundly humanistic ethic of love and
> concern for all mankind. He exhorts us
> time again to throw ourselves into the strug-
> gle for man against everything in nature, or
> history that would impair his unforfeitable
> dignity.

---

[1]Hanna, The Thought and Art of Albert Camus, p.
30.

[2]The Myth of Sisyphus, pp. 21-37.

But, intriguing as this notion of the absurd hero doubtless is, it can hardly define a real possibility, whether for thought or for existential choice. If all our actions are in principle absurd, the act of heroically resisting their absurdity must also be absurd. It, too, is _ex_ _hypothesi_ a totally meaningless response and can be supposed not a bit more fitting than the various attempts to flee from absurdity that Camus so unsparingly condemns. Or, to take the other side of the dilemma, insofar as resistance for the sake of man _is_ a meaningful act—is somehow fitting as the alternatives to it are not—the absurdity of our existence cannot be unrelieved as was originally alleged.[1]

Ogden observes in a footnote that a collection of Camus's shorter writings, _Resistance_, _Rebellion_, _and_ _Death_, is a good example of Camus's "profoundly humanistic ethic of love and concern for all mankind."[2] Ogden views this ethic as an example of Camus's confidence in the final or abiding worth of life, and therefore conformable to his argument that Camus, too, evidences the faith in the abiding worth of existence which—by Ogden's definition—means faith in God. If such is to be true, Ogden, while ignoring the import of the title _Resistance_, _Rebellion_, _and Death_, must also ignore such statements within the work itself as: "Man is mortal. That may be; but let us die resisting; and if our lot is complete annihilation, let us not behave in such a way that it seems justice."[3]

As for me, I feel rather as Augustine did before becoming a Christian when he said: 'I tried to find the source of evil and I got nowhere.' But it is also true that I, and a few others, know what must be done, if not to reduce evil, at least not to add to it. Perhaps we cannot prevent this world from being a world in which children are tortured. But we can reduce the number of tortured children.[4]

---

[1]The _Reality_ of _God_, pp. 41-42.
[2]_Ibid._, p. 67, footnote 67.
[3]Camus, _Resistance_, _Rebellion_ _and Death_, p. 26.
[4]Camus, _Resistance_, _Rebellion_ _and Death_, p. 73.

From The Myth of Sisyphus through his latest
writings, Camus stresses that what value is to be
realized is to be realized in the present. Even the
rebel does not escape the condemnation of death. Nor
does he trade the "we are" for the "we shall be." One
can trace the development of Camus's thought from the
realization of the absurdist position--i.e. man condemned to death without any appeal beyond his experience to overcome the finality of death--to the position of man-in-revolt and the present value entailed
if the position is carried to its conclusion. This is
not to imply that Camus abandons the absurdist position
and turns to a different position, that of revolt; but
it does mean that Camus's man moves from the absurdist
position as a starting point to the position of man-
in-revolt, affirming life here and now even though he
knows that he is condemned to death. Not only does
his early literature--The Myth of Sisyphus, The
Stranger,[1] The Misunderstanding,[2] and Caligula[3]--expli-
cate the absurdist position, but also his later literature, the literature of revolt--The Plague,[4] The State
of Seige,[5] The Just Assassins,[6] and The Fall.[7] Exemplary of this contention is the fact that The Fall
which explicates a position much like that of the
Christian understanding of "the fall," nevertheless,
ends on a note--if not of despair--at least on that of
seeing no hope for assuaging the guilt experienced by
all men. The portrait of the central character of the
novel, Jean-Baptiste Clamence, is a portrait of "fal-
len man" and it is an "image of all and of no one."[8]

---

[1]Camus, The Stranger. New York: Vintage Books,
1942.

[2]Camus, "The Misunderstanding," in Caligula and
Three Other Plays. New York: Vintage Books, 1958,
pp. 75-134.

[3]Camus, Caligula and Three Other Plays, pp. 1-75.

[4]Camus, The Plague. New York: The Modern Library, 1948.

[5]Camus, "The State of Siege," Caligula and Three
Other Plays, pp. 135-232.

[6]Camus, "The Just Assassins," Ibid., pp. 233-302.

[7]Camus, The Fall. New York: Vintage Books, 1956.

[8]Ibid., p. 139.

This is a new theme in Camus's thought. Previously, he had been interested to assert the basic innocence of man. In The Stranger he depicts man struggling against an unjust legal and social order, and dying in his struggle. In The Plague innocent man struggles against the horror of natural evil. Again, the struggle is to no avail, as revealed by the words of Dr. Rieux to Father Paneloux on the occasion of a child's death of the plague: "Ah! That child, anyhow, was innocent, and you know it as well as I do!...No, Father. I've a very different idea of love. And until my dying day I shall refuse to love a scheme of things in which children are put to torture."[1] In The State of Siege man struggles against the enslavement of a totalitarian regime. But in The Fall, the innocence of man is questioned openly. Camus well shows that all men are guilty. Remaining consistent with his philosophy of absurdity and revolt, he does not absolutize guilt or innocence, but maintains both. Nor does he bring in something from outside man's experience to alleviate the guilt. Jean-Baptiste Clamence attempts to lessen his own guilt by confessing in such a way that all others who hear him will thereby realize their own guilt. The question nevertheless remains: how is one's guilt lessened merely by making others realize their guilt? Camus asserts the guilt of all men, but he posits no hope for overcoming such guilt. If one attempted to do so, Camus--even here in his later writings--would respond in the words in which Thomas Hanna has summed up Camus's thought: "For the honest man, a reality, no matter how bitter, can never be traded for an illusion or hope, no matter how redemptive."[2] Even the man who realizes his guilt or who revolts is still "in a campaign in which he is defeated in advance."[3] This, too, is evidenced in Camus's later writings, when, in the closing pages of The Plague, Camus writes of two lovers who were reunited after having been separated by the long months of the plague: "They knew now that if there is one thing one can always yearn for and sometimes attain, it is human love."[4] But Camus immediately continues: "But for

---

[1]Camus, The Plague, pp. 196-197.
[2]Thomas Hanna, The Lyrical Existentialists, p. 263.
[3]Camus, The Myth of Sisyphus, p. 68.
[4]Camus, The Plague, p. 271.

those others who aspired beyond and above the human individual toward something they could not even imagine, there had been no answer."[1]

The preceding brief description of Camus's position indicates that whatever confidence Camus expresses is of a preliminary sort and not one which would entail an assertion in the 'final,' 'abiding' or ultimate' worth of man's existence which Ogden asserts as necessary and universal. For Camus, the very fact that there is no final or abiding meaning or hope frees man to live in the present, the arena in which whatever knowledge there is is to be utilized. That the assertion of final, abiding, and ultimate meaning is absent from Camus's later work is evidenced by a statement from the very work which Ogden uses as exemplary of Camus's assertion of final confidence. Camus says: "If Christianity is pessimistic as to man, it is optimistic as to human destiny. Well, I can say that, pessimistic as to human destiny, I am optimistic as to man."[2]

---

[1] Ibid.

[2] Camus, *Resistance, Rebellion, and Death*, p. 73. Yet, even this "optimism as to man" must be viewed in the light of two other previously mentioned assertions from *Resistance, Rebellion, and Death*: "Man is mortal. That may be; but let us die resisting; and if our lot is complete annihilation, let us not behave in such a way that it seems justice." (p. 26.). "As for me, I feel rather as Augustine did before becoming a Christian when he said: 'I tried to find the source of evil and I got nowhere.' But it is also true that I, and a few others, know what must be done, if not to reduce evil, at least not to add to it. Perhaps we cannot prevent this world from being a world in which children are tortured. But we can reduce the number of tortured children." (p. 73.). On the page preceding this one, Camus's position is indicated when, in answering the question: "What can Christians do for us?," he says: "I believe...that M. Gabriel Marcel would be well advised to leave alone certain forms of thought that fascinate him and lead him astray....What M. Marcel wants is to defend absolute values, such as morality and man's divine truth, when the things that should be defended are the few provisional values..." (*Resistance, Rebellion, and Death*, p. 72.).

208

All of this is considered not to say that Camus's position is an adequate analysis of existence while Ogden's is not. But it is to assert, however, that Ogden's criticism of Camus is unwarranted, for Camus does not abandon his original position. He knows that the rebel's lot is death, just as is the lot of the one who chooses resignation. Ogden, however, maintains that Camus's stance is invalid, and he does so on the grounds of a questionable presupposition. Ogden presupposes that any decision between alternatives is a decision asserting the final, abiding and ultimate value of the alternative chosen. It may well be that any choice among alternatives affirms the greater value of the alternative chosen, but such does not entail an assertion of ultimate worth regarding the alternative affirmed--even if one takes the position, as Ogden does, that one cannot "rationally decide" the nullity of his choices.[1] Ogden argues that even for one to decide to commit suicide is an affirmation of the faith or confidence in the final worth of his decision,

[1]Of Ogden's position, Delwin Brown observes: "But that one cannot 'rationally decide' his own actions to be ultimately pointless does not imply 'that moral thought and action are (logically or) existentially possible only because their roots reach down into an underlying confidence in the abiding worth of life.' Even if reality in toto were deemed meaningless, one could still arbitrarily erect spheres of discourse with arbitrarily selected assumptions and rules. Ethics might be so regarded. 'Though life is meaningless,' one might say, 'I now decide that one should be moral and that being moral means following the rules I arbitrarily decide upon.' This same ethical 'game' can be participated in by all who agree to the same rules, and conversations about what actions are implied in these rules are meaningful within the confines of the game. No problem arises so long as the rules are accepted and no one asks 'Why should I be moral?' Yet even if this limiting question were asked, one would not logically be driven to religion because the entire affair may be viewed as an arbitrary construct outside of which all is objectively meaningless, i.e. it has no rational ground in objective reality. Given its own assumptions, this account of ethics is both complete and self-consistent. (Delwin Brown, "God's Reality and Life's Meaning: A Critique of Schubert Ogden," Encounter, Vol. 28, Summer 1967, pp. 259-260.

since the one deciding, by choosing death over life
affirms the significance and meaning of death.[1] Yet,
Ogden fails to realize that man does not decide to
have existence, but rather finds himself already in
existence, an existence which carries with it the necessity of deciding within a limited context. Man
finds himself in existence. He is thereby faced to
make decisions, often with no choice not to choose.
He finds himself in the midst of life, but he did not
choose to be so. Ogden's assumption that any decision
is an affirmation of confidence in the final worth of
life, that any decision entails an evaluative assertion
of the final significance of the alternative chosen
fails to account for the fact that were man given the
choice not to choose, he may in fact not choose. That
man is forced to make decisions in the context of a
life in which he finds himself without having chosen
life, does not entail that any decision-making whatsoever affirms one's "ineradicable confidence in the
final worth of our existence."[2] Camus, Ogden to the
contrary, represents the one instance requisite to
challenge adequately Ogden's contention of the univer-
sality of such a confidence.

Closely connected with the problem which arises
with Ogden's transformation of the common denominator
of human existence from that of "affirmation of life
here and now" to "basic confidence in the abiding
worth of life," is his acceptance of Toulmin's definition of religion on the one hand coupled with a rejection of Hick's concept of "eschatological verification"
on the other.

As has been noted, Ogden relies heavily upon
Toulmin's description of the function of religion.
Ogden points out that for Toulmin: "The purpose of
'religion'...and thus of the kind of language and reasoning that can be called 'religious' or 'theological,'
is to give answers to the questions that naturally
arise at the limits of man's activities as moral actor

----

[1]By choosing death, one could, of course, be affirming the significance of his decision; yet, this
hardly seems identical with affirming "an underlying
confidence in the abiding worth of life" (Cf. The
Reality of God, pp. 37-38) of which Ogden speaks so
much.
    [2]The Reality of God, p. 37.

and scientific knower."[1] Agreeing with Toulmin that
religion does indeed function to give answers to
questions which arise at the limits of man's activities, he asserts, with Toulmin, that a good religious
answer will involve the following:

> a good religious answer 'will give us a re-
> assurance which will not be disappointed;
> will allay our fear of "the eternity before
> and behind the brief span" of our lives,
> and "of the infinite immensity" of space;
> will provide comfort in the face of distress;
> and will answer our questions in a way which
> will not seem in retrospect to have missed
> their point.'[2]

Moreover, Ogden agrees with Toulmin's analysis of the
function of religion, which is:

> 'Over the matters of fact which are not to
> be "explained" scientifically (like the
> deaths on their birthdays of three children
> in one family), the function of religion
> is to help us to resign ourselves to them--
> and so feel like accepting them. Likewise,
> over matters of duty which are not to be
> justified further in ethical terms, it is
> for religion to help us embrace them--and
> so feel like accepting them'[3]

Ogden's acceptance of Toulmin's description of
"a good religious answer" involves several problems
relative to his own attempt to explicate an adequate
theology. For Ogden, an adequate theology must be both
meaningful, warranted by man's common experience, and
logically consistent. The first problem has to do with
the incompatibility of man's commom experience of affirmation of life here and now and Ogden's understanding of the role of resignation, acceptance, and "in
retrospect" in religion. The one thing which all men
have in common, and therefore the one thing to which

---

[1]Ibid., p. 30.

[2]Ibid., p. 32; Cf. above p. 171; also, Toulmin,
An Examination of the Place of Reason in Ethics, pp.
212-213.

[3]The Reality of God, p. 31; Cf. above, p. 170.

theology must be relevant, according to Ogden, is man's "affirmation of life here and now in the world in all its aspects and in its proper autonomy."[1] Yet, his understanding of "a good religious answer" seems to have a place neither for "affirmation" nor for the "here and now." Instead of affirmation, he speaks in terms of acceptance of things which one cannot understand; instead of the "here and now" he speaks in terms of the religious answers "which will not seem in retrospect to have missed their point."[2] Ogden's modern man" who affirms life "here and now in the world" would be more apt to accept Camus's philosophy of rebellion than Ogden's religion of acceptance and resignation. Moreover, his idea of a good religious answer as being one "which will not seem in retrospect to have missed the point" admits the possibility of entertaining "eschatological verification," a "device" which Ogden himself holds as "untenable."[3]

A second problem in Ogden's understanding of religion, a problem which is crucial in a doctrine of God, is his understanding of religion as functioning merely to answer "limiting" questions, questions which cannot be answered scientifically or ethically. Ogden means to affirm God in the midst of life, in the here and now, just as man affirms life here and now. But to reserve the function of religion to that of answering man's questions which cannot be answered scientifically or ethically is to view the God whom men worship as functioning only in those areas. In short, the stopgap God, the deus ex machina, is introduced in this definition of religion, the Chestovian God whom Camus has rejected.[4] How does such a God function any

---

[1]The Reality of God, p. 20.

[2]Ibid., p. 32.

[3]Ibid., p. 76.

[4]Cf. Camus, The Myth of Sisyphus in which Camus rejects Chestov's contention that "The only true solution is precisely where human judgment sees no solution. Otherwise, what need would we have of God? We turn to God only to obtain the impossible. /Like, for example, "the deaths on their birthdays of three children in one family," of which Ogden speaks? Cf. above, p. 256; The Reality of God, p. 31./ As for the possible, men suffice." (The Myth of Sisyphus, p. 25).

differently from the way in which Ogden views the
function of the God of classical theism, the God whom
Ogden attempts to reject? Ogden does not mean to affirm such a concept of God. Like Bonhoeffer, Ogden
wants to speak of God's activity in the midst of life,
at life's center. He would probably say with Bonhoeffer that:

> We are to find God in what we know, not in
> what we do not know; God wants us to real-
> ize his presence not in unsolved problems,
> but in those that are solved. That is true
> of the relationship between God and scientific
> knowledge, but it is also true of the wider
> human problems of death, suffering and guilt
> ....God is no stop-gap; he must be recognized
> at the center of life, not when we are at the
> end of our resources; it is his will to be
> recognized in life, and not only when death
> comes; in health and vigour, and not only in
> suffering; in our activities, and not only
> in sin.[1]

Ogden would probably agree with these words from the
pen of Bonhoeffer, for both his doctrine of God and
that of Cobb's, developed from a Whiteheadian-Hartshornean base, allow a philosophical explication of a
doctrine of God who acts in the midst of life, at life's
center. Ogden's description of the function of religion is incompatible with his philosophical stance insofar as it is in danger of pushing God to the periph-
ery only to be called upon as a "filler" for man's lack
of knowledge.

Some clarification would be helpful with regard
to the way in which Ogden understands the compatibility
of three related strands of his thought, namely, his
understanding of faith, his definition of theology, and
his demand that theology must be logically consistent.
On the one hand, Ogden's broad definition of faith, as
referred to above, defined faith as "our ineradicable
confidence in the final worth of our existence."[2]

---

[1]Dietrich Bonhoeffer, Letters and Papers from
Prison. (Revised edition, Eberhard Bethge, ed.). New
York: The Macmillan Company, 1967, p. 164.
  [2]The Reality of God, p. 37.

Such "confidence" is really faith in God, for "God" is
the word the primary function of which is to refer to
the objective ground in reality of this ineradicable
confidence.[1] On the other hand, Ogden's definition of
theology requires that what he means by theology be
understood as specifically Christian theology. In his
definition[2] of "theological thinking and speaking" he
asserts that: "theological thinking and speaking are
a more or less distinguishable type or level of thinking and speaking about God as apprehended through the
witness of faith of Jesus Christ."[3] With regard to
these understandings respectively of faith and theology, some clarification is necessary. Ogden understands any faith in the final worth of life to have
as its referent what is properly meant by the word
"God." Yet, he asserts that his proposition--that "all
theological thought and speech are thought and speech
having the God of Jesus Christ as their object or referent"--is not convertible. One could take this to
mean that not all talk about God is theological, but
only that talk about God as known through Jesus Christ.
Hence, Ogden seems to be saying that all faith is somehow faith in God, while not all God-talk is theological. On the one hand, one could therefore ask Ogden
for some clarification regarding the relation of his
understanding of faith in the general sense to what
could be understood as specifically Christian faith, in
the sense, for example, of Paul's understanding of
faith in the God of Jesus Christ as "obedience," "confession," "hope," "fear," and "confidence."[4] On the

---

[1]Ibid.

[2]Of his definition, Ogden observes: "I propose
the following preliminary definition of how 'thinking'
and 'speaking' are to be taken when used in connection
with the undertaking properly designated 'theology.'
I assume, naturally, that the sense of the word 'theology' appropriate here is not the generic sense with
which we might properly use it in other contexts, but
the specific sense explicitly conveyed by the words
'Christian theology.'" (The Reality of God, p. 72.).

[3]The Reality of God, p. 72.

[4]Cf. Bultmann, Theology of the New Testament, Vol.
II, for a phenomenological description of Paul's understanding of faith as obedience, confession, hope,
fear and confidence, pp. 314, 317, 319, 320, and 322-
323, respectively.

other hand, one could inquire of Ogden--since he demands that theology be philosophically sound and logically consistent--regarding the philosophical justification for asserting that all theological thinking and
speaking is to be understood as "thinking and speaking
about God as apprehended through the witness of faith
of Jesus Christ." Can one justify philosophically that
only that speaking of God which is "apprehended through
the witness of faith of Jesus Christ" is to be considered to be "theology?"

That the problem of the indispensability of the
witness of Christ is crucial for Ogden's understanding
of theology is to be seen in his criticism of Bultmann's program of demythologization. Ogden contends
that Bultmann does not carry out his existentialist
interpretation,[1] and hence his demythologization consistently.[2] The point at which Bultmann fails, according to Ogden, is his claim "that authentic human existence is factually possible solely in consequence of
God's unique act in Jesus Christ."[3] Ogden stresses
that the "solely in consequence of God's unique act in
Jesus Christ" remains mythological insofar as the "only
in Jesus Christ" is retained. Ogden contends, therefore, that if the existentialist interpretation is to
be maintained one must affirm "not that God acts to
redeem only in the history of Jesus and in no other
history, but that the only God who redeems any history
--although he in fact redeems every history--is the
God whose redemptive action is decisively re-presented
in the word that Jesus speaks and is."[4] This seems
to carry thoroughly the existentialist interpretaion
which Bultmann and Ogden demand. Yet, Ogden does not
escape the pitfall which he sees in Bultmann's thought,
for when he interprets what he means by "decisive act
of God," he says: "to say of any historical event that

---

[1]Ogden also criticizes Bultmann for the "one-
sidedly existentialist character" (Cf. above, p. 225;)
of his solution, but this particular criticism is not
under consideration at this point.

[2]The Reality of God, p. 170; Cf. above, p. 227.

[3]Ibid., p. 173; Cf. above, p. 227.

[4]Ibid.; Cf. above, p. 227.

it is the 'decisive' act of God can only mean that,
in it, in distinction from all other historical events,
the ultimate truth about our existence before God is
normatively re-presented or revealed."[1] However, to
say that the act of God in Jesus Christ "in distinction
from all other events" contains the ultimate normative
truth about our existence is once more to assert the
"only in Jesus Christ" which Ogden claims is the point
at which Bultmann fails to carry out consistently his
existentialist interpretation.

It is, of course, permissable for a Christian
theologian to affirm his stance in faith and to say
that the only God who redeems history has acted decisively in Jesus Christ, which act becomes the criterion
by which all other purported revelations of God are
adjudicated. But on what philosophical grounds can
such a claim be made? The Whiteheadian-Hartshornean
philosophy offers excellent possibilities for explicating the possibility of God's acting uniquely in a
particular entity. Hence, this philosophy can be an
important aid in helping Christian theology to understand its faith relative to the doctrine of the Incarnation as well as the doctrine of God.[2] Yet, Ogden
has ceased to be a philosopher and has become strictly
speaking a Christian theologian when he begins to affirm that the history of Jesus Christ is the "final"
revelation,[3] the criterion by which all other revela-

---

[1]Cf. Ogden. "How Does God Function in Human
Life," op. cit.; Ogden, "What Sense Does It Make To
Say, 'God Acts In History,'" op. cit.; Cobb, "A
Whiteheadian Christology," (unpublished); Cobb, "The
Finality of Christ in a Whiteheadian Perspective,"
op. cit.

[2]For example, the Incarnation may be viewed from
a Whiteheadian standpoint as Jesus' accepting the possibility of revealing God's love to man; while the
crucifixion may be seen as man's negative prehension
of such a possibility; and the Resurrection the working of God's patience in offering another possibility
of love.

[3]Ogden utilizes the Tillichian sense of the word
"final." For Tillich "final" means "last" only in the
sense of "the last genuine revelation." "But final
revelation means more," asserts Tillich, "than the last
genuine revelation. It means the decisive, fulfilling,

216

tions are to be adjudicated. Odgen can, with the
philosophical tools at his disposal, delineate a doctrine of God in relation to God's action in Jesus
Christ which is logically consistent and greatly bene-
ficial to one's attempt to understand the Christian
faith. One can even elaborate philosophically, as
both Ogden and Cobb do, how God's action in Jesus
Christ is to be considered unique. Yet, whether one
can maintain--on philosophical grounds alone--that the
purported revelations of God are to be ascertained
still remains in abeyance, for Ogden--merely on the
basis of his philosophical explication--has not accomplished this. Just as Whitehead maintained that the
transition from the attempt to explicate philosophical
first principles to the grasping of these principles
required an "imaginative leap,"[1] so also must the
Christian theologian remain aware of the fact that
while the Christ event is not unknowable, is capable of
being captured "by a flash of insight," nevertheless,
"an imaginative leap" is required between systematic
description and existential appropriation. What
Whitehead has said of philosophical attempts to formulate metaphysical first principles is applicable also
to the theologian's attempt to delineate his understanding of the Christ-event: "Words and phrases must
be stretched towards a generality foreign to their
ordinary usage; and however such elements of language
be stabilized as technicalities, they remain metaphors
mutely appealing for an imaginative leap."[2]

---

unsurpassable revelation, that which is the criterion
of all the others." And the basic criterion of this
final revelation is: "a revelation is final if it
has the power of negating itself without losing itself." (Tillich, Systematic Theology, Vol. I., pp.
132-133.).

[1]In Whitehead's words: "Philosophers can never
hope finally to formulate these metaphysical first
principles. Weakness of insight and deficiencies of
language stand in the way inexorably. Words and
phrases must be stretched towards a generality foreign
to their ordinary usage; and however such elements of
language be stabilized as technicalities, they remain
metaphors mutely appealing for an imaginative leap.
"There is no first principle which is in itself
unknowable, not to be captured by a flash of insight."
(Whitehead, Process and Reality, p. 6.).

[2]Whitehead, Process and Reality, p. 6.

III.   Conclusion: The Theologies of Cobb
       and Ogden as Complementary

     The mere fact that any two theologians both enter-
tain the affirmation that the doctrine of God is the
central theological problem in contemporary theology
is not enough--in and of itself--to link these two
theologians as allies in the theological enterprise.
One only needs to glance at the work of such men as
van Buren, Hamilton, and Altizer on the one hand, and
Ogden, Cobb, Gilkey, and Macquarrie on the other hand
to realize this. Yet, the fact that both Ogden and
Cobb view the central problem of contemporary theology
to be that of the doctrine of God, the problem of the
reality of God, does serve as an initial point of
contact for the two theologians. In the case of Ogden
and Cobb, however, this initial point of contact--as
should well be evidenced by now--is accompanied by
other points of similarity which make their total
endeavors highly compatible. Not only does the fact
that the two theologians are favorably oriented toward
philosophical theology provide another link, but, what
is more, both Ogden and Cobb have a deep appreciation
for and reliance upon the philosophies of Whitehead
and Hartshorne. With this realization, one comes to
the point which indicates that the philosophical-theological attempts of both Cobb and Ogden will be highly
compatible throughout, and this point of compatibility
is at the point of the primary demand of the Whiteheadian doctrine of God.

     The primary demand which Whitehead makes of any
adequate doctrine of God is summed up in the following:
"God is not to be treated as an exception to all metaphysical principles, invoked to save their collapse.
He is their chief exemplification."[1] The acceptance of
this principle pervades all attempts on the part of
both men in their development of a doctrine of God that
is philosophically responsible and existentially acceptable. Cobb's primary attempt, as has been shown,
is that of developing a doctrine of God based on the
thought of Whitehead. In fact, he says of most of his

---

[1]Whitehead, Process and Reality, p. 521.

work: "I have identified myself fully with the position I have expounded on Whitehead's authority...Whitehead's philosophical reasons for affirming God and his attempt to show that God is not an exception to all the categories appear to me philosophically reasonable and even necessary."[1] Moreover, when Cobb begins to develop his own Whiteheadian doctrine of God, he does not mitigate or alter the Whiteheadian demand, but rather attempts to apply the principles with more rigor than did even Whitehead himself. He says of his approach: "I undertake to develop a doctrine of God more coherent with Whitehead's general cosmology and metaphysics than are some aspects of his own doctrine."[2] Then, as Cobb develops his doctrine of God, he recalls: "The attempt is to explain the way in which God is related to actual occasions, eternal objects and creativity in such a way that at no point do we attribute to him a mode of being or relation inexplicable in terms of the principles operative elsewhere in the system."[3] Hence, pervasive throughout Cobb's theology is the application of the Whiteheadian principle that God is not to be treated as an exception to all metaphysical principles, but as their chief exemplification.

The same primary demand is characteristic of Ogden's overall attempt to develop a neoclassical doctrine of God. His rejection of the classical doctrine of God as well as the traditional analogia entis is

---

[1]Cobb, A Christian Natural Theology, p. 176.

[2]Ibid. Of Cobb's dependence on Whitehead at this point Langdon Gilkey observes: "The dependence of the philosophical theology (a better term, it seems to me, than natural theology for what is presented to us) outlined in this book on Whitehead's system cannot be overemphasized. Whenever Cobb seeks, as he frequently does, to criticize and so to 'improve' on Whitehead's stated views, he does so by showing us an interpretation more, not less, in accord with the basic categorial structure of the system. In other words, it is Whitehead, the man, not his system, that can be at fault." (Langdon Gilkey, "A Christian Natural Theology by John B. Cobb, Jr.," Theology Today Volume 22, January 1966, Number 4, pp. 532-533.

[3]Cobb, A Christian Natural Theology, p. 179.

based on the contention that in them God is treated
as an exception to the categories descriptive of other
entities, and his alterations of classical theism and
the traditional analogia entis are aimed at the attempt
to overcome the incoherence by interpreting God in
such a way that he is not viewed as an exception to
the metaphysical categories, nor merely one example of
such, but rather their chief exemplification. Ogden
observes that the "crucial insight" of neoclassical
metaphysics is Hartshorne's contention that "God is to
be conceived in strict analogy with the human self or
person,"[1] and he notes that this means: "The force of
the word 'strict' is that God, as Whitehead says,
is not to be treated as an exception to metaphysical
principles, but rather is to be understood as exemplifying them."[2] That Ogden keeps this "crucial insight"
at the center of his theology has been shown in the
preceding discussion. The insight is present in his
rejection of traditional theism, in his discussion of
the objectivity of God, and especially in his discussion of the temporality of God and the way in which
God functions in human life.

The acceptance of Whitehead's contention that God
is to be considered the chief exemplification of all
metaphysical principles places Ogden and Cobb together
in Protestant theology in a renewed emphasis on natural
theology. The primary characteristic of the last generation of theologians was what Ogden has called "its
exaggerated reaction against so-called 'natural theology.'"[3] The reaction against natural theology in all
its forms was summed up by Karl Barth, the dominant
figure in the movement which reacted against natural
theology, when he said:

> The logic of the matter demands that, even
> if we only lend our little finger to natural

---

[1]Ogden, The Reality of God, p. 175.

[2]The Reality of God, p. 175; Cf. Process and
Reality, p. 521.

[3]Ogden, "A Review of John B. Cobb's New Book: A
Christian Natural Theology," The Christian Advocate.
Vol. IX, No. 18 (September 23, 1965), p. 11.

theology, there necessarily follows the
denial of the revelation of God in Jesus
Christ. A natural theology which does
not strive to be the only master is not
a natural theology. And to give it place
at all is to put oneself, even if unwit-
tingly, on the way whch leads to this
sole sovereignty.[1]

Already[2] Barth had rejected natural theology in rejecting metaphysics as being a part of religion, which he
defined as the highest human possibility in contrast
to grace considered as man's divine possibility.[3] Of
religion, which includes metaphysical speculation or
"natural theology" Barth says: "What then is religion,
if it be not the loftiest summit in the land of sin."[4]
Bonhoeffer followed Barth's teaching at this point, and
he, too, launched an attach on religion as opposite to
Christianity. He, too, included in his attack a rejection of metaphysics and natural theology.[5] Although
many continental theologians and not a few American
theologians were greatly influenced by the Barthian
rejection of natural theology, the eclipse of natural
theology during the past four decades has proved to
be temporary. The first signs of new strength for
natural theology came in 1955 in Great Britain with the
appearance of New Essays in Philosophical Theology.[6]
Since that time there have been signs that natural
theology or philosophical theology may have a future as
well as a past, and John B. Cobb and Schubert Ogden

---

[1]Karl Barth, Church Dogmatics: The Doctrine of
God, Vol. II, Part I. New York: Charles Scribner's
Sons, 1957, p. 173.

[2]Cf. Karl Barth, The Epistle to the Romans.
(Translated from the sixth German edition by Edwyn C.
Hoskyns.), London: Oxford University Press, 1933, pp.
229-270.

[3]Barth, The Epistle to the Romans, p. 242.

[4]Ibid.

[5]Bonhoeffer, Letters and Papers from Prison, pp.
143-145, 167-172.

[6]Anthony Flew and Alasdair MacIntyre. New Essays
in Philosophical Theology, New York: The Macmillan
Company, 1964. (First Published, 1955.).

stand together in support of such a future. But their rejection of traditional theism and Ogden's rejection of the traditional analogia entis indicates that the future of natural theology is not to be a mere return to the natural theology which Barth rejected.

While Ogden and Cobb stand together in their attempt to develop a Christian philosophical-theology, and while both attempt to meet the demand that God not be treated as an exception to the metaphysical principles but as their chief exemplification, they also stand together in their attempt to speak to modern man in the life-situation in which he finds himself. Neither theologian views his philosophical attempt as esoteric and foreign to the understanding of twentieth-century man. On the contrary, they attempt to speak to men in relation to man's own experience of reality. They present their attempts as possibilities for communicating understandably with men who are unable to understand, accept and identify with the theological speculation of traditional theism. They present their theologies as visions of reality and doctrines of God which will "make sense" to man today. Both theologians attempt to speak to men who have experienced the demise, eclipse, and even death of God. This is shown through Cobb's acceptance of Whitehead's emphasis that the experience is the concrete. Of this Cobb notes:

> Whitehead alters the locus of concreteness as over against modern common sense. Especially with the decay of idealism, modernity has identified concreteness either with things presented to us in sense experience or with the sense data themselves. Whitehead declares this to be 'the fallacy of misplaced concreteness.' What is concrete is experience as such, just as it occurs in each particularized moment. Whitehead's 'actual occasions of experience' has close affinities with the 'shining present' of Brightman and the 'Dasein' of Heidegger.[1]

---

[1]Cobb, "From Crisis Theology to the Post-Modern World," Toward a New Christianity. (Thomas J. J. Altizer, ed. New York: Harcourt, Brace and World, Inc., 1967), p. 247.

Moreover, it is the attempt to speak meaningfully to modern man which leads Ogden to reject the conceptuality of traditional theism and attempt to wed the understanding of existence explicated by Bultmann's existentialist interpretation on the one hand with Hartshorne's neoclassical metaphysics on the other.

The two theologies of this study coincide insofar as Ogden and Cobb view the doctrine of God as the central theological problem, accept the central demand of Whitehead that God is to be interpreted as the chief exemplification of all metaphysical categories, attempt to speak to modern man who has experienced the death of God, and in so doing attempt to present a total vision of reality. It would seem that the two theologians, therefore, would be highly redundant. That many of the specific elements of their theologies coincide is not to be questioned. Both develop a bipolar view of God; both speak of God's relation to the world in a way which clearly admits of God's affecting the world as well as being affected by it, that is, both develop a panentheistic view of God's relation to the world; both men, in their efforts to depict a wholistic view of reality attempt to account for both history and nature, act and being. But this is not to say that their theologies are redundant nor that a study of the two involves mere repetition. Rather, the two theologians complement each other in significant ways. Weaknesses or omissions on the part of one are often overcome by the other. This is not to question the significance of the work of either of these theologians alone, but rather merely to recognize that no one man can consider any one problem--especially that of the doctrine of God--in its entirety. The complementariness referred to has to do with pre-systematic considerations on the one hand and the development of the systematic response to the pre-systematic considerations on the other. What is meant by "pre-systematic" consideration in this case is merely the examination of the various questions, situations, and world-views which make the doctrine of God problematic. Such an examination is pre-systematic insofar as it is a consideration of the background from which issues the current problem of the reality of God and in terms of which the systematic answer is developed. It is at the point of the pre-systematic considerations on the one hand and the systematic explication on the other that the complementariness of Ogden's and Cobb's doctrines of God may be seen. On the one hand, much of

Ogden's efforts are directed toward "setting up" the
contemporary problem of the doctrine of God as he sees
it, and pointing to the resources which are available
for its solution. He has not yet systematically developed fully the doctrine which could serve as the
successor to the traditional theism he has rejected as
incoherent and existentially irrelevant.[1] On the
other hand, the main thrust of Cobb's work has been
that of painstaking, precise, systematic development
of a Whiteheadian doctrine of God, a doctrine which
draws almost entirely upon the very resources which
Ogden sees as capable of providing the solution to the
problem of God in our day. His published work to date
does not concern itself as explicitly with an analysis
of the problem itself as does that of Ogden. Such a
consideration is virtually absent from Cobb's primary
systematic development A Christian Natural Theology.

That Ogden's published work to date is largely
devoted to a consideration of what Ogden understands
to be the reasons for the rejection of God in the
contemporary world can be seen by noting the consideration given the problem in Part II. of this study.
Although some of his essays do point toward systematic
development of the doctrine--for example, "The

---

[1]In the preceding, (Part II) Ogden's work regarding the development of his doctrine of God to date has
been explicated. Noticeably absent from this delineation is a systematic explication of the doctrine
similar to that of John Cobb's (Part I). Such an
absence is easily accounted for. Ogden has not yet
delineated his doctrine systematically and fully as
Cobb has done--or rather, is still doing. Cf. Cobb's
God and the World in which his major concern is the
problem of the relation of God and the world. He
says: "This is not a book about God, nor is it a book
about the world. It is a book about how God is in the
world and how the world is in and from God...Against
those who see us as being forced to choose God or the
the world, I am affirming that we must choose God and
the world. To choose one against the other is in the
end to reject both." (Cobb, God and the World, p. 7.).

225

Temporality of God,"[1] "How Does God Function in Human Life?,"[2] and "What Sense Does It Make to Say, 'God Acts in History?'"[3]--the essays remain fragmentary and Ogden concludes merely by pointing to the resources available for the solution to the problem he has explicated.

Virtually any one of Ogden's essays will support this contention. Consider only a few. After referring briefly to the resources found in Hartshorne's philosophy, Ogden, in an essay entitled "Beyond Supernaturalism" concludes:

> These brief remarks of course, hardly establish the validity of the philosophical alternative Hartshorne has explored and developed...Nevertheless, the task of receiving a fair hearing for such thinking is a formidable one, and what has been said here can do little more than point to the task and suggest its possible fruitfulness for our continuing reflection.[4]

In concluding the essay "The Christian Proclamation of God to Men of the So-Called 'Atheistic Age'" Ogden asserts that "the Christian proclamation of God to the men of our age both can and should be freed from its particular formulations in classical theism."[5] Moreover, he notes that the neoclassical metaphysics of Whitehead "provides an appropriate conceptuality" for speaking of "the double reality of our own existence as free and responsible persons and of the existence

---

[1]Ogden, "The Temporality of God," The Reality of God, pp. 144-163.
[2]Ogden, "How Does God Function in Human Life?," Christianity and Crisis, Vol. 27, May 15, 1967, pp. 105-108.
[3]Ogden, "What Sense Does It Make To Say, 'God Acts in History?'" The Reality of God, pp. 164-187.
[4]Ogden, "Beyond Supernaturalism," op. cit., p. 15.
[5]Ogden, "The Christian Proclamation of God to Men of the So-Called 'Atheistic Age,'" op. cit., p. 97.

of God as the eminently personal ground of ourselves and of the world," and thus "overcomes the usual objections to traditional metaphysics, but it also relativizes the judgment of Pascal about the Deus philosophorum."[1] But with this statement, Ogden concludes the essay, and there is no explanation of the neoclassical metaphysics which he contends contains the resources for the solution of the theistic problem.[2] At about the midpoint of another article "Love Unbounded: The Doctrine of God," Ogden observes that "the crucial question, then, is whether there can be any form of genuine theistic belief other than that represented by classical Christian theology."[3] His answer to the question is that "we already have before us a way of conceiving the reality of God, in comparison with which the theism of our classical tradition can be seen to be but a first and rather rough approximation."[4] Yet, Ogden only sketches[5] the insights of this view, while a response to the "crucial question" requires some full explication. In another article, "Toward a New Theism," Ogden presents the same analysis of the problem of traditional theism and indicates that the solution to the problem is to be found in a neoclassical theism similar to that of Whitehead and Hartshorne. Yet, again no developed explication is given. Of the essay, Ogden himself concludes: "The most I can have accomplished by it is to have suggested a somewhat un-

---

[1] Ibid.

[2] Concluding an essay in Dean Peerman's Frontline Theology, Ogden virtually repeats the conclusion just noted. He says: "my revered teacher in philosophy, Charles Hartshorne, has established the significance of this new metaphysical position /i.e. neoclassical metaphysics/ for the philosophy of religion or natural theology.' He has succeeded in working out a neoclassical conception of God which not only is capable of meeting the usual objections to traditional theism but also indicates that ours has become a situation in which Pascal's tragic saying can no longer be the final verdict about the God of the philosophers." ("Faith and Truth," Frontline Theology, p. 133.).

[3] Ogden, "Love Unbounded: The Doctrine of God," op. cit., p. 10.

[4] Ibid., p. 11.

[5] The explication consists of four pages.

conventional approach both to the problem that Christian faith in God raises today and to the way in which it might possibly be solved."[1] In "Theology and Philosophy: A New Phase of the Discussion," Ogden reviews some of the basic ideas of Hartshorne's The Logic of Perfection and Other Essays In Neoclassical Metaphysics. Of this work he says: "at long last the attention of the larger theological community may be directed to a philosopher whose thought at least seems to have an unusual relevance for Protestant theology."[2] A full explication, however, is still not given. Finally, in the lead and lengthy essay of Ogden's collected essays, "The Reality of God," Ogden concludes his analysis by asserting: "That I have not even tried to develop such a theology here is consistent with the critical, analytical emphasis of the whole understanding. Yet, I have at least sought to show how it might be developed by pointing to the philosophical resources that seem to me adequate to the task."[3]

In contrast to Ogden's failure to carry out the explication of neoclassical metaphysics which, he observes, contains--together with Bultmann's existentialist interpretation--the resources for the solution of the theistic problem, John Cobb has developed a doctrine of God based on the neoclassical metaphysics of Whitehead. To this extent he complements the work Ogden has only begun. He does not, however, focus specifically on the problem which makes a new direction in the doctrine of God necessary.[4] It is in this

---

[1]Ogden, "Toward a New Theism," op. cit., p. 17.

[2]Ogden, "Theology and Philosophy: A New Phase of the Discussion," op. cit., p. 3.

[3]The Reality of God, p. 97.

[4]To date, Cobb has not specifically focused on this problem in his published works to the extent that Ogden has. That he is giving more attention to the problem is indicated by his essay "The Possibility of Theism Today," which, at the time of this writing, is not yet published, and in his theological work God and the World, the first chapter of which indicates some of the problems of traditional theology's doctrine of God. Regarding Cobb's attempts to date, Langdon Gilkey bemoans his failure to correlate his philosophical explication with traditional theology. Of Cobb's A

respect that Ogden complements the work of Cobb. He
provides an analysis of the problem to which Cobb's
systematic development provides one possible solution.
And since the solution provided by Cobb is the solution
Ogden himself introduces, but never fully develops,
Cobb's work complements that of Ogden. Hence, although
the theologies of the two men have many similarities,
they are not merely repetitive nor redundant but rather
complementary.

To say that Cobb does not focus his primary in-
terest on explicating the question of the problem of
God today is not to say that he fails to consider it,
just as observing that Ogden does not fully develop
the neoclassical conceptuality does not mean that he
engages himself in no development of the conceptuality
whatsoever. That Ogden does, in fact, introduce the
development of the neoclassical conception of God has
already been indicated. That Cobb is very much aware

Christian Natural Theology, Gilkey writes: "Since this
book is, as we have said, almost entirely about Whitehead's view of the world, man, and God, it is in effect an argument for Whitehead, not for Christianity or
even for peculiarly Christian notions about things.
Cobb seems in other words to assume that if a philosophical interpretation on 'Christian subjects' is
presented by a man who lives within the community of
Christianity, the resulting set of ideas will be
'Christian.' Surely it is not my wish to deny this out
of hand. But equally surely some appeal to such classical Christian authorities and sources as Scripture,
traditional theology either Catholic or Protestant, or
the general mind of the contemporary church is in some
sense called for if the word 'Christian' is to be used
descriptively....And can one talk of a Christian notion
of God with no mention of Scripture, the teachings of
Jesus, traditional Christian concepts, or contemporary
theological movements? Continually I was forced to
ask myself, not so much because of what was said but
because all reference to Christian authorities was
omitted: 'On what basis does this book call itself a
Christian natural theology?'--and because of these
omissions, I found no satisfactory answer. (Langdon
Gilkey, "A Christian Natural Theology, by John B.
Cobb, Jr." Theology Today, Vol. 22, Number 4, January
1966, p. 531.).

of the problem which faces contemporary theology[1] in
its attempt to develop a doctrine of God is indicated
by his forthcoming book. He indicates five features
which have played prominent roles in the past in man's
speaking about God. First, he notes that men have
reflected on the kind of unity requisite for the whole
of which they and other entities are parts, and so have

---

[1]Gilkey contends that Ogden's analysis of the
problem facing contemporary theology's attempt to develop a doctrine of God is inadequate insofar as he
sees the factors which give rise to the problem as
being limited merely to an antiquated metaphysics. Of
Ogden's position, Gilkey says: "Whatever 'God' the
average secularized product of Baptist, Methodist,
Disciple, Congregational, or Presbyterian church life
is now negating, it is certainly not the actus purus
of medieval theology. If, therefore, this static,
metaphysical God is the only one who has died, this
demise raises few real theological issues for modern
theology, since Hegel, Schleiermacher, and Ritschl on
the one hand, and Barth, Brunner, and the Niebuhrs on
the other, had as little discernible relation to or
dependence on this classical metaphysical view of the
divine as have the process thinkers; and all alike have
spent most of their time excoriating its influence.
It is, I believe, neither good historical nor
good apologetical theology to blame our present real
problems on the now tattered remnants of medievalism,
questioned and even repudiated by much present Roman
theology itself. And it is surely unwise to blunt the
real threats of the secular spirit by believing that
this is the only God radically challenged by modernity.
There is latent here a fallacy of misplaced intellec-
tualism, the tendency to think that an entire cultural
Geist has been created by one philosophical ontology,
especially one recently represented only by a weaken-
ing ecclesiastical tradition. No, the dynamic factors
responsible for secularism lie far deeper than partic-
lar philosophies of the past, which expressed rather
than created these cultural moods...As they say over
and over, it is the category of God, dynamic or static,
independent or dependent, unrelated or related, ontological and impersonal and 'out there,' which is
radically questioned by the modern mood." (Gilkey,
"A Theology in Process: Schubert Ogden's Developing
Theology," Interpretation, Vol. 21, pp. 449-450.).

been led to speak of God.[1] Other aspects of experience which have led men to speak of God are: "reflection on the order they observe and which is revealed to
them in increasing intricacy by the advances of the
sciences;"[2] man's sense of absolute dependence;[3] the
confrontation in moral experience by an absolute
ought;[4] and finally, distinctive religious experience.[5]
These five approaches may lead to a different way of
viewing God, but the views need not be incompatible,
and no one approach need exclude the others.[6] Cobb's
view is that "the case for theism can be considerably
strengthened if the mutual compatibility of all these
grounds for belief is displayed in a single coherent
doctrine of God and God's action in the world and in
history."[7] Cobb, however, realizes the problems of the
attempt at synthesis. He discusses four of these:
"First, these traditional ways of thinking about God
have only a tenuous foothold in contemporary experience."[8] Second, the traditional thought about God
is not distinctively or centrally Christian.[9] Third,
the traditional understanding of God is not compatible
with the experience of the world.[10] Finally, the
traditional ideas of God have often operated against
the attainment of full humanity.[11]

Reference is made to these aspects of Cobb's
thought merely to indicate that explication of the

---

[1]Cobb, God and the World, p. 21.

[2]Ibid.

[3]Ibid.

[4]Ibid.

[5]Ibid., p. 22.

[6]Ibid.

[7]Ibid., p. 23.

[8]Ibid.

[9]Ibid., p. 24.

[10]Ibid., p. 25.

[11]Ibid., p. 27. Ogden would contend that traditional theism is subject to all of the problems.

231

theistic problem is not absent from his published
work, although he does not give it the primary consideration which Ogden does.[1] He presents, in his forthcoming book, a doctrine of God which is basically
Whiteheadian, thus again utilizing the resources which
Ogden indicates as requisite for a solution to the
contemporary theistic problem. Again, the theologies
can be viewed as complementary.

---

[1]Ogden's continued consideration of the theistic
problem accompanied by little development of the resources is dangerously close to mere repetition and
redundance. This may indicate one of the problems of
writing theology merely in fragments or essays, for
under such circumstances full systematic development--
which Ogden calls for, but never really gives--is not
possible. Cobb, on the other hand, shows evidence of
a developing theology with each work supplementing
rather than repeating past publications. One would
look forward to the appearance of the neoclassical
theistic solution the necessity of which Ogden affirms.

BIBLIOGRAPHY

BIBLIOGRAPHY

Altizer, Thomas J. J. Toward A New Christianity:
    Readings in the Death of God Theology. New York:
    Harcourt, Brace and World, 1967.

Ayer, A. J. Language, Truth and Logic. New York:
    Dover Publications, Inc., 1952.

Balthasar, Hans Urs von. The God Question and Modern
    Man. New York: The Seabury Press, 1967.

Barth, Karl. Church Dogmatics: The Doctrine of the
    Word of God. Volume I., Part 2, (G. W. Bromiley
    and T. F. Torrance, eds.). New York: Charles
    Scribner's Sons, 1956.

_____. The Epistle to the Romans. (Translated
    from the Sixth Edition by Edwyn C. Hoskyns.).
    London: Oxford University Press, 1933.

Bartsch, Hans Werner (ed.). Kerygma and Myth, Vol. II.
    London: S.P.C.K., 1962.

_____. Kerygma and Myth: A Theological Debate.
    New York: Harper Torchbooks, Harper and Row,
    Publishers, 1961.

Beardslee, William A. America and the Future of
    Theology. Philadelphia: The Westminister Press,
    1967.

Blackstone, William T. The Problem of Religious
    Knowledge. Englewood Cliffs, N. J.: Prentice-
    Hall, 1963.

Bonhoeffer, Dietrich. Act and Being. New York:
    Harper and Row, Publishers, 1956.

_____. Letters and Papers From Prison. New
    York: The Macmillan Company, (New Edition
    Revised and Enlarged) 1967.

Bree, Germaine. Camus: New Brunswick, New Jersey:
    Rutgers University Press, 1959.

_____. (ed.). Camus: A Collection of Critical Essays. Englewood Cliffs, N. J.: Prentice-Hall, Inc., 1962.

Bultmann, Rudolf. Existence and Faith: Shorter Writings of Rudolf Bultmann. (Selected, translated and introduced by Schubert M. Ogden.). New York: Meridian Books, Inc., 1960.

_____. Theology of the New Testament, Volume I. New York: Charles Scribner's Sons, 1951.

Callahan, Daniel. The Secular City Debate. New York: The Macmillan Company, 1966.

Camus, Albert. Caligula and Three Other Plays. (Stuart Gilbert, translator.). New York: Vintage Books, 1958.

_____. Exile and the Kingdom. (Justin O'Brien, trans.). New York: Vintage Books, 1965.

_____. The Fall. (Justin O'Brien, trans.). New York: Vintage Books, 1956.

_____. "The Just Assassins," Caligula and Three Other Plays. (Stuart Gilbert, trans.). New York: Vintage Books, 1958.

_____. "The Misunderstanding," Caligula and Three Other Plays. (Stuart Gilbert, trans.). New York: Vintage Books, 1958.

_____. The Myth of Sisyphus and Other Essays. (Justin O'Brien, trans.). New York: Vintage Books, 1956.

_____. Notebooks 1935-1942. (Philip Thody, trans.). New York: The Modern Library, 1965.

_____. The Plague. (Stuart Gilbert, trans.). New York: The Modern Library, 1948.

_____. The Possessed. (Justin O'Brien, trans.). New York: Vintage Books, 1964.

_____. The Rebel. (Anthony Bower, trans.). New York: Vintage Books, 1964.

_____. _Resistance, Rebellion and Death_.
(Justin O'Brien, trans.). New York: Alfred A.
Knopf, 1961.

_____. "The State of Siege," _Caligula and Three
Other Plays_. (Stuart Gilbert, trans.). New
York: Vintage Books, 1958.

_____. _The Stranger_. (Stuart Gilbert, trans.).
New York: Vintage Books, 1942.

Cauthen, Kenneth. _Science, Secularization and God_.
New York: The Abingdon Press, 1969.

Christian, William A. _An Interpretation of Whitehead's
Metaphysics_. New Haven: Yale University Press,
1959.

Cobb, John B., Jr. _A Christian Natural Theology_.
Philadelphia: The Westminister Press, 1965.

_____. _God AND The World_, Unpublished Manuscript
(to be published by Westminister.).

_____. _Living Options in Protestant Theology_.
Philadelphia: The Westminister Press, 1962.

_____. _The Structure of Christian Existence_.
Philadelphia: The Westminister Press, 1968.

_____. _Varieties of Protestantism_. Philadel-
phia: The Westminister Press, 1960.

Cox, Harvey. _The Secular City_. New York: The
Macmillan Company, 1965.

Dillenberger, John and Claude Welch. _Protestant Chris-
tianity_. New York: Charles Scribner's Sons,
1954.

Edwards, David L. (ed.). _The Honest to God Debate_.
Philadelphia: The Westminister Press, 1963.

Ely, Stephen Lee. _The Religious Availability of
Whitehead's God: A Critical Analysis_. Madison:
The University of Wisconsin Press, 1942.

Ferre, Frederick. _Basic Modern Philosophy of Religion_.
New York: Charles Scribner's Sons, 1967.

_____. _Language, Logic and God_. New York: Harper and Row Publishers, 1961.

Flew, Antony. _God and Philosophy_. New York: Dell Publishing Company, Inc. (by arrangement with Harcourt, Brace and World, Inc.), 1966.

Funk, Robert W. and Gerhard Ebeling (eds.). _Journal for Theology and the Church: Translating Theology into the Modern Age_. New York: Harper and Row Publishers, Inc., 1965.

Funk, Robert W. _Language, Hermeneutic and Word of God_. New York: Harper and Row, Publishers, 1966.

Gilkey, Langdon. _Maker of Heaven and Earth: The Christian Doctrine of Creation in the Light of Modern Knowledge_. New York: Doubleday and Company, Anchor Books, 1959.

Haggis, Donald. _Albert Camus: La Peste_. New York: Barron's Educational Series, Inc., 1962.

Hanna, Thomas. _The Lyrical Existentialists_. New York: Atheneum, 1962.

_____. _The Thought and Art of Albert Camus_. Chicago: Henry Regnery Company, Gateway Editions, 1968.

Hartshorne, Charles. _Anselm's Discovery: A Re-examination of the Ontological Proof for God's Existence_. La Salle, Illinois: The Open Court Publishing Company, 1965.

_____. _Beyond Humanism: Essays in the New Philosophy of Nature_. New York: Willett, Clark and Company, 1937.

_____. _The Divine Relativity: A Social Conception of God_. New Haven: Yale University Press, 1948.

_____. _The Logic of Perfection and Other Essays in Neoclassical Metaphysics_. La Salle, Illinois: Open Court Publishing Company, 1962.

_____. _Man's Vision of God and the Logic of Theism_. New York: Willett, Clark and Company, 1941.

238

_____. A Natural Theology for Our Time. La
   Salle, Illinois: Open Court Publishing Company,
   1967.

Hartshorne, Charles and William L. Reese (eds.).
   Philosophers Speak of God. Chicago: The University of Chicago Press, 1953.

Heidegger, Martin. Being and Time. London: SCM Press
   Ltd., 1962.

Herzog, Frederick. Understanding God: The Key Issue
   in Present-Day Protestant Thought. New York:
   Charles Scribner's Son's, 1966.

Hick, John (ed.). The Existence of God. New York:
   The Macmillan Company, 1964.

Hick, John. Philosophy of Religion. Englewood Cliffs,
   New Jersey: Prentice-Hall, Inc., 1963.

King, Magda. Heidegger's Philosophy, A Guide to His
   Basic Thought. New York: The Dell Publishing
   Company, 1964.

Kirkpatrick, Dow (ed.). The Finality of Christ.
   Abingdon Press, 1966.

Kline, George L. Alfred North Whitehead: Essays on
   His Philosophy. Englewood Cliffs, New Jersey:
   Prentice-Hall, Inc., 1963.

Leclerc, Ivor. Whitehead's Metaphysics: An Introductory Exposition. New York: The Humanities Press,
   1965.

Lewis, H. D. (ed.). Religious Studies. Volume 4,
   No. 1, 1968. ("Special Part on the Ontological
   Argument".). London: Cambridge University Press,
   1968.

Lowe, Victor. Understanding Whitehead. Baltimore:
   The Johns Hopkins Press, 1962.

Macquarrie, John. An Existentialist Theology: A
   Comparison of Heidegger and Bultmann. New York:
   Harper and Row, Publishers, 1965.

_____. New Directions in Theology Today: God and Secularity. Philadelphia: The Westminister Press, 1968.

Martin, Gottfried. An Introduction to General Meta-physics. (Translated by Eva Schaper and Ivor Leclerc.). London: George Allen and Unwin, Ltd., 1961.

Marty, Martin E. and Dean G. Peerman (eds.). New Theology No. 1. New York: The Macmillan Company, 1964.

_____. New Theology No. 2. New York: The Macmillan Company, 1965.

_____. New Theology No. 3. New York: The Macmillan Company, 1966.

Matson, Wallace I. The Existence of God. Ithaca, New York: Corness University Press, 1965.

Michalson, Carl. Worldly Theology: The Hermeneutical Focus of an Historical Faith. New York: Charles Scribner's Sons, 1967.

Ogden, Schubert M. Christ Without Myth: A Study Based on the Theology of Rudolf Bultmann. New York: Harper and Row, Publishers, 1961.

_____. The Reality of God and Other Essays. New York: Harper and Row, Publishers, 1966.

Peerman, Dean G. (ed.). Frontline Theology. Richmond, Virginia: John Knox Press, 1967.

Peters, Eugene H. The Creative Advance: An Introduc-tion to Process Philosophy as a Context for Christian Faith. St. Louis, Missouri: The Bethany Press, 1966.

Plantinga, Alvin (ed.). The Ontological Argument: From St. Anselm to Contemporary Philosophers. New York: Anchor Books, Doubleday and Company, Inc., 1965.

Price, Lucien (recorder.). Dialogues of Alfred North
    Whitehead. New York: The New American Library,
    Mentor Books, 1954.

Ramsey, Ian T. Religious Language: An Empirical
    Placing of Theological Phrases. New York: The
    Macmillan Company, 1957.

Reese, William L. and Eugene Freeman (eds.). Process
    and Divinity: The Hartshorne Festschrift. La
    Salle, Illinois: Open Court Publishing Company,
    1964.

Robinson, James M. and John B. Cobb, Jr. New Frontiers
    in Theology, Vol. I.: The Later Heidegger and
    Theology. New York: Harper and Row, Publishers,
    1963.

_____. New Frontiers in Theology, Vol. II.:
    The New Hermeneutic. New York: Harper and Row,
    Publishers, 1964.

_____. New Frontiers in Theology, Vol. III.:
    Theology as History. New York: Harper and Row,
    Publishers, 1967.

Robinson, John A. T. Exploration into God. Stanford,
    California: Stanford University Press, 1967.

_____. Honest To God. Philadelphia: The
    Westminister Press, 1963.

Schilpp, Paul Arthur (ed.). The Philosophy of Alfred
    North Whitehead. Chicago: Northwestern Univer-
    sity, 1941.

Sherburne, Donald W. A Key to Whitehead's Process
    and Reality. New York: The Macmillan Company,
    1966.

Stace, W. T. Religion and the Modern Mind. New York:
    J. B. Lippincott Company, 1952.

Teilhard de Chardin. The Divine Milieu. New York:
    Harper Torchbooks, Harper and Row, Publishers,
    1960.

Thody, Philip. Albert Camus: A Study of His Work. London: Hamish Hamilton, 1957.

Tillich, Paul. Perspectives on 19th and 20th Century Protestant Theology. (Carl F. Braaten, ed.). New York: Harper and Row, Publishers, 1967.

_____. Systematic Theology. Volume I. Chicago: The University of Chicago Press, 1951.

_____. Systematic Theology. Volume II. Chicago: The University of Chicago Press, 1957.

Toulmin, Stephen. Reason in Ethics. Cambridge: The University Press, 1964.

_____. The Uses of Argument. Cambridge: Cambridge University Press, 1958.

Treash, Gordon Spencer. Actuality and Social Order: Whitehead's Theory of Societies. Atlanta: Emory University, (doctoral dissertation.), 1968.

Van Buren, Paul M. The Secular Meaning of the Gospel: Based on an Analysis of Its Language. New York: The Macmillan Company, 1963.

Whitehead, Alfred North. Adventures of Ideas. New York: The Free Press, 1933.

_____. Modes of Thought. New York: The Macmillan Company, 1938.

_____. Process and Reality. New York: Harper and Row, Publishers, 1957.

_____. Religion in the Making. New York: The World Publishing Company, Meridian Books, 1954.

_____. Science and the Modern World. New York: The New American Library, Mentor Books, 1925.

Williams, Colin. Faith in a Secular Age. New York: Harper and Row, Publishers, 1966.

ARTICLES

Allan, George and Merle F. Allshouse. "Current Issues
    in Process Theology: Some Reflections." The
    Christian Scholar. Vol. 50, Number 3, Fall, 1967,
    pp. 167-176.

Anderson, R. T. "Reality of God." Journal of the
    American Academy of Religion. Vol. 35, September,
    1967, pp. 294-296.

Bespaloff, Rachel. "The World of Man Condemned to
    Death." (Eric Schoenfeld, trans.). Esprit,
    January, 1950, pp. 1-26.

Brown, Delwin. "God's Reality and Life's Meaning: A
    Critique of Schubert Ogden." Encounter, Volume
    28, Summer, 1967, pp. 256-262.

_____. "Recent Process Theology." Journal of
    the American Academy of Religion, Volume XXXV,
    March, 1967, Number 1, pp. 28-41.

Bultmann, Rudolf. "On the Question of Philosophical
    Theology." Union Seminary Quarterly Review, Vol.
    20, March, 1965, pp. 261-263.

Christian, William A. "A Discussion on the New Meta-
    physics and Theology." The Christian Scholar,
    Volume 50, Number 3, Fall, 1967, pp. 304-315.

Cobb, John B., Jr. "Affirming God in a Non-theistic
    Age." Unpublished.

_____. "Can Natural Theology Be Christian?"
    Theology Today, Vol. 23, April, 1966, pp. 140-142.

_____. "Christian Natural Theology and Christian
    Existence." Christian Century, March 3, 1965,
    Vol. 82, pp. 265-267.

_____. "Christianity and Myth." Journal of
    Bible and Religion, Vol. 33, October, 1965, pp.
    314-320.

_____. "Consultation on Hermeneutics." The Christian Century, Vol. 79, Part 1, 1962, pp. 783-784.

_____. "The Intrapsychic Structure of Christian Existence." Journal of the American Academy of Religion, Volume XXXVI, Number 4, December, 1968, pp. 327-344.

_____. "Nihilism, Existentialism, and Whitehead." Religion in Life, Vol. 30, Autumn, 1961, pp. 521-533.

_____. "The Objectivity of God." Christian Advocate, March 9, 1967, Vol. 11, pp. 7-8.

_____. "On Being 'Post-Christian.'" Christian Advocate, Volume 7, June 6, 1963, pp. 13-14.

_____. "Ontology, History and Christian Faith." Religion in Life, Vol. 36, Spring, 1967, pp. 28-39.

_____. "'Perfection Exists:' A Critique of Charles Hartshorne." Religion in Life, Volume 32, Spring, 1963, pp. 294-304.

_____. "The Philosophic Grounds of Moral Responsibility: A Comment on Matson and Niebuhr." The Journal of Philosophy, July 2, 1959, pp. 619-621.

_____. "The Possibility of a Universal Normative Ethic." Ethics, October, 1954, pp. 55-61.

_____. "The Possibility of Theism Today." Unpublished.

_____. "The Post-Bultmannian Trend." Journal of Bible and Religion, January, 1962, pp. 3-11.

_____. "Protestant Theology and Church Life." Religion in Life, Volume 25, Winter, 1955-56, pp. 65-75.

_____. "Some Thoughts on the Meaning of Christ's Death." Religion in Life, Vol. 28, Spring, 1959, pp. 212-222.

_____. "Speaking about God." Religion in Life, Spring, 1967, pp. 28-39.

_____. "Teilhard de Chardin: The Great Yes-Sayer." Christian Advocate, Voulume 9, March 11, 1965, pp. 7-8.

_____. "Theological Data and Method." The Journal of Religion, July, 1953, pp. 212-223.

_____. "A Theological Typology." The Journal of Religion, July, 1959, pp. 183-195.

_____. "Toward Clarity in Aesthetics." Philosophy and Phenomenological Research. December, 1957, pp. 169-189.

_____. "A Whiteheadian Christology." Unpublished.

_____. "Whitehead's Philosophy and a Christian View of Man." Journal of Bible and Religion, Vol. 32, July, 1964, pp. 209-220.

Crosby, Donald A. "Language and Religious Language in Whitehead's Philosophy." The Christian Scholar, Volume 50, Number 3, Fall, 1967, pp. 210-221.

Ford, Lewis S. "Christian Natural Theology." The Journal of Bible and Religion, Vol. 34, January, 1966, pp. 60-64.

_____. "Divine Persuasion and the Triumph of Good." The Christian Scholar, Volume 50, Number 3, Fall, 1967, pp. 235-250.

Freeman, Kenneth D. "Self-Identity and Responsibility in Process Philosophy." Proceedings of the Iowa Philosophical Society. Volume I., Grinnell, Iowa: Grinnell College, 1965.

Fuller, B. A. G. "The Theory of God in Book Lambda of Aristotle's Metaphysics." Philosophical Review, Volume 16, 1907.

Gilkey, Langdon. "A Christian Natural Theology by
    John B. Cobb, Jr." Theology Today, Volume 22,
    Number 4, January, 1966, pp. 530-545.

_____. "Social and Intellectual Sources of
    Contemporary Protestant Theology in America."
    Daedalus, Winter, 1967, pp. 69-98.

_____. "A Theology in Process: Schubert Ogden's
    Developing Theology." Interpretation, Volume 21,
    October, 1967, pp. 447-459.

Griffin, David. "Schubert Ogden's Christology and the
    Possibilities of Process Philosophy." The Chris-
    tian Scholar, Volume 50, Number 3, Fall, 1967,
    pp. 290-303.

Guthrie, W. K. C. "The Development of Aristotle's
    Theology--I." The Classical Quarterly, Volume 27,
    1933, pp. 162-171. (R. Hackforth and J. D.
    Denniston, eds., New York: G. E. Stechert and
    Company, 1933.).

Guthrie, W. K. C. "The Development of Aristotle's
    Theology--II." The Classical Quarterly, Volume
    28, 1934, pp. 90-98. (R. Hackforth and J. D.
    Denniston, eds., New York: G. E. Stechert and
    Company, 1934.).

Guy, Fritz. "Comments on a Recent Whiteheadian Doc-
    trine of God." Andrews University Seminary
    Studies, Vol. 4, July, 1966, pp. 107-134.

Hanna, Thomas. "Albert Camus and the Christian Faith."
    The Journal of Religion, Vol. 36, 1956, pp.
    224-233.

Hartshorne, Charles. "Abstract and Concrete Approaches
    to Deity." Union Seminary Quarterly Review, Vol.
    20, March, 1965, pp. 265-269.

_____. "The Idea of God--Literal or Analogical?"
    The Christian Scholar, Vol. XXXIX, Number 2,
    June, 1956, pp. 131-136.

_____. "What Did Anselm Discover?" Union
    Seminary Quarterly Review, March, 1962, pp. 213-
    222.

Hocking, Richard. "The Polarity of Dialectical History and Process Cosmology." The Christian Scholar, Volume 50, Number 3, Fall, 1967, pp. 177-183.

Johnson, W. A. "Reality of God." Union Seminary Quarterly Review, Vol. 22, March, 1967, pp. 285-289.

Jones, B. E. "Christian Natural Theology." London Quarterly And Holborn Review, Vol. 192, July, 1967, p. 264.

Kelly, Allen D. "Christian Natural Theology." Anglican Theological Review, Vol. 47, October, 1965, pp. 449-452.

Kelly, A. D. "Reality of God." Anglican Theological Review, Vol. 49, July, 1967, pp. 313-314.

Leclerc, Ivor. "The Problem of the Physical Existent." International Philosophical Quarterly, Vol. 9, No. 1, March, 1969, pp. 40-62.

Macquarrie, John. "Reality of God." Theology Today, Vol. 24, April, 1967, pp. 116-117.

Martland, T. R. "Is A Theology of Dialogue (of Process) Permissible?" The Christian Scholar, Vol. 50, No. 3, Fall, 1967, pp. 197-209.

Merlan, Philip. "Aristotle's Unmoved Movers." Traditio, Vol. 4, 1946, pp. 1-30. (Stephan Kuttner and Anselm Strittmater, eds., New York: Cosmopolitan Science and Art Service Company, Inc., 1946.).

Norman, Ralph. "Steam, Barbarism, and Dialectic: Notations on Proof and Sensibility." The Christian Scholar. Vol. 50, Number 3, Fall, 1967, pp. 184-196.

Ogden, Schubert M. "Beyond Supernaturalism." Religion in Life, Vol. XXXIII, (1963-1964), pp. 7-18.

_____. "A Christian Natural Theology." The Christian Advocate, Volume IX, Number 18, September 23, 1965, pp. 11-12.

_____. "The Christian Proclamation of God to
Men of the So-Called 'Atheistic Age.'" Concilium:
Theology in the Age of Renewal, Volume 16: Is
God Dead. New York: Paulist Press, 1966, pp.
89-98.

_____. "The Debate on 'Demythologizing.'" The
Journal of Bible and Religion, Volume XXVII, 1959,
pp. 17-27.

_____. "Faith and Truth." Frontline Theology,
(Dean Peerman, ed.). Richmond: John Knox Press,
1967, pp. 126-133.

_____. "God and Philosophy." Journal of
Religion, Vol. XLVIII, No. 2, April, 1968, pp.
161-181.

_____. "How Does God Function in Human Life?"
Christianity and Crisis, Vol. 27, May, 1967, pp.
105-108.

_____. "Love Unbounded: The Doctrine of God."
The Perkins School of Theology Journal, Vol. XIX,
Number 3, Spring, 1966, pp. 5-17.

_____. "Myth and Truth." McCormick Quarterly,
Volume 18, January, 1965, pp. 57-76.

_____. "The Possibility and Task of Philosoph-
ical Theology." Union Seminary Quarterly Review,
Vol. 20, March, 1965, pp. 271-279.

_____. "II.--Systematic Theology," from
"Symposium: The Situation in Contemporary Protestant Theology," The Perkins School of Theology
Journal, Volume XII, Number 2, Winter, 1959, pp.
13-20.

_____. "Theology and Philosophy: A New Phase
of the Discussion." Journal of Religion, Volume
XLIV, Number 1, January, 1964, pp. 1-16.

_____. "Toward a New Theism." Theology in
Crisis: A Colloquim on the Credibility of 'God.'
New Concord, Ohio: Muskingum College, 1967, pp.
3-18.

_____. "Welch's Polemic: A Reply." Theology Today, Volume 22, July, 1965, pp. 275-277.

Ogletree, Thomas W. "A Christological Assessment of Dipolar Theism." The Journal of Religion, Volume 47, Number 2, April, 1967, pp. 87-99.

Parsons, Howard L. "History as Viewed By Marx and Whitehead." The Christian Scholar, Volume 50, Number 3, Fall, 1967, pp. 273-289.

Priebe, D. A. "Reality of God." Dialog, Vol. 6, Summer, 1967, p. 229.

Rahner, Karl. "Atheism and Implicit Christianity." Theology Digest, Sesquicentennial issue, February, 1968, pp. 43-56.

Reinelt, Herbert R. "Whitehead and Theistic Language." The Christian Scholar, Volume 50, Number 3, Fall, 1967, pp. 222-234.

Rust, E. C. "Christian Natural Theology." Review and Expositor, Volume 64, Fall, 1967, pp. 555-557.

Schmidt, P. F. "Christian Natural Theology." Zygon, Vol. 2, June, 1967, pp. 206-209.

Sherburne, Donald W. "Whitehead Without God." The Christian Scholar, Volume 50, Number 3, Fall, 1967, pp. 251-272.

Smart, Ninian. "Reality of God." Church Quarterly Review, Vol. 168, July, 1967, pp. 361-362.

Stokes, Mack B. "The New Quest for a Credible Theism." Religion in Life, Winter, 1968, pp. 572-590.

Tillich, Paul. "Existential Philosophy." Journal of the History of Ideas, January, 1944, pp. 44-70.

Williamson, C. M. "Reality of God." Encounter, Vol. 28, Spring, 1967, pp. 185-186.

249

Wolfson, Harry Austryn. "The Knowability and
    Describability of God in Plato and Aristotle."
    Harvard Studies in Classical Philology, Volume
    LVI-LVII, 1947, pp. 233-249, Cambridge: Harvard
    University Press, 1947.

Young, W. "Reality of God." Christianity Today,
    Vol. 11, February 3, 1967, pp. 35-36.